Food for Thought

Food for Thought

ancient visions and new experiments of rural people

Bertus Haverkort and Wim Hiemstra (eds)

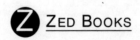

Published in 1999 by ETC / COMPAS in association with Books for Change
and Zed Books Ltd.
ETC / COMPAS, P.O. Box 64, 3830 AB Leusden, The Netherlands.
Books for Change, 28 Castle Street, Ashok Nagar, Bangalore, 560 025, India.
Zed Books Ltd, 7 Cynthia Street, London N1 9JF, United Kingdom
and Room 400, 175 Fifth Avenue, New York, NY10010, United States.
Distributed in the USA exclusively by St Martin's Press, 175 Fifth Avenue,
New York, NY10010, United States.

Food for Thought
ancient visions and new experiments of rural people
Bertus Haverkort, Wim Hiemstra (eds)
Leusden: ETC / COMPAS
Bangalore: Books for Change
London: Zed Books
1999

India ISBN 81 87380 06 3
UK / US ISBN 1 85649 722 4 hb
UK / US ISBN 1 85649 723 2 pb

A catalogue record for this book is available from the British Library.
Keywords: sustainable agriculture, health, culture,
indigenous knowledge, on-farm experimentation, cosmovision

PREFACE

'*There was a little bird living in a huge beautiful green forest. The forest contained many other animals, trees and plants. One day, the forest was set on fire. All the animals fled to the edge of the forest to save their lives. The smallest of all birds went to a small pond and picked a minute droplet of water in its tiny beak and flew back to the fire. The big animals looked strangely at the little bird. "What do you think you can do with such a small droplet?" they asked. But the bird smiled, took another droplet and flew back to the burning forest, saying to the other animals: "This is all I can do and I should do it".*'
[Gloria Miranda Zambrano, COMPAS partner in Peru]

Indigenous knowledge and cultural diversity is increasingly being put under pressure as the process of modernisation reaches into every corner of the world. Rapid changes are taking place in land use practices, farming methods, health care and the cultural ethos and rituals of indigenous peoples. Fortunately, in recent years much work has been done to come to a better understanding of indigenous knowledge and its relevance for sustainable development. Today the products of indigenous knowledge are better understood. However, our understanding of the concepts of life or cosmovisions of rural people, the processes of indigenous learning and experimentation and the roles of spiritual leaders and other traditional institutions is less advanced. This book shows the wealth of knowledge that people are prepared to share, if outsiders show respect and sincere interest for them.

COMPAS is an initiative to understand and support the processes and concepts of indigenous knowledge through field experimentation and intercultural dialogue. At present, COMPAS involves ten countries in Asia, Africa, Latin America and Europe and consists of fourteen NGOs and one university. It aims to become an open platform with national, regional and global membership and activities.

Taking the cosmovision of the rural people as a point of departure for development, taking spirituality seriously, looking for ways to test and improve traditional practices and rituals and looking at development cooperation as an intercultural dialogue is a fairly new approach. We are grateful to the funding agencies, NEDA, Novib and SDC, who have provided the means necessary to help COMPAS to develop this new approach. We hope to publish another book in 4 years time recording the new insights and experiences gained by the COMPAS programme.

We feel that the COMPAS approach is both challenging and relevant. There is a great need to learn together, to inform each other and to maintain intercultural dialogue on the different sources of knowledge present within the rich diversity of human cultures.

Freddy Delgado, Gustavo Saravia and Jaime Delgadillo, AGRUCO; *Cosmas Gonese,* AZTREC; *Joke de Jonge,* BD-Union; *David Millar,* CECIK; *Shyam Sundar and A.V. Balasubramanian,* CIKS; *G.K. Upawansa, Kalyani Palangasinghe and Rukman Wagachchi,* ECO; *Maheswar Ghimire,* ECOS; *Bertus Haverkort and Wim Hiemstra,* ETC-COMPAS; *Darshan Shankar,* FRLHT; *Vanaja Ramprasad, Krishna Prasad and Gowri Gopinath,* GREEN Foundation; *Gowtham Shankar,* IDEA; *Mary Shetto,* IDIKS; *Upendra Shenoy, Purushothama Rao, Aruna Kumara and A.S. Anand,* KPP; *Gloria Miranda Zambrano and Raúl Santana Paucar,* TALPUY; *Johan Kieft and Marthen Duan,* TIRD-P.

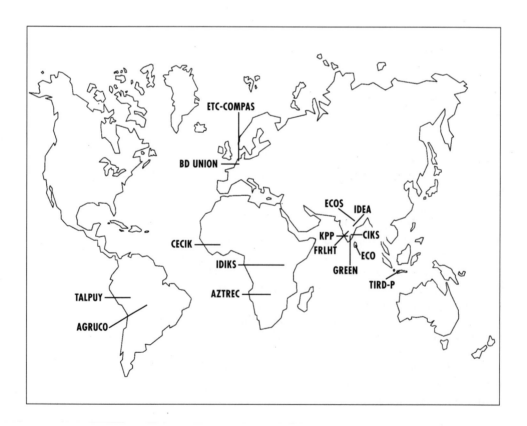

Present COMPAS Partners (1998)

AGRUCO - Centre for Agroecology of the University of Cochabamba
    Cochabamba, Bolivia

AZTREC - Association of Zimbabwean Traditional Environmental Conservationists
    Masvingo, Zimbabwe

BD-UNION - Union of Bio-Dynamic Farming
    Driebergen, The Netherlands

CECIK - Centre for Cosmovision and Indigenous Knowledge
    Tamale, Ghana

CIKS - Centre for Indian Knowlege Systems
    Madras, India

ECO - Ecological Conservation Organization
    Nawalapitya, Sri Lanka

ECOS - Ecological Services Centre
    Narayangarh, Nepal

ETC-COMPAS - Comparing and Supporting Endogenous Development
    Leusden, The Netherlands

FRLHT - Foundation for the Revitalisation of Local Health Traditions
    Bangalore, India

GREEN Foundation - Genetic Resource Ecology Energy Nutrition Foundation
    Bangalore, India

IDEA - Integrated Development and Environmental Awakening
    Visakapatnam, India

IDIKS - Initiative for the Development of Indigenous Knowledge
    Mbeya, Tanzania

KPP - Krishi Prayoga Pariwara
    Shimoga, India

TALPUY - Research and Development Group on Andean Science
    Huancayo, Peru

TIRD-P - Timor Integrated Rural Development Programme
    Kefamananu, Indonesia

CONTENTS

Photographic sequences

COMPAS: SUPPORTING ENDOGENOUS DEVELOPMENT

The COMPAS network for comparing and supporting endogenous development began in 1995 when NGOs and universities in India, Sri Lanka, Ghana, the Netherlands, Norway, Mexico, Bolivia and Peru agreed to take a fresh look at the farming communities they were working with. They were concerned about the quality of the development activities they were supporting. The development organisations that became partners in the COMPAS programme had gone through a variety of experiences. In the early stages, many had been involved in efforts to enhance agricultural production by the application of fertilisers, hybrid seeds and mechanisation in monocultures. Most of them had realised the limitations of this approach in the rainfed farming areas in which they were working and had subsequently built up experiences with agriculture using lower levels of external inputs that made better use of locally available resources. They became engaged in activities such as agroforestry, soil and water harvesting, the use of botanical pesticides, organic manure, multiple cropping and the improvement of local seed. In these efforts they realised that, in most cases, the farming communities themselves had a great wealth of knowledge about the physical and biological environment in which they lived. Farmers know their own soil, their own climatic conditions, their own land races, have learned to manage local water resources and have observed the effects of local herbs on animal health and when used as botanical pesticides. Therefore, many of the technologies developed were largely based on farmers' knowledge.

But the partners also learned that rural communities have their own processes for testing new practices and that in seemingly traditional societies, farmers are continuously adapting their farming practices in the light of their experiences. This insight led to many experiences with Participatory Technology Development (PTD), an approach in which farmers and outside agencies cooperate to develop new farming techniques, and where the experimental capacity of farmers determines the choice of topic for experimentation and the criteria for success and failure. The outcome of PTD activities are generally better insights into the possibilities and limitations of new techniques, as well as an improved capacity amongst farmers and outsiders to develop technologies that are appropriate to the local conditions.

Working within the cultural context of the rural people, starting with their knowledge, their technologies, and some of their tools, and trying to evolve together with them was a rewarding approach for development agencies. In general, these approaches led to enthusiasm amongst partners and the farmers with whom they worked. It also led to a better relationship between the farming community and outside agencies. In this process, however, several partners also realised that their professional background made it difficult to free themselves from conventional approaches. It proved difficult for them to fully appreciate the real meaning of indigenous knowledge. Formal science was the dominant paradigm and a pace-setter for development. From the formal perspective, indigenous knowledge and rural peoples' cultures matter in so far as they fit into this dominant paradigm. Indigenous technical knowledge was given attention, validated, processed and judged by the standards, criteria and rules of conventional science. 'It is only when we have proof for farmers' knowledge that it is scientific'. And rural peoples' knowledge was only considered relevant to the extent that it could be understood within the dominant paradigm.

Participatory Technology Development often meant that farmers participate in processes of technology development that were defined by outsiders. Development intervention based on conventional science often has a negative perception of indigenous knowledge: it is seen as traditional, obsolete, irrelevant, a curiosity or folklore of romantic value. Sometimes, in relation to the use of herbal medicine, it is seen as a source of extraction or as partially useful. Indigenous knowledge is rarely seen as a source of learning and a basis for the exchange of ideas. Of herbal medicines, for example, only the recipes are seen as interesting. This notion led a number of organisations to look deeper into the basic features of indigenous knowledge.

Understanding farmers' cosmovisions

Historical perspective. The experiences of COMPAS partners first led to an understanding that apart from the western based concepts of science that emerged with the work of Descartes in the seventeenth century, there were many other scientific traditions, past and present.

Since mankind became engaged in agriculture, some 10,000 years ago, people have taken an active position towards nature. This required an explicit concept of nature and a definition of the relationship between mankind and nature. In different parts of the world people developed their own interpretation and in the course of history the Chinese, the ancient Indians, peoples from South America, Africa, Middle East, Australia, Greece and Europe developed their own science. The early scientists' main goal was to understand the meaning of things, rather than to predict and control. Questions relating to divine beings, the human soul and ethics were considered to be of the highest significance.

Only in the seventeenth century did western science replace the notion of an organic, living and spiritual universe with the notion of the world as a machine. The new methods of enquiry, as advocated by Bacon and developed by Descartes and Newton, involved a mechanistic and mathematical description of nature and an analytical method of reasoning. Descartes concluded that 'mind' and 'matter' were two separate and fundamentally different things. To make it possible for scientists to describe nature mathematically, they had to restrict themselves to studying the essential properties of matter: those that could be quantified by shapes, weights, numbers and movement. Other properties, like colour, sound, taste or smell were considered subjective mental projections and were neglected or excluded from the scientific domain. Aspects related to the mind such as the spiritual worlds, gods, the human soul and emotions were no longer considered part of science, and were left to priests. As the social sciences as we know them today began to develop, they initially applied the same mechanistic approach in these domains. Since the eighteenth century Europe and western countries have adopted an approach to science that reduced the perception of the world to that of a machine. Science became organised in highly specialised disciplines, each focusing on a narrowly defined part of the material world.

In the course of the 20th century scientists like Einstein (physics), Heisenberg (quantum physics), Sheldrake and Lovelock (biology), Jung (psychology) and Prigogine (chemistry) brought forward research results and insights that made major corrections to the Cartesian materialistic-mechanistic approach. New concepts include the laws of thermodynamics, chaos theory, the world as a living entity (Gaia), synchronicity (event A and B happen 'when the time is ripe for it, and not necessarily as a consequence of a particular cause'). These new concepts in fact have again brought together 'mind' and 'matter' as part and parcel of one entity. These scientific insights make or rather restore the bridge between the material world and the spiritual world.

It should be emphasised that also in the West, in addition to mainstream scientists, agronomists and farmers, there have always been those who maintained a more holistic and spiritual worldview. Examples in Europe are Gnostic movements such as the Catarhs in southern France, who were fought by the church, and other ecospiritual movements such as the Franciscans who were accepted by it. In the late eighteenth and early nineteenth century, Goethe, the German botanist and poet, developed a holistic and organic approach to research. In this phenomenological natural science, skills like observation, lively imagination, identification, observing living interconnections, were meant to revive the cognitive powers of scientists (and farmers). At the end of the nineteenth century, Rudolf Steiner developed the theory of cognition from Goethe's investigations in nature. Steiner and his 'spiritual science' also inspired the anthroposophic movement with its biodynamic way of farming.

Cartesian scientific concepts and technology have undoubtedly had a great impact on the world and have led to a great number of technological breakthroughs. In agriculture, they enabled a clearer understanding of the influence of the biological processes involved in the growth of plants and animals, the biological and physical processes taking place in the soil and the mechanics of farm labour. The exploitation of fossil energy sources supported the development of machines that in turn created the possibility of developing mechanical implements for farm work. Chemistry led to technologies such as chemical fertilisers and pesticides. Farmers became part of a market economy that changed their locally oriented economy to an open one, in which production and consumption became increasingly separated. In this vision of market economy, economic growth is an important goal.

In temperate climates such as Europe and North-America and in irrigated tropical areas, agricultural productivity has increased considerably. However, the environmental impact of this external-input-oriented agriculture is increasingly seen as unacceptable. Pesticides and nitrates from fertilisers pollute the groundwater in many regions and the resistance of pests to pesticides is seen as a very serious problem. Underground acquifers have become exhausted, irrigation systems silt and soils become salinated. Biodiversity is rapidly decreasing and the use of fossil energy is considerable, contributing to the greenhouse effect whereas agriculture has the potential to be a net producer of energy. Farmers are increasingly faced with economic problems. The prices of external inputs are rising faster than the off-farm prices for their agricultural products. These concerns have led many farmers in western countries and irrigated tropical areas to adopt alternative farming practices with the goal of reducing the cost of farm inputs, preserving their resource base and protecting human health. Agriculture in rainfed tropical areas faces a generally poor infrastructure and depends on irregular rains. Agricultural development programmes have, in most cases, been a failure here, as production did not increase. These approaches often led to an erosion of soils, of indigenous knowledge and genetic diversity. These rainfed areas include an important part of the tropics and probably between 1.5 and 2 billion people rely on them for their livelihood. Farming systems here are complex, the environment is diverse and the agricultural production is carried out under conditions of considerable risk.

The above insights have called for a reorientation of science and technology development. Worldwide there is an acceptance that major changes are required to achieve sustainable agricultural development. This acceptance culminated in 1992, when there was considerable attention to the problem and the political will to do something. The United Nations Conference on Environment and Development in Rio de Janeiro, Brazil, concluded that: '... *there is a need to intensify agriculture by diversifying the production systems for maximum efficiency in the utilisation of local resources, while minimising environmental and economic risks.*' The section on biodiversity states: '*Governments [...] should recognise and foster the traditional methods and knowledge of indigenous people and their communities, emphasising the particular role of women, relevant to the conservation of biological diversity and the sustainable use of biological resources, and ensure the opportunity for participation of those groups in economic and commercial benefits derived from the use of such traditional methods and knowledge*'.

Rediscovering cosmovisions. In many tropical environments holistic and spiritual worldviews continue to be of major importance for farmers and rural and urban people, despite efforts of religious organisations, colonial powers, formal science and education to neglect, forbid or ridicule them. Thus, when COMPAS partners started to look into the background, internal logic and deeper meaning of indigenous knowledge, they encountered many holistic worldviews and scientific systems. Juan San Martin, Stefan Rist and Freddy Delgado and their colleagues of AGRUCO working in rural communities in Bolivia, initially tried to promote European concepts of organic farming in the Andean highlands. In working together with rural communities the technicians learned that farmers in their tradition were not only practising organic farming, but that their knowledge was based on a comprehensive philosophy that was the result of a worldview or cosmovision that was much richer than expected. Nature has a sacred meaning and has a reciprocal relationship with humans.

To improve the work of Participatory Technology Development, David Millar of CECIK made a study of the way farmers in Northern Ghana teach, learn and experiment. In studying the dynamics of indigenous knowledge he found that even in the most traditional communities farmers carried out experiments. But, the context of these experiments, the criteria for drawing conclusions and the actors involved in them initially puzzled him. He could only understand the traditional experimental practices once the cosmovision of the rural population and the role of the traditional spiritual leaders was accepted and understood. Spirits and ancestors play a major role in the cosmovision of the farmers in Ghana.

Upawansa of ECO in Sri Lanka and Gowtham Shankar of IDEA in India worked together with rural and tribal people. In the course of time they learned that spiritual practices were part and parcel of farming activities. Many activities such as land preparation, ploughing, pest control and harvesting were accompanied by rituals performed by traditional spiritual leaders. Taking a closer look at these traditional practices revealed here too that these practices were the result of a comprehensive worldview that was held by many farmers, despite their apparent materialistic or commercial behaviour. Also partners from other parts of India, Mexico, Norway and the Netherlands were involved in this initial stage of COMPAS and carried out case studies on the cosmovision of farmers in their areas. Many partners recognised that spirituality is a vital part of farmers' indigenous knowledge. However, the development agencies cannot understand or deal with it because, from the scientific view, it is irrelevant and considered as 'metaphysics'. Various NGOs have tried to deal with culture, but the rural people's own vision, their concept of life or worldview has generally been missed out.

After revisiting the farmers, and by looking at indigenous knowledge as part of a more comprehensive philosophy and worldview, the experience of the COMPAS partners is that once an outsider takes the traditional cosmovision seriously, a wealth of knowledge, vision and wisdom is revealed. Learning from these permits development workers to improve their professional knowledge and interaction with communities. That was the main reason for starting COMPAS: offering a space for a deeper understanding of farmers' visions and enabling a dialogue between the development organisations that shared this concern. The main activities, therefore, were initially to clarify the main concepts relating to indigenous visions on nature and on agriculture; to document farmers' cosmovisions in different cultures and to establish a space for dialogue between organisations and individuals.

Cosmovision was chosen as a key concept. It refers to the way a certain population perceives the world or cosmos. Cosmovision includes assumed relationships between the spiritual world, the natural world and the social world. It describes the roles of supernatural powers, the way natural processes take place and the relationship between mankind and nature. Furthermore, the cosmovision makes explicit the philosophical and scientific premises behind the farmers' intervention in nature. Another key concept was *endogenous development*. This refers to development from within, based on the values and the dynamics of people and the resources available in a particular area. The knowledge, values, resources and choices of the people determine the course and direction of development.

Participating in the first phase of COMPAS (1995-1996) enabled the partner organisations to go back to the farming communities. In dialogue with the farmers, they have tried to understand the farmers' worldview, their notions of cause-effect relation-ships and the relationship between society and nature. They also accepted the traditional and spiritual leaders in the communities as partners in this dialogue. In doing so, they generally discovered that these leaders play an important role in farm-related rituals, as well as in decision making on community matters such as land ownership, use of water resources and agriculture. In this way, they came across a diversity of visions that in many respects are different from the conventional vision on the relationship between mankind and natuture.

Lessons learned from indigenous cosmovisions

In April 1996 a workshop was organised in the Andean mountains of Cochabamba, Bolivia and hosted by AGRUCO, the Bolivian partner in COMPAS. COMPAS partner organisations gathered in a Quechua community called Capellani and lived for one week among the farmers. This not only enabled the experience of nature with its sacred places, it also created a favourable environment for partners to exchange cosmovision experiences. Partners from all over the world were welcomed by the farmers. The visitors took part in rituals to invoke the spirits, and ask blessings for the workshop. Posters were made with drawings, pictures and cultural expressions which helped participants to visualise the different cultures. The workshop showed that in spite of clear differences, there are many similarities amongst holistic perspectives in agriculture. Agricultural practices are subject to an elaborate set of rules and rituals that reconfirm the relationship between nature, mankind and the spiritual world. The different case studies provided material to make a number of generalisations and conclusions:

□ In all countries, major changes in demography, economic and cultural integration, technological innovations, exposure to mass media and degradation of environmental resources have taken place and are leading to an erosion of indigenous cultures, knowledge and cosmovisions.

□ At the same time, despite the South's apparent acceptance of the dominant technologies, beliefs and values, below the surface a persistent core of indigenous culture survives and a wealth of indigenous knowledge on natural resource use still exists. This determines the values and decision making of rural populations.

□ Many cosmovisions of indigenous farming communities are based on a holistic concept: the reality in which farming takes place generally encompasses the natural

First COMPAS-workshop in Capellani, Bolivia (1996).

Many rural people have sophisticated ways of explaining the reality in which they live. For them, a good harvest and good health can only be obtained if farming is practised in harmony with the laws of nature, the regulations of the community, and the rules set by the gods and other spiritual beings. ◆

1-1 Mr. Don Philoris Wijenayaka, the shaman or Kapu Mathattaya, *performs a kem ritual in Sri Lanka.*

In recent years, considerable work has been done to understand the products of indigenous knowledge. Most development activities, however, consider indigenous knowledge to the extent that it can be understood and explained in Western concepts derived from the basic sciences. ◆

1-2 Waru-waru in southern Peru has been redis-covered by scientists who found it a very effective way of water management and one that reduces the damage done to crops by frost.

1-3 Farmers in eastern Burkina Faso share with the community the result of an experiment with a new groundnut variety.

1-4 Bolivian farmers and outsiders discuss the results of potato variety trials.

Rediscovering cosmovisions

Rural people often find that there is a lack of understanding for their indigenous concepts and institutions, especially as far as non-material aspects are concerned. Therefore indigenous communities have learned not to express their worldviews openly to outsiders and some indigenous institutions may have gone underground. ◆

1-5 Mahadevaia Belalam, traditional priest and farmer in Thalli, southern India, offering pooja *to the village deity Basaweshara.*

1-6 COMPAS partner Upawansa shares the Sri Lankan cosmovision with Bolivian farmers in Japo.

A peoples' understanding and description of their spiritual world is frequently rich, diverse and structured. It is experiential and can be based on the teachings of persons with visions, such as spirit mediums or shamans or expressed in classical texts such as the Indian Vedas. ◆

1-7 Cover of a publication of the Asian Agri-History Foundation [Andhra Pradesh, India. 1996]: the original Sanskrit text and its english translation of Surapala's Vrikshayurveda, the science of plant life.

1-8 Sri Brahamanda Swamigal of Coimbatore in his library with ola scripts in ancient languages.

Rediscovering cosmovisions

world, the human world and the spiritual world. Mankind, the spiritual world and nature are often seen as having a reciprocal relationship. If nature is not treated well, it may react by treating the people badly, for example, a plague, a drought or a bad harvest. If the spirits are respected they will ensure good life for living creatures. People, therefore, look upon farming not only as an activity in the natural world, but also as an activity in the spiritual world.

☐ The peoples' understanding and description of the spiritual world is frequently rich, diverse and structured. It is experiential and can be based on teachings of persons with visions, such as spirit mediums or shamans. It can be expressed in classical texts such as the Veda's, or in linguistic or artistic symbols. The spiritual world is seen as containing a creating force and a destructive force. There may be a polarity of good and bad forces, and there are often different spiritual beings such as gods, spirits, and ancestors. These spiritual beings may express themselves in nature and through living creatures.

☐ In many cosmovisions, nature is considered sacred. This finds its expression in concepts like Mother Earth, sacred mountains, rivers, trees and animals. Animals, plants and especially trees are often considered to be linked with the spiritual world and should be treated with respect. The sacred character of nature and the spirituality of the people often lead to the need to conduct rituals during agricultural activities. Some of these relate to spiritual beings or ancestors.

☐ Cosmic influences are frequently dealt with by using astrological information that determines the moments when different agricultural activities can take place. Thus, in many cases, the agricultural calendar and the ritual calendar are linked and they guide social, natural and spiritual activities.

☐ Indigenous communities organise themselves on the basis of their cosmovision. Many indigenous institutions regulate the use of land, water and biological resources as well as the way farmers learn, teach and experiment. Traditional leaders often combine their political powers with spiritual skills and functions.

☐ The way farmers learn and experiment is based on their own concepts, values and criteria.

☐ Many development activities and conventional systems of education and technology development neglect or reject the importance of cosmovision, culture and indigenous knowledge and suggest the superiority of dominant western science. This western scientific system tends to be less holistic and more materialistic than indigenous knowledge systems.

☐ There is no reason to romanticise cosmovisions. It cannot be concluded that indigenous cosmovisions and traditional practices have always been effective in preventing overexploitation of soils, overgrazing, deforestation, pollution of water, erosion or environmental disaster. Nor have they always led to maintaining social stability or equity.

☐ Indigenous knowledge is not always equally spread in the communities, some persons may monopolise and misuse certain knowledge.

☐ For development organisations to be effective, there is a need for them to support endogenous development. This is development that is based on locally available biological and physical resources and the values and knowledge of the local population. This implies a good understanding of the diversity of cultures and the characteristics and dynamics of indigenous knowledge systems and cosmovisions; cooperation with traditional leaders; an appreciation of the potentials and limitations of locally available resources for agriculture, health and nature management, and of their possible role in the local economy; and finally a diversity of approaches to endogenous development that can be applied by local NGOs and governmental organisations for research and development.

The partners agreed that 'development' should be understood from the perspective of native cosmovision that implies the integration of spiritual life in social and material life. Yet there was a clear difference in the way the different partners, acting as development agencies, could work with them. In the traditional communities in Bolivia and Ghana and the tribal areas in India, traditional cosmovisions are still quite intact. Agricultural production involves bio-physical as well as spiritual activities. The agricultural calendar and the ritual calendar coincide. Here, the only way to have a good relationship with the rural population is to understand and appreciate their cosmovision and collaborate with indigenous institutions.

In the rural areas in India, in Sri Lanka and in Peru, the traditional cosmovisions have been subjected to considerable erosion and it is difficult to get a good picture of the rural people's cosmovision. It is a mixture of traditional and modern ideas that may differ from village to village and from year to year. In these areas, it was noticed that in initial discussions with farmers, traditional concepts are frequently not expressed. However, after further probing beyond the surface, many elements of the traditional cosmovisions gradually began to emerge. Farmers are used to the fact that outside agencies do not understand, respect or tolerate traditional practices or cosmovisions. Therefore, they talk with the outsider with empathy, in the language or concepts they think the outsider appreciates. They have learned that outsiders do not appreciate their cosmovision, and thus they do not openly express their own concepts and views. There is reason to assume that in traditional societies, but also in countries where traditional cosmovisions are subject to erosion, traditional cosmovision and spirituality is more widespread and prevalent than assumed by outsiders in general. This means that working with traditional institutions is relevant and requires tact and social skills. In the Netherlands and Norway and to a certain extent also in central Mexico, it seems that traditional cosmovisions and spirituality have almost completely disappeared. There is a widespread discontent about the materialistic way of modern farming and a small number of farmers want to restore agriculture's spiritual vision. In such cases indigenous institutions may no longer exist and, therefore, new institutional allies may have to be sought.

In essence, the partners concluded that a focus on rural peoples' cosmovisions can make it possible to re-connect their work with rural people's indigenous knowledge in its full significance. It is within their cosmovision that farmers interpret (agricultural) development and within this context they define their relationships with outside agencies. Development workers, are now challenged to go beyond validating indigenous technical knowledge. Farmers' concepts of life - and the practices based on them - are a reality to which they must relate. This relationship can only be genuine when respect is given to the unknown concepts and traditional institutions. It also provides an opportunity for mutual learning.

Implications for development agencies

Holistic professionalism. It is obvious that outsiders who want to work with the farming community in order to enhance their endogenous development, need to have the attitudes and skills that allow them to build up a good understanding with traditional leaders. They should not only accept and respect the decision making and community processes particular to these communities, but also be prepared to take part in them. This can mean taking part in rituals, carrying out experiments together with farmers and accepting or seeking cooperation with spiritual leaders such as traditional priests, healers, soothsayers or shamans.

If outsiders want to learn from and with spiritual leaders in a culture that is different from their own, they must find an answer to important questions: How to approach the people so that I can tell my story? And, how can I make myself available to hear theirs? Most people are satisfied when they succeed in contacting the spiritual elders and leave it at that. However, there is another question that might be of much greater importance than 'How do I relate to the elders'. This is: 'How do I personally relate to the spiritual powers these people represent?' Most people will not ask themselves this second question seriously. The spiritual world is not really taken into account and professionals have not learned how to relate to it. Field staff of development agencies should have an open mind and might need to develop a spirituality that is personally their own and which is compatible with that of the community.

Farmers are the main actors in the use of indigenous knowledge. They go through their own learning experiences irrespective of the presence and involvement of outsiders. External agents can function as catalysts to stimulate specific processes of learning and to revalidate indigenous knowledge. They can learn a great deal from the interaction with traditional knowledge and cosmovision. External agents are generally trained by formal education and employed by formal development organisations. Before joining these organisations, they had to undergo 'an initiation' in the formal system of thinking and reasoning. There is a need to be de-schooled and retrained to be open for indigenous wisdoms.

The objectives of development programmes may need to be reformulated in order to allow for activities that can bridge the gap. Rather than a top-down or centrally planned development approach, decentralisation is required to allow for location specific priorities and unexpected events. Such a change of attitude, skill, planning and organisation is not easy to achieve within existing organisations. Church-based NGOs may have problems in accepting the indigenous spirituality of the local people. Universities may have difficulties in accepting the scientific value of spirituality. Government-based research and extension programmes are generally centrally planned and have a technical and commercial focus that is connected to government policies. Endogenous development frequently contradicts their policies. To maximise the impact and to receive inspiration and motivation, it is important for external agents to have strategic alliances with like-minded individuals in other organisations.

To bridge the gap between farmers and outsiders or between indigenous, cosmovision-related knowledge and conventional science, outsiders 'have to learn to walk in two worlds'. Bridging is more of a problem for them than it is for the farmers. As children, villagers have been educated in their own cosmovision and have learned to deal with outside sources of knowledge. Indigenous knowledge is their mainstream and their aim is often to strengthen this mainstream. They will then decide what parts of conventional knowledge to include in their knowledge. Present scientific methods advocate the objectivity and non-involvement of the researcher. Yet, it seems that actor-involvement is a crucial aspect of understanding how a system works. Most cosmovisions advocate involvement of all members of the community in rituals and festivals to foster or restore the balance between mankind, nature and the spiritual world. It is not the quantity of the homogeneous variables that is important as in the case of formal scientific research, but the quality, the attitudes and skills to relate to the spiritual world and to influence the natural world through spiritual practices.

In order to enable a dialogue of complementarity between inside and outside knowledge, several conditions have to be fulfilled. Outsiders and farmers need to work on an attitude of mutual trust. Outsiders should understand the intricacies of the local language, understand the concept of life of farmers as well as their own and accept that the farmers have their own knowledge which is coherent with the context of their reality. As outsiders are not trained for such roles, they have to be prepared to dialogue without competition, without the seeking of dominance over the other. In this way, indigenous and external knowledges will be strengthened and the potentials of the community will be mobilised.

Relating to power and hierarchies.
The issue of power and hierarchies in society is a challenge when dealing with cosmovisions. In dealing with power relations, important points to be observed are: what are the interests of the state in relation to local authorities, of clans in relation to families, and families in relation to individuals, of elite in relation to the marginalised, the collective in relation to the private, the clergy in relation to commoners and male in relation to female? Another issue deals with class and caste differences. How do they affect access to knowledge and to its dynamics within the community?

Supporting endogenous development may have to contain activities to overcome differences caused by class, caste, ethnic, financial, academic or intellectual position. An important point for development workers is to be aware of their own power position in their relation to rural people. How can they overcome differences in status, caste, class and build a relationship based on confidence?

Enhancing traditional resource rights.
How to ensure that activities of development organisations, like documentation of cosmovision, guarantee the local population's property rights to their knowledge and their biological resources? In other words: how is it possible to ensure or strengthen intellectual property rights and avoid piracy of biological resources or of local knowledge? The notion of intellectual property rights (IPR) is an issue in the power relations between North and South. As technology has advanced, legal ownership of knowledge and genetic materials is expressed in farmers' rights, breeders' rights and patent rights. These rights have become issues for life forms such as seeds, genes and plant extracts. The actual plant or organism as such cannot be patented, but an extract or part of the plant (such as a gene) can. There are a few criteria for recognition in a patent: it should be a technological novelty; its generation is not obvious; its application should be useful; and it should be possible to give a detailed description of the technical aspects of the tech-

nique involved in production.

The intensification of the activities of international companies in prospecting the potentials of indigenous biological resources for medical, agricultural and commercially interesting potentials should put COMPAS partners on the alert. The mechanism of patenting can lead to claims for property rights on knowledge developed by indigenous people. An international resolution (FAO 1989) recognised that the owners of germ plasm, through the concept of Farmers' Rights, should be compensated for their contributions to the enhancement of the genetic resources. There are several practical problems in compensating farming communities. The biggest is knowing who to compensate. The notion of ownership rights relating to knowledge or the use of genetic resources is often non-existent in the local communities. Genetic resources and knowledge about the use of biological resources are the products of generations of improvement by indigenous farmers. In addition, farmers rarely have the expertise and power to negotiate a fair exchange.

There are a number of international agreements that regulate intellectual property rights: The International Convention for the Protection of New Plant Varieties (UPOV), The General Agreement on Tariffs and Trade of the World Trade Organisation (GATT/WTO), Convention of Biological Diversity 1992. Also national legislation in the USA such as the Plant Patent Act (PPA) and the Plant Variety Protection Act (PVPA) are important. These regulations are the domain of controversy and negotiation between states, commercial companies, indigenous peoples and farmers' representatives. Participation in these negotiations is generally not a task for NGOs such as COMPAS who work with rural communities. However, for such NGOs another aspect is important: the protection of knowledge and biological resources at community level and strengthening the communities' capacity to negotiate. At the moment there is no way to patent a plant in its wild state. It is not always possible to prove that certain knowledge belongs to a certain population. Once it has been documented and published, it belongs to the public domain and patenting is not possible. But a modification of indigenous knowledge and practices can be patented if the innovator can prove that it is a real innovation. Further, the application of indigenous knowledge in commercial enterprises cannot be prevented. From the above it is clear that the property rights of genetic resources and indigenous technologies is a sensitive issue. The COMPAS partners should be very careful in publishing local information. A code of conduct would, therefore, be good. A beginning of such a code of conduct has been formulated in the last chapter of this book.

Handling conflicting values. Cosmovision can have both positive and negative effects on human rights, women rights, equity, land use and sustainability. Some of the positive effects in the eyes of outside agencies may be practices that enhance equity, democracy, women's rights, conservation of soil or biological resources. Looking at the way traditional societies function, COMPAS partners have observed some positive effects. Sacred groves in Africa create nature reserves; the sacred status of certain trees and animals in India and other Asian countries have helped to protect them; recycling nutrients in organic agriculture enhances sustainability; and the reciprocal relationship with sacred nature in Bolivia and Peru is considered a good basis for land management. In addition the redistribution of wealth through feasts in Peru and Mexico can be considered positive.

However, effects have been observed that can be considered negative. Tribal wars and disputes over land use in Ghana are supported by calling on the intervention of gods or ancestors. The problem of pollution in the River Ganges remains unresolved because the river is considered sacred and should not be touched. Women often do not have the same rights as men, especially when it comes to traditional and spiritual leadership. The cosmovision of conventional Dutch farmers allows a bioindustry that keeps thousands of animals under inhumane conditions. In some countries animals and even humans are used in sacrifices.

It is extremely risky for an outsider to have a negative or positive value judgement when there is no thorough understanding of the total cosmovision. Outsiders can only change negative effects by having a respectful dialogue that leads to awareness about the positive and negative aspects of the cosmovision and spiritual and cultural practices and subsequently to modifying the judgements of rural people. However, through this dialogue and a better understanding of the cosmovision, outsiders may also come to reconsider their value judgements.

Considering gender roles. In most, if not all indigenous societies the positions and roles of men and women in the indigenous institutions are different. Men usually have more positions in the political and spiritual leadership and play a major role in decision making. In many cases there is inequality in decision making and access to natural resources such as land and irrigation water. Women often contribute more to farm labour and receive fewer benefits from farm produce. In many cases women have less access to services such as credit, irrigated land, education and extension. So far gender studies have not given much attention to gender differences in the cosmovision perspective. What is generally little known is the question of how far gender differences in household decision making and economic position are based on worldview and cosmovision. Also the position of women in spiritual institutions and their roles in spiritual practices have not received much attention.

It is likely that women have a different interpretation of the cosmovision of their community and that they may have a different knowledge about the spiritual world, the social world and the natural world. It is important to know this worldview and how it translates into the indigenous knowledge of the men and women, and to anticipate ways and means to use that insight in subsequent activities such as local experiments, farmer to farmer exchange, training and networking and advocacy.

Some of the partners dealt with gender roles in their documentation. In Ghana, there are only a few female soothsayers and there are rules that discriminate against women becoming spiritual leaders. In India, the ritual of Agnihotra as promoted by KPP, can be performed by women as well as by men, but in practice it is generally performed by men. In many countries a dowry system exists which determines and frequently limits the rights of women. There are cases where women who are menstruating are not allowed to plant or harvest or take part in rituals. In many cases women are not allowed to perform functions in spiritual practices, in other cases women have special roles, complementary to those of men. They are confined to their houses to prepare food and offerings for the divine beings and ancestral spirits during most of the major festivals. There are also tribal communities in which women are not allowed to express their feelings. IDEA in India found that women have more knowledge about sacred trees than men. This was used in strategies for environmental protection.

Gender roles are deeply rooted in the belief system of a society. One should treat this subject with care. If a development agency concludes that it is good to try to change the position of the women viz a viz the position of the men, in order to enhance equity, a study should first be made of the cosmovision of the society concerned. A well-intended effort to enhance equity by focusing on the material and social aspects of gender relations, without understanding its spiritual aspect, may easily be misunderstood or misinterpreted as a western idea. Its impact may be very limited. Once gender roles are understood from a cosmovision perspective, the way to deal with them in subsequent activities may become clear. Cooperation with spiritual leaders and an open dialogue may be an important first step.

Learning from health. In India, there is a rich body of classical knowledge described in the Vedas. These are classical texts written in Sanskrit or other languages. Even though there was an initial link between the theories in the Vedas and the way farming is practised, today the link has been lost. This is not the case in health, where there appears to be more openness when it comes to using classical knowledge. Ayurveda, the traditional approach to health, is accepted in India and Sri Lanka by conventional medical science. There are Ayurvedic hospitals and universities. These carry out research, update their own knowledge and also selectively integrate some elements of western medical technology. FRLHT works with local health traditions and Ayurveda.

Why is there no such recognition of indigenous knowledge within agriculture? In agricultural science, hardly any attention has been given to classical texts even though classical texts on animal health and crop production and protection do exist. It would appear that there is an under-utilisation of the stock of knowledge available for testing and development. A recent development is that some Indian researchers are trying to revive this link and they are confident that the future of sustainable agriculture can benefit from the ancient principles described in the Vedas. CIKS, KPP and GREEN Foundation work with classical texts in agriculture. It is hoped that crucial lessons can be learned from the openness in health for the development of sustainable agriculture. It is also possible that the health sector may learn from interactions with agriculture.

Testing and experimenting

Taking indigenous knowledge seriously, means that outsiders should be prepared to learn from it, study it, try to understand it, and in challenging it, look for ways of developing it further. Perhaps this can be done by carrying out field tests based on cosmovision. We realise that the statement 'study', 'understand' and 'test' can easily be interpreted in terms of a positivist scientific approach, as just another, albeit semantically upgraded, anthropological approach, or another way of technology research. Therefore, it is important to state that 'study' and 'understanding' implies in-situ experiencing and learning about reality by and with the indigenous people. COMPAS partners hope to build up a relationship with the rural population and understand the enigmas of their survival, their practices as these relate to nature, their site-specific insights and problems. On this basis, it may be possible to provide the basis for real dialogue, mutual learning and experimentation. In this process, outsiders need to be open to rural experiences that combine the mind, the spirit and the heart of rural people.

Testing indigenous knowledge within a cosmovision perspective may pose problems. In the positivist view, knowledge can only be derived from sensory experience. Metaphysical speculation, subjective or intuitive insight and even purely logical analysis are rejected. Therefore, quantitative methods are used to falsify hypothesis about the real, that is the measurable, the material world. Taking indigenous knowledge seriously means accepting the concepts, the metaphysical explanation, the intuitive insights and also mythical and magical explanations as a basis for a respectful dialogue.

Mambima Pangananda

This does not mean that we should accept everything as true, but we should definitely not categorise this body of knowledge as savage, decadent, pagan or unenlightened. Mambima Pangananda, a Buddhist monk in Sri Lanka said: '*It is always good to test the effectiveness of indigenous practices. Yet this testing should not limit itself to the quantitative measuring of material data. It is important to provide the farmers with the opportunity to reflect on the use of spiritual practices and to test their efficacy. They should be given the chance to draw their own conclusions based on their intuition, their perception of the reality and their values. Persons with a good personal and spiritual development will draw the right conclusions as they are sensitive to the laws of harmony in nature, the balance between different powers and long-term sustainability.*' [Field notes Bertus Haverkort, November 1997].

Respectfully appreciating and, where it occurs, also respectfully disagreeing and subsequently looking for ways to come together by testing and improvement is the key to intercultural dialogue. This intercultural dialogue abstains from hierarchical notions as pertained in 'top-down' and 'bottom-up' approaches. In ethnocentric, eurocentric and exploitative approaches, different levels and thus a distinction between 'top' and 'bottom' is relevant. It is good to express clearly that for COMPAS partners, no inherent superiority exists between cultures or knowledge systems. This does not mean that in certain aspects there cannot be advantages or superiority, but as long as no society has shown a categorical and permanent paradise for all people and other beings in the biosphere, we should be careful to confine ourselves to a particular worldview, paradigm or epistemology.

There may be various goals for experimentation. For example, there are farm-level experiments to test the effectiveness of local practices. After testing, a distinction needs to be made between effective practices and doubtful practices. Practices may be doubtful if they are based on superstition or the abuse of power by spiritual leaders. Testing makes it possible to avoid the pitfall of romantic fantasy and can lead to better technologies. Many COMPAS partners are carrying out activities in this domain. Also the ecological, economic and cultural costs and benefits of traditional practices can be determined through experiments. Moreover, possibilities for upscaling certain local practices in the same cultural or ecological zone can be determined. IDEA wants to extend the activities to other tribal areas in India. This makes prior testing a necessity. Astrology is important in Sri Lanka, the Andes and in biodynamic agriculture. Ancestors play an important role in Africa, Indonesia and in India. Testing and comparing may determine possibilities for the transcultural translation of practices to other ecological, spiritual and social systems.

How can a degree of complementarity be found between local practices and science-based technologies and how can synergetic combinations be developed? Complementarity is not only sought in biological and physical techniques, but spiritual technologies are also included and explicit cooperation may be sought with indigenous institutions. KPP is aiming to achieve a scientific validation of indigenous practices. FRLHT will test the effectiveness of herbs used by local herbalists and Ayurvedic doctors, healers from the Siddha system, Tibetan medicine, the Unani system of medicine, and by western bio-medical scientists.

How can the potential of cosmovision-related farming be released to improve the use of natural resources and agricultural practices? In Zimbabwe, AZTREC carried out a survey on the role of pre-colonial indigenous knowledge in the conservation of natural resources including the rehabilitation of wetlands, gully reclamation, and woodland management. The spirit mediums guide the communities in their choice of location, tree species and ways of implementation and setting up the laws enforced by the chiefs. The effects on erosion, biodiversity, water retaining capacity and a revival of traditional laws, norms and values need to be established. The use of environmental protection and development groups by IDEA is based on the same principle.

Testing may improve the experimental capacities of the local population and of indigenous institutions. The testing of the framework for Empathic Learning and Action (ELA) as is foreseen by CECIK in Ghana is one example of this. KPP in India is an interesting example of a farmers' organisation that organises farmers' experiments independent of the formal research system. AGRUCO in Bolivia will enhance the experimental capacity of rural people and in Sri Lanka efforts will be made to include Buddhist spiritual leaders in the field testing of spiritual technologies such as the use of *mantras* and *yantras* in agriculture. In Zimbabwe, the spirit mediums, village chiefs and others will work together to develop local ways for environmental management.

The results of experiments may help to explain the effectiveness of indigenous technologies by building a theory that combines the material with the spiritual approach. A systematic presentation of the main concepts, principles and methods of verification and its internal logic, in other words, the scientific paradigm of other than western-based sciences is scarce. This is no small task and it is far beyond the capacity and ambition of COMPAS. Yet, where a contribution by COMPAS can be made, it should be tried.

Intercultural dialogue

The first phase of COMPAS ended with the main conclusion that there is a need for a better understanding of cultural diversity, indigenous knowledge systems and cosmovisions. A continued intercultural dialogue between representatives of different knowledge systems, between southern-based cultures and western-based cultures was, therefore, considered important. There are several reasons why an intercultural dialogue on endogenous development and cultural diversity is relevant.

First of all, after several decades of development intervention it is still not widely accepted that a true understanding of local culture is a precondition for good communication between development workers and the local populations. Intercultural exchange between organisations that build up experiences in this domain is important as it will allow for mutual support, the exchange of methods and concepts and may provide support in regional training activities. Dialogues are important in the search for a synergy between cultures and the avoidance of struggle and domination. We can learn from each other, agree with each other, or respectfully disagree. We can feel free to challenge foreign cultures or assumed positive and negative customs. At the same time, we should be prepared to be challenged. Thus, intercultural dialogues can help partners in drawing the right conclusions from their work.

COMPAS partners from Tanzania and Nepal visiting Dutch biodynamic farmers.

An intercultural dialogue is also a precondition for fair international cooperation. In scientific circles worldwide, positivist science and technology are generally regarded as the only valuable approach. An intercultural dialogue can help overcome the implied primacy of western-based approaches and bring partners from different background together in a platform that can search for more holistic paradigms and systems for technology development that build on the traditions of science and wisdom from different cultures both past and present. In this way, the intercultural dialogue can be seen as an effort to overcome the scientific, commercial and political domination that is part of the present processes of globalisation. It can subsequently support processes of regionalisation and endogenous development, the counter-weight to globalisation.

Intercultural dialogues can create space for suppressed and marginalised cultures and prevent reactions such as fundamentalism, violence, silence and inferiority complexes. Such reactions can be observed in many places, and we feel that they can be interpreted as the understandable reaction of people who have experienced ridicule, suppression and injustice. Taking the basic concepts of others seriously and encouraging a dialogue between equal partners is one way of reducing international pressure.

We can only work in this direction if we start with ourselves. This includes holistic development as organisations, as professionals and as individual persons. It requires a process that involves the development of our intellectual, emotional and spiritual capacities; down to earth and with compassion. Communication is essential in any dialogue. This is not just the exchange of words and rational concepts. Communication has to do with exchange of feelings, meanings, interpretations, doubts, dreams, hopes and despairs. Therefore, this we have to combine the exchange of rational language as is being practised in science and development, with the exchange of symbolic expressions as found in dreams, art, love, protest and worship. In other words we need to enhance the use of both parts of our brains. The left side with its rational capacities and the right side with its capacities for emotion, creativity and spirituality. COMPAS partners realise that we cannot rely on and only use rational scientific reasoning. The challenge is to complement this rational reasoning with emotions, with the use of symbols, with awe, with the acknowledgement of our ignorance and our desire to learn.

COMPAS is a an exciting initiative to bring together different insights and experiences. We hope to provide a basis for joint learning and action based on mutual respect and reciprocity. We would like to contribute to a global movement of those seeking new, holistic solutions. In nature, there is an ecological niche for combinations of specific plants and animals: in COMPAS we are looking for complementary and synergistic partnerships of the organisations within COMPAS. We hope to develop a style of working together in which there are no secrets and important information is accessible to those who request it.

This books presents case studies of the partners currently involved in COMPAS. The cosmovisions of different peoples, the roles of indigenous institutions and some specific spiritual practices are described. In the partners' work plans, cooperation with indigenous leaders is being sought and local concepts are included in field experiments. We have no intention to test cosmovisions, but we do want to carry out field experiments within their framework. All partners will gain experiences with enhancing endogenous development. In the last section of the book, there are some reflections on possible methods for carrying out local level experimentation within the perspective of the cosmovision.

COSMOVISIONS IN HEALTH AND AGRICULTURE IN INDIA

Prabha Mahale and Hay Sorée

There are two major cosmovision traditions in India. The 'Great Tradition', which represents the Sanskrit or classical tradition described in the Vedas and the 'Folk Tradition', representing popular Hindu tradition and the tradition of the tribal peoples. The rituals and practices of the Hindu tradition, both classical and folk, is a continuing history. They both represent a living cult that is deeply ingrained in social, religious and cultural traditions, both in the orthodox and the popular sense. Generally they converge, occasionally they diverge. There is also the indigenous system of the original inhabitants, the tribal people who have another history and knowledge base.

The Vedas are a collection of hymns, *mantras* and prayers written in Sanskrit, that communicate the sacred knowledge of the cosmic order visioned by the *rishis* or seers. Thus, *rishis* are exalted beings who manifest divine wisdom and include the visionary sages of ancient India to whom the Vedas were intuitively revealed. A *rishi* or seer has a perfectly subjective and objective mind, because it is free from the six prejudices: lust, anger, greed, intoxication, delusion, jealousy. Because of this he is able to make full use of the five senses and his mental capacity. The senses naturally move out to see, hear, touch, smell and taste, whereas the mind can move outward with the senses and move inward and experience an inner non-sensory world. For a seer, the way to understanding nature is to become one with it. Vedas cover diverse branches of learning, such as astrology, medicine, law, economics, agriculture and government. The Vedic tradition is the root of cosmology and knowledge for the vast majority of Indians, Hindus and Jains. In India's traditional thought, there is no distinction between the sacred and the profane: everything is sacred. The essence of this tradition is to live in partnership with, rather than to exploit nature. The most complete holistic perspective of the universe was evolved by Vedic culture about 6000 to 8000 years ago, and has been sustained by Indian civilisation throughout the millennia. The Vedas have played a major role in bringing together mankind and faith in nature and have guided man through Rta, the cosmic morality. The cosmology, the total worldview, had the relationship between the Human and Nature as its core. All life is believed to be interrelated and interwoven. According to Hindu mythology Brahma is the creator, Vishnu the conserver and Shiva the destroyer of the universe.

The basic theory of cosmovision is known as Siddhanta. The Sarva Tantra Siddhantas cut across all areas of traditional Indian science. The following elements are important for health and agriculture:
- Understanding the composition of all material, animate as well as inanimate, in terms of the five primordial elements, the Pancha Mahabhutas: *vayu* (air), *jala* (water), *prithvi* (earth), *agni* (fire) and *akasha* (ether, sky or space).
- Understanding the properties and action of human beings, animals and plants, in

33

terms of three biological factors: *vaata*, *pitta* and *kapha*. *Vaata*: slender, light and averse to sunlight. *Pitta*: medium size, abundancy and fond of sunlight. *Kapha*: stout and bulky, abundant flowers and fruits, housing many creepers.
- Understanding the fundamental existential principles of *dravya* (matter), *guna* (quality) and *karma* (action).

All living beings are born and evolve from the five Mahabhutas earth, water, fire, air and space. In death they go back to them. The Mahabhutas are the primary natural resources essential for all life forms. Through myths and rituals mankind is ever reminded of his duty (*dharma*) to sustain these elements.

Gods and Goddesses from the Great Tradition

The cosmovision of ancient India can be illustrated by a quotation from an Ayurvedic text: '*The basic aim of the concepts and fundamental principles of all the sciences is to establish happiness in all living beings. But a correct and thorough knowledge of the basic principles of the universe and the (human) body leads to the correct path to happiness, while deceptive knowledge leads to the wrong path.*'

The cosmic forces were personified in the form of various gods and goddesses, whose influence or failure to maintain cosmic morality was considered the main cause of an imbalance in health. They play a role in healing and thus it was the responsibility of every individual to observe the prescribed rules. Most of the Vedic rituals are institutionalised in Hindu Dharma and are a part of the day-to-day life of the people. Varuna is the God of waters and all the rivers. Ganga, Yamuna, Saraswati and Kaveri are deities of the vast water cosmogony. No ceremony of birth, death or marriage is complete without the ritual purification of water. Vegetative and animal life forms such as lotus, coconut, mango, snake, tiger and cow are central in Hindu myths. Cows, which are a symbolical representation of the earth, have traditionally been objects of great worship and reverence. The killing of the cow is listed as one of the major sins in Hinduism: '*All that kill, eat and permit the slaughter of the cow will rot in hell for as many years as there were hairs on the body of the cow.*' [Artha Shastra of Kautilya].

The teachings in ancient scripts such as the Upanishads, emphasise the importance of trees. Reverence for trees is expressed in the various tree worships related to the Ficus species. Trees have also been linked with penance, education and religious activities. Prithvi, the Mother Earth, is the divine mother who sustains plant and animal life. She is perceived to be a powerful Goddess for the world as a whole. The cosmos itself is seen as a great being, a cosmic organism. Different parts of the world are identified as parts of her body. The earth is called her loins, the oceans her bowels, the mountains her bones, the rivers her veins, the trees her body hair, the Sun and Moon her eyes and the lower worlds her hips, legs and feet. *Vayu* (air) in the Vedic pantheon is associated with Indra, the God of the firmament, the personified atmosphere. He is *prana*, the pure breath of life. Finally the sun, the great ball of fire is the energiser, the life giver.

The Goddesses too illustrate important ideas in Hindu philosophy. For example, Prakriti denotes physical reality. It is nature in all its complexity, orderliness and intensity. The Goddess Sri, or Lakshmi, is today one of the most popular and widely venerated deities. In early Vedic literature she was invoked to bring prosperity and abundance. In the Sri-Sukta (an appendix to the Rig Veda dating from pre-Buddhist times) she is described as moist in cow dung. Clearly, Sri is associated with growth and the fecundity of moist, rich soil. Villagers, particularly women, worship Sri in the form of cow dung on certain occasions. Lakshmi is associated with the lotus (symbolising vegetative growth) and the elephant (whose power brings fertilising rains). Together they represent the blossoming of life. Durga is one of the most formidable Goddesses of the Hindu Pantheon. Her primary mythological function is to combat the demons who threaten the stability of the cosmos.

Deities of villagers

In the villages, these goddesses are worshipped by upper caste Hindus. The 'Great Gods and Goddesses', though acknowledged to be in charge of distant, cosmic rhythms, are only of limited interest to most village people. Every village has its own village deities. They often share the names or epithets of deities in the Sanskrit pantheon but they do not necessarily have any similarity with 'the Great Tradition' Goddesses. Unlike the 'Great Gods' whose worship is often restricted to certain castes, these deities are the goddesses of the whole village. All over southern India, these village deities are almost exclusively female. They are not usually represented by anthropomorphic images but by uncarved natural stones, trees or small shrines. The village and its immediate surroundings, therefore, represent for the villagers a more or less complete cosmos. The central divine power impinging on, or underlying this cosmos is the vil-

Munishewara, positioned in farmers field. Farmers believe that their fields are protected by this deity.

lage goddess. The extent to which order and fertility dominate the village cosmos is determined by the relationship between the goddess and the villagers. Their relationship is localised and aims not so much at individual welfare but at securing the welfare of the village as a whole. In return for their worship, the goddess ensures that the villagers have good crops, timely rain, fertility and protection from diseases, spirits and untimely death.

The entire ritual complex built around agricultural operations involves protective, prohibitive and promotional values. For example, the villagers in Pachara (West Bengal) propitiate Lakshmi and Manasa a number of times each year. While Manasa is worshipped generally during the cultivation season, Lakshmi is worshipped during pre-harvest or post-harvest periods. Furthermore, many of the rituals performed for living human are also being extended to Mother Earth. The Adi Perukku agricultural festival is celebrated in Tamil Nadu. On the eighteenth day of the Tamil month of Adi (between mid-July and mid-August) this festival hails the arrival of the monsoon. Reverence is paid to the River Goddess and farmers are encouraged to sow seeds. An important aspect of this festival is the sowing of nine varieties of seeds: wheat, paddy, *toordal*, green gram, groundnut, bean, sesame, black gram and horse gram (Navadanya) in a pot. It is called Mulaipari and is a forerunner of the present germination test.

Apart from the festivals of the village goddess, there are a number of ritual performances that directly or indirectly relate to the various stages of managing agriculture production and consumption. These are observed by individual families and by particular caste communities. These rituals vary from region to region and from community to community. But the ultimate goal is the same: the worship of deities, implements, bullocks, and spirits in the fields to ensure a good harvest.

Classical Indian Agricultural Science

In the Vedas, particularly Rig Veda and Atharva Veda a great deal of attention is paid to agriculture, implements, cattle and other animals, and the rains and harvests. Ancient texts relating to agriculture are the Vrkshayurveda (Ayurveda of plants) and the Krshisastra (science of agriculture) and Mrgayurveda (animal science). They provide a wealth of knowledge on such subjects as the collection and selection of seeds, germination, seed treatment, soil testing and preparation, methods of cultivating plants, pest control and crop protection, the rearing of cows and the care of draught cattle, for example.

Outbreaks of disease and pest attacks on plants are viewed as being based on the same principles as the epidemics that affect the human and animal species. The basic understanding is that epidemics occur because of imbalances in the ecosystem. One of the major causes of such inbalance is human error or living in the wrong way which leads to an incorrect intervention in natural processes. The main protection against epidemics is a thorough knowledge of nature which makes it possible to avoid causing serious imbalances in the ecosystem.

Vrkshayurveda - the science of plant health - was accorded a prime position in the history of agriculture in India. The three major ancient texts that provide the basis for Vrkshayurveda were compiled by Varahamihira, Chavundarya and Sarangadhara.

Western science focuses on the analysis of matter, time and space. In Ayurveda, understanding of the world is not limited to the five senses because these only convey reality in its grossest manifestations. To reach good understanding the mind must be freed from the six prejudices of lust, anger, greed, intoxication, delusion and jealousy. ◆

2-1 Sri Brahamanda Swamigal at his temple with Hindu goddesses. He is a healer with expertise in alchemy, pharmacology and spirituality.

Except for scattered documentation by anthropologists and ethno-botanists, no systematic documentation and assessment has been made of Indian local health traditions. The Foundation for Revitalisation of Local Health Traditions (FRLHT) aims to make a fairly comprehensive documentation of the living health traditions in southern India. It found that the application of herbs is usually combined with mantras, meditation or other forms of spiritual healing. ◆

2-2, 2-3 Meeting of local healers, Ayurvedic and bio-medical doctors to discuss the effectiveness of herbs according to each of their own experiences and theories.

2-4 Barefoot doctor of the Centre for Indigenous Medicine and Health Care in Coimbatore in a botanical garden. The herbs that cure snake bites are grown in an environment that includes a sacred grove.

Living health traditions and Ayurveda

Ayurvedic prescriptions may look promising, but in some cases the knowledge is only textual and needs to be field tested. The Centre for Indian Knowledge Systems (CIKS) intends to make a description of traditional farming practices. There is a reciprocity between the moral behaviour of a community and the care of spiritual beings for a healthy crop and good harvest. ◆

2-5, 2-6 Staff of CIKS dialogue with farmers of the Women's Welfare and Development Association: why are rains failing to fall, soils less fertile and crops increasingly attacked by pests and diseases? Farmers have opted for natural farming, the collection of indigenous seed varieties and natural pest control.

2-7 Meeting farmers at CIKS' experimental plot with traditional rice varieties.

CIKS documented the relevance of astrology for agriculture in the first phase of COMPAS. Sowing dates, but also other farm operations are determined by moon phases and astrological constellations. ◆

2-8 Farmers in Chengalpet district share the astrological calendar, on which the Panchangam (a farmers' almanac) is based, with staff of CIKS.

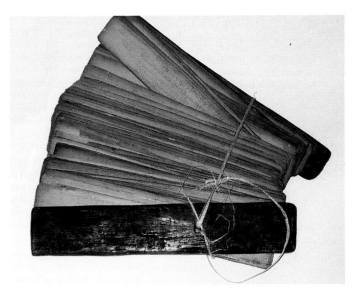

2-9 Ola scripts on palm leaves is the way knowledge has been recorded since ancient times. There are scripts for future prediction, agriculture, folk poetry and some may be 2000 years old.

Living health traditions and Ayurveda

These texts provide indications of an integrated approach to controlling crop pests and diseases through soil, seed, plant and environmental treatment. These different methods have several characteristics in common and can be used to launch a multi-pronged attack on pests and diseases; to improve plant health and increase resistance; to enrich the soil with nutrients and increase useful microbial activity, and finally to ensure a broad spectrum effect on pests and diseases.

Folk knowledge

Farmers' perception and understanding of ecology, crops, land, labour, livestock and agricultural implements has a profound bearing on the strategy they adopt in their day-to-day agricultural operations. Their ideas about climate, crops, the optimum climatic conditions required for cultivation and beliefs relating to crops and fruits are the results of the knowledge they received from their ancestors and their own long experiences in the natural laboratory of their fields. Farmers have the ability to identify various types of seeds and seedlings and this is often based on morphological characteristics. By looking at the nature of the flowers on a plant, an estimation of the yield can be made.

The technically useful items of indigenous agricultural practices are often documented without reference to the symbolic or ritual matrix in which they occur. It is a debatable point whether, by looking at these practices from a mere scientific and rational perspective does not devalue them. Despite the fact that farmers have been subject to external influences, they still continue to experiment and make innovations, sometimes adapting external knowledge to indigenous knowledge and sometimes revitalising their own knowledge.

There are indigenous institutions that regulate community administration, decision-making, elements of farming and the rites and rituals related to cosmovison. In the villages, religious functionaries such as Brahmin priests, and in the tribal communities of the Eastern Ghats traditional functionaries such as the Naiks and Disaris play an important role (see Gowtham Shankar in this publication). The functioning and strength of the institutions that kept the environment protected, depends on how successfully future citizens are introduced to the heritage that generates respect for these institutions. Knowledge systems cannot grow if traditional cultural anchors are not properly located. Culture provides a 'grammar', while technology provides new words. The meaning of life can only be discovered if both are blended together.

Synthesis of local and external knowledge

There is a close-knit relationship between cosmovision, or the way the relation between mankind and nature is viewed in the widest sense, and agricultural practices. Folklore, proverbs and songs are the vehicles of this process. This, however, does not necessarily mean that farmers always have a thorough insight into what they are doing or why. Traditional knowledge often seems to imply that rites, practices and customs are continued out of sheer habit or out of an undefined fear of the effects of bad influences if they are abolished. This could mean a slide towards superstition, which means there is a kind of mysterious belief. A constant review of any knowledge

41

system is essential for further development.

The advantage of modern science is that it is analytical and tries to arrive at general truths by discovering the parts of the whole. The advantage of indigenous knowledge is that it is location specific, holistic and relates to diversity. The disadvantage of modern agricultural science is that it deals with parts only and is obsessed with the general. But knowledge systems are not static, they are dynamic. They change. Farmers and researchers experiment.

Is a synthesis of local and external knowledge, or traditional and western-based knowledge possible? In our opinion a synthesis is not possible if traditional knowledge is viewed as an 'alternative' to external knowledge. Both have their own bases and both have their limitations. Influencing each other would involve changing fixed paradigms and the creation of new ones, which no doubt would bring about major improvements and changes and involve a readiness to question one's own system and the courage to enter into a dialogue with the other. There are quite a number of indications that there is at least a growing interest in indigenous knowledge systems and their integration into conventional science. COMPAS is one example.

REVITALISING LOCAL HEALTH TRADITIONS

Darshan Shankar

Non-western knowledge systems have so-far failed to establish their right to endogenous development. Their epistemology, or 'theory of the method of knowing', lies unexplored outside of their traditional worlds. Their universal attributes lie unrecognised. It may be alarming to learn that they are, in fact, being rapidly eroded and face destruction due to the political and economic effects of a globalisation process that has its intellectual and philosophical roots in mainstream western cultures. This destructive process began with colonisation and continues today.

Many people have a fairly mature understanding of the nature of indigenous traditions in various applied fields such as agriculture, health, food, nutrition, veterinary care, the performing arts, architecture, metallurgy and also in theoretical fields like mathematics, linguistics, astronomy and logic. For them it is clear that the marginalisation of the indigenous cultures during the last two centuries has essentially been due to oppressive political and economic processes rather than their alleged disfunctioning, inherent inadequacy or irrelevance. Indigenous traditions continue to be alive, are evolving, changing and adapting, as does life itself. Only dead things do not evolve and do not change. A living tradition evolves.

The concern for revitalisation of indigenous cultures must, therefore, not be viewed as a concern for reviving the past. It should rather be seen as a serious attempt to broaden and deepen the scope, quality and content of modern civilisation. Unfortunately, this process has, over the last two centuries, become wedged in a narrow monocultural track and resulted in world-wide cultural uniformity. This cultural uniformity is extremely dangerous for the survival and evolution of civilisations. Uniformity narrows down the alternatives and options available to the peoples of the world and their capacity to cope with the present and the future.

All cultures have a potential stake in supporting the revitalisation of the worlds' many indigenous cultures because world civilisation as a whole stands to gain from a state of 'flourishing' cultural diversity. The key to appreciating 'cultural plurality' is an acceptance of the fact that cultures are guided by their own epistemologies. It seems to be necessary for our understanding of the epistemological differences between knowledge systems to appreciate the historical fact that various knowledge systems have had their genesis and basic evolution in specific cultural spaces in time. Modern science, as we know it today is, in this context, definitely, a product of European culture, with its Greek antecedents. Science, despite its universal attributes, (which are also a feature of non-western knowledge systems), is a cultural product. Science, therefore, cannot be viewed, except from an Eurocentric viewpoint, as the only universal epistemology or way of studying and knowing nature.

In the medical field, particularly in the countries of Asia, Africa and Latin America, there are living medical knowledge systems that are indigenous and have been evolving in these societies for generations. These medical cultures have epistemological foundations that are very different from western bio-medicine. There is an urgent social reason for promoting these indigenous cultures because, in the context of public health, the 'modern' health system, based on western bio-medicine, is unable to meet the basic health needs of the majority of the people. In the Indian context for example, the modern medicine health system is only able to offer primary health care to about 30% of the rural population. Revitalisation of indigenous health cultures based on locally available biological resources and local knowledge, has the potential to provide health security to millions.

Epistemology of Ayurveda

To gain an understanding of indigenous non-western health systems, such as Ayurveda in India, it is necessary to be familiar with its epistemological traditions. The Ayurvedic worldview is based on the Sankhya school in which the manifest world (*vyakt*) emerges from the unmanifest world (*avyakt*). One flows into the other. Observer and observed are one, just as subject and object are one. The way to understand nature is, therefore, to become one with it. This is achieved by the five senses and the mind. Sight, hearing, touch, taste and smell make it possible to decipher the world around while the mind moves both inwards and outwards. A mind free of prejudice is both perfectly objective and subjective. This is perfect oneness with nature and is termed as the mental state of Brahma from which Ayurvedic Shastra was pro-pounded.

In the western tradition, the scientific temper is limited to the use of analytical disciplines. But in Ayurveda it means freeing the mind of the six prejudices of *kam* (lust), *krodh* (anger), *lobh* (greed), *madh* (intoxication), *moh* (delusion) and *matsar* (jealousy). The western tradition restricts itself to the concepts of matter, time and space. But Ayurveda is based on the recognition of fundamental *padarthas* or existential principles such as *dravya* (existential principles of 9 types), *guna* (qualities of 41 types), *karma* (action of 5 types), *samanya* (generic), *vishesha* (distinctiveness) and *samvya* (inseparability).

Dravya encompasses nine categories of being from *atma* (soul) to *prithvi* (earth), which means it covers a range from subtle to gross, from consciousness to solid earth. They are simultaneously different and linked, one devolving into the other. Consciousness devolves into the mind, because the mind's qualities like innumerability (*sankhya*), magnitude (*parimana)*, uniqueness (*prthaktva*), conjunction (*samyoga*), disjunction (*vibhaga*), nearness (*paratva*), remoteness (*aparatva*), impression (*samskara)* causal relations (*yukti)* and repetitive expression (*abhyasa*), create the notions of time and space on the mental plane. The mind further devolves into the five states of matter: *akasha* (space like), *vayu* (wind like), *agni* (fire like), *ap* (water like) and *prithvi* (solid earth like). An understanding of the world is not limited to the five senses which only convey reality in its grossest manifestation. Complete awareness only comes from a level of perception at which the observer both reaches out and looks within, thereby establishing a subjective flow which connects the observer and the observed.

FUNDAMENTAL EXISTENTIAL PRINCIPLES (PADARTHAS) OF AYURVEDA

DRAVYA: existential entities	GUNA: qualities		KARMA: action
	VISHESHA: distincitiveness	SAMANYA: generic	
Prithvi: solid state	Ghanda - *smell*	Sita - *cold / temperature* Guru - *heavy / weight* Snigdha - *oil, moist / emolliency* Manda - *slow, dull / intensity* Sthira - *stable / fluidity* Sandra - *solid / viscosity* Kathina - *hard / rigidity* Khara - *rough / texture* Sthula - *gross / density*	
Ap: fluid state	Rasa - *taste*	Sita, Guru, Drava - *liquid / viscosity* Snigdha, Manda, Sara - *mobile / fluidity* Mrdu - *soft / rigidity* Sthula, Picchila – *sticky / adhesion*	Spatial temporal displacements applicable to all the first five *dravyas*. Utksepana - *upward movement*
Tejas: transforming state	Rupa - *form*	Usna - *hot / temperature* Laghu - *light / weight* Ruksa - *dry / emolliency* Tiksna – *intense / intensity* Cala - *mobility* Suksma - *subtle / density*	Apaksepana - *downward movement* Akuncana - *centripetal* Prasarana - *centrifugal*
Vayu: state of motion	Sparsa - *touch*	Sita, Laghu, Ruksa, Suksma, Cala Visada - *clear / adhesion* Khara	Gamana -*multidirectional*
Akasha: state of pervasiveness	Sabda - *sound*	Sita Laghu Slaksna - *smooth / texture* Visada	
Kala: time			
Dik: directions	Sankya – *enumerability*, Parimana - *magnitude* Prthakvta – *uniqueness*, Samyoga - *conjunction* Vibhaga – *disjunction*, Paratva - *nearness* Aparatva – *remoteness*, Samskara - *impression* Yukti - *causal relations*, Abhyasa - *repetitive expression*		
Mana: mind			
Atma: consciousness	Iccha – *inclination*, Dvesa - *aversion* Sukha – *pleasure*, Dukha - *pain* Prayatna – *aversion*, Buddhi - *intelligence*		

The western tradition in theoretical sciences is founded in the logic of Aristotle and the deductive and axiomatic method of theory construction as evidenced in Euclid's elements, which have been further refined in the course of work in logic and mathematics during the last hundred years. The Ayurvedic *shastras* (sciences), by contrast, are based on the Indian school of logic called the Nyaya-Vaisesika Darsanas. Western logic deals with a study of 'propositions', especially their 'logical form' as abstracted from their 'content' or 'matter'. It deals with 'general conditions of valid inference'. Whereas one of the main characteristics of the Indian 'formal' logic is that it is not logic at all, in the sense that it is generally understood. Indian logic refuses to totally detach form from content. It takes great care to exclude terms that have no referential content, from logical discourse.

The difficulty in making comparisons between epistemologies can be illustrated when one attempts to compare their internal parameters. For example, there is no conceptual correlation available between the three basic physiologic parameters of Ayurveda: *kaph*, *vat* and *pith* and western physiologic parameters like hormones, blood pressure, lipid levels and blood. Quantitative parameters in Ayurveda are not given the same importance as they are in western traditions. Although measurement and quantification are used, they differ in form from western systems of knowledge. Most measurements in the traditional medical science are made using units 'normalised' to an individual. That is, while assessing a person's height or the length of his or her limbs, the measurement is expressed in units of *anguli*, the dimension of a finger of the individual concerned rather than in an arbitrary standard external to the individual, such as the international meter. Such normalised units exist not only for measurement of length but also for volume and time. Qualitative parameters and natural language have been given far more importance and support the rigour and accuracy of Indian tradition.

Ayurveda has three standards for validation. *Aptoupdesh* is knowledge regarding principles and practice through the statements of authorities that are in the most evolved state of mind, free of the six prejudices which colour perception. The others are *anuman* which stands for inference and *pratyaksha* which is direct perception, including intuitive cognition. *Aptoupdesh* is seen as a departure from the western tradition in that it is a recognition of the various levels of perception which may be acquired by a learned practitioner of the science. Ayurveda defines health as *swasthya* or to be established in one's self. This is when the body, mind, tissues, metabolism, awareness, and senses are all in equilibrium.

Living health traditions

Moving from epistemology to social reality in the practical world, the traditional health culture of India functions through two streams. One is the 'codified' stream, which includes well-developed systems of medicine like Ayurveda, Siddha, Unani and Tibetan. The other is the ethnic community-based and ecosystems-rooted 'folk' stream, which is referred to in this article as 'local health traditions'.

The 'codified' stream consists of medical knowledge with sophisticated theoretical foundations expressed in thousands of regional manuscripts covering treatises on all branches of medicine and surgery. Today in India there are around 600,000 licensed practitioners of the codified stream and they manage a whole range of common, chronic and sometimes even acute conditions as well as preventive and promotive healthcare.

The Siddha systems is one of the oldest systems of medicine in India. The term 'siddha' means achievement. Siddha literature is in Tamil and the system is practiced in the Tamil-speaking areas of India. It is a system largely therapeutic in nature and specialises in pharmacy: the use of mercury and sulphur as well as other minerals and metals alongside plant and animal parts. It was practiced by *siddhars*, a Shaivite sect who aimed at maintaining perfect health in order to achieve *siddhi* or heavenly bliss. The *siddhars* were saintly figures who achieved results in medicine through the practice of yoga. The root belief of Siddha is an intimate link between human beings and their environment. Man is seen as a microcosm constructed of all the elements found in nature. Just as the earth is susceptible to natural calamities and epidemics, the human organs are influenced by food, poison, the seasons and mental stress. The principles and doctrines of this system are similar to Ayurveda. The difference is more linguistic than doctrinal. The diagnosis of disease involves identifying its causes. This is done by examining the pulse, urine and eyes, studying abnormal sounds, the colour of the body and tongue and, above all, the status of *agni* (the digestive system of the body). Treatment is not oriented simply towards disease, but has to take into account the patient, his or her environment, meteorological conditions, age, sex, race, habits, mental frame, habitat, diet, appetite, physical condition and physiological constitution. Thus, treatment has to be normalised to the individual to reduce the chances of error.

The Unani system of medicine, with its origin in Greece, has a long and impressive record in India. It was introduced by the Arabs and Persians around the eleventh century. Today, India is one of the main areas where it is practised. It also has the largest Unani educational, research and health care institutions. In India, the Unani system closely interacts with Ayurvedic and other local medical systems. After subjecting it to its own tests, the Unani system absorbed what was best in the native medical systems. Special attention was paid to the medicinal herbs found in India. Several books on the therapeutic qualities of these herbs were written by Arab physicians. Gradually, a number of schools were set up to impart instruction in the system of medicine, and hospitals and dispensaries were established in the large cities where the sick could be treated.

Tibetan medicine in India is, in a sense, a regional manifestation of Ayurveda in the Trans-Himalayan regions and in parts of Northeastern India. The Tibetan people through long and serious effort absorbed and assimilated Ayurveda via Buddhism and built upon its principles and resources. Tibetan medicine has its origins largely in Ayurveda, in the local traditions of people living in the ecosystems in the Trans-Himalayas and to a lesser extent in Chinese medicine. Tibetan medical literature is available today in the Tibetan language. Its main teaching institutions are in Dharamshala (Himachal Pradesh), but clinics have been established in several parts of the country.

Local health traditions which are linked to village based ecosystems are purely empirical. They represent a highly decentralised system of knowledge of health care which is community specific, local resource dependent and hence region specific.

Millions of households, practise home remedies and possess knowledge of local foods and nutrition. More than 600,000 traditional birth attendants manage over 90% of rural deliveries. Thousands of herbal healers, monks, bone-setters, tribal doctors and a host of specialists in various areas attend to a variety of rural health problems. All these local, community-based actors are the carriers of local health traditions. According to the Anthropological Survey of India, there are 4,639 ethnic communities in India and each ethnic community has its own health culture.

Except for scattered documentation by anthropologists and ethno-botanists of the ethno-medical traditions of many tribal, and fewer non-tribal communities in different regions, no systematic documentation and assessment has been made of the entire spectrum of India's local health traditions. Thus the knowledge and resource base of this stream has not been fully documented or understood.

COMPAS: Documentation and formal assessment of local health practices

Our proposal within the COMPAS programme on the revitalisation of indigenous health cultures is a limited approach based on a strategic plan to promote the revitalisation of local health traditions in pockets of southern India. The approach has to be limited because today the resources, human and financial are limited, but we expect that this limited approach and modest investment into the revitalisation program, will give rise to further investments and more comprehensive approaches from others inspired by the results of this work.

The proposal has two objectives. Today the existence of local health traditions is not recognised in official health policy as it has not been systematically documented and presented in an objective manner. Therefore, the first objective is to conduct a fairly comprehensive documentation of living health traditions in five locations in southern India, from Kerala to Maharashtra. Each of these five locations is an administrative unit or Taluka and may have a population of some hundred thousand and a geographical size of about 100 square kilometres. The documentation would be done in a participatory way involving the local carriers of the health traditions as well as representatives of local community organisations. The documentation could cover the knowledge base, resource base and the sociological features of the health tradition. Also the worldview of the tradition, the range of its functional medical knowledge, the type of health conditions which it manages and the epistemology of the tradition will be included. Plants, animals and minerals used in the local tradition and the purposes for which these resources are used will be recorded. Also cultural aspects like the season in which particular herbs and plants are collected, favourable astrological times for collection and the rituals associated with collection will be indicated. Sociological information will also be assembled: the ethnic background of the carriers, the mode of transmission of knowledge from one generation to the other, the extent to which the tradition is accepted socially and the size of the tradition. The purpose of the documentation is to build up a fairly detailed picture of the functioning of local health traditions in southern India. The report could be used to inform policy makers and community health organisations about the nature, scope, relevance and culture of local health traditions.

The second objective of the FRLHT-COMPAS proposal is to select some limited aspects of the traditions and subject them to a rapid assessment. The local communities will be involved through self-assessment, but also medical professionals from the codified medical traditions (Ayurveda, Siddha, Unani and Tibetan) and from the western bio-medicine system. The first level of assessment in this project will be carried out by the community itself on the basis of its own experiences. Other local professionals will be consulted to provide a formal confirmation of evidence about the validity of the tradition, to contribute suggestions for improvement or to provide suggestions to other medical traditions about the wider applications of local health traditions. In this exercise only those aspects of local health traditions will be selected that are amenable to rapid assessment. For example, in southern Indian villages a plant, known as *Phyllanthus Niruri* is used in the treatment of hepatitis. Local experience is positive. There is also formal confirmation from the experiences of codified medical systems like Ayurveda, Unani, Siddha and the Tibetan system of medicine about the efficacy of this plant for hepatitis. There is also corroborative evidence from western bio-medical workers, based on the work of a Nobel prize winner Baruch Bloomberg, about the efficacy of *Phyllanthus Niruri* in combating the hepatitis virus. This rapid assessment exercise would initiate a meeting between local health practitioners and other medical professionals to discuss specific medical practices such as the example of *Phyllanthus Niruri* and hepatitis mentioned above. The objective of doing this rapid assessment is to reinforce the community's confidence in its own traditional knowledge, and, where necessary to supplement local practices if they are seen as being incomplete. In some cases practices may even be discouraged. The reports of this rapid assessment workshop would be published and widely distributed to local, regional, national and international organisations. The methodology for carrying out this rapid assessment systematically would be refined during the course of project implementation.

One very important approach that will be used for the documentation and rapid assessment is the participatory approach. It is not the outsiders who are going to document or assess. It will be a team of insiders and outsiders, working in a relationship of mutual respect. The outcome of this work is expected to create an awareness of the relevance of local health traditions in the community and amongst public health institutions and policy makers. The awareness created will hopefully not only relate to the medical relevance of the traditions, but also to their cultural uniqueness and appropriateness.

Bio-prospecting

What happens when one culture pirates the intellectual and biological resources of another culture? Issues like bio-prospecting will also be addressed. An attempt will be made to broaden the debate on bio-prospecting and explore its implications from an endogenous development perspective. Bio-prospecting initiatives are often controversial because of a general failure to acknowledge sources of materials and information and the frequent absence of equitable benefit sharing agreements. Practical problems arise when seeking to identify the 'rightful' owners of indigenous knowledge in attempting to reward the holders of indigenous knowledge, and the owners of the resources. Most often traditional knowledge about a particular resource is widely distributed beyond the community concerned. This can be seen in the case of the plant *Phyllanthus Niruri* whose use for treatment of infectious hepatitis is known throughout South India. The Fox Chase Research Centre in the USA has filed a patent claim on a hepatitis drug developed from this plant. The practical problem in such cases is how to share benefits with a widely distributed owner constituency. One possible solution is to place the benefits in a common community biodiversity fund. This proposal raises further issues, such as who would control the biodiversity fund and how to ensure it would be applied equitably.

A central issue missed in these debates is the serious cultural erosion that takes place when one culture prospects the intellectual and biological resources of another. In effect, science and its carriers (the western knowledge system) are prospecting traditional knowledge system of non-western origin. One culture is considered advanced and the other viewed as essentially backward. One culture is assumed to be the creator of new and superior knowledge and products; the other the donor of raw material and imperfect, crude and unrefined knowledge which is only good enough to provide 'leads'. Economic and political power lies within the prospecting culture, whereas the donor culture belongs to a society that is politically and economically weak. Given the domination of the prospecting culture, intellectual property rights (IPRs) are only defined in terms of the parameters of one cultural tradition. The parameters, categories and concepts of diverse ethnic knowledge systems cannot be applied to claim IPRs under the rules of the currently expanding global market. When bioprospecting is viewed as a cross-cultural transaction, the question that arises is: Can any financial 'compensation' and reward to the donor ethnic culture for permitting itself to be prospected upon - and thus demeaning its own integrity, identity and the value of its heritage - make up for the erosion and loss of its own culture? Whereas mutually respectful exchanges across cultures are to be welcomed, the political, sociological and epistemological foundations for such cross-cultural dialogue have not yet been established, and bioprospecting represents a typical example of a one-sided transaction.

The message from the COMPAS-FRLHT project would be that southern countries should act politically to change the terms of cross-cultural discourse, especially in the context of 'globalisation'. The challenge within globalisation today is threefold. Firstly, to involve multi-cultural exchange of diverse cultural goods and services. Secondly, to promote substantial economic investments in the diverse social cultures of the world, so that they can retain their integrity and creativity. And finally, to promote a modern world order where cultural diversity can flourish and global unity is founded not on a 'uniformity' of economic, political, social and technological forms, but on a sharing of diversity.

Globalisation based on such a sharing would perhaps reduce the size of the world market and encourage local markets and even non-market (nature-culture) relations to re-manifest themselves amongst the ecosystem peoples of the world.

AYURVEDA,

COSMOVISION AND TRADITIONAL AGRICULTURE

K.M. Shyam Sundar and A.V. Balasubramanian

How does one comprehend the cosmovision of a people? There could be two approaches. One is to look at the living traditions and reality of present day rural people and the other to look at what has been written and recorded. Indian tradition offers a structure for viewing and understanding by describing two 'levels' of understanding and knowledge. They are Sastriya Parampara, the classical or textual tradition and Lok Parampara, the folk or oral tradition. It is important to realise that these two traditions are not 'opposed' to each other or in conflict: their relationship is symbiotic. They are in fact the two ends of a continuum. At one end we may have scholars well versed in Sanskrit texts and at the other end we may have a totally unschooled, village bone setter. Various intermediate positions are possible. One can be a practioner of Ayurveda who only knows the local language and has never learned Sanskrit. He or she may be familiar with Tamil texts of Ayurveda or the translations. But it is also possible that there is a local healer who may know and quote bits and pieces of texts or verses in a local dialect even though he may be unlettered.

As already indicated by Mahale and Sorée in this publication, in the Vedas, a great deal of attention is paid to agriculture, implements, cattle, rains and harvests. Texts of Vrkshayurveda or the 'Science of plants' give a detailed description of different aspects of plant life. They encompass areas such as collection, selection and storage of seeds; germination, sowing, various techniques of plant propagation, grafting, nursing and irrigation; testing and classification of soil and selection of soils suitable for various plants or types of plants; manuring; pest and disease management, preventive and promotive care to build up disease resistance and to cultivate healthy plants; nomenclature, taxonomy, description and classification to suit varied purposes; favourable and unfavourable meteorological conditions for various plants, and the use of plants as indicators of weather, water and minerals.

How does this cosmovision relate to the reality of our people's lives? In what way can it contribute to comprehend, enhance and enrich traditional knowledge? These are matters to be addressed during our participation in COMPAS.

Field location for action research

The Kancheepuram district is the northern most district in the state of Tamil Nadu. It is located in the northeastern corner of the state. Its borders are the Bay of Bengal on the eastern side, Pondicherry and Villupuram districts on the southern side and Andhra Pradesh on the northern side. Its western borders are the two neighbouring districts of Tamil Nadu, namely Vellore district and Thiruvannamalai district. Historically,

Kancheepuram has formed a part of Thondaimadalam which is one of the major sub-divisions of the ancient Tamil country. Kancheepuram, one of the bigger towns of the district, has been famous since Puranic times as a major centre of pilgrimage and learning. Even today Kancheepuram has important religious shrines and leaders associated with Saivite, Vaishnavite, Buddhist and Jain religions. At various points in history it has been the capital of the Chola and the Pallava kingdoms.

The district has an area of about 7,800 square kilometres and is sub-divided into twelve *taluks*. The field area selected for our participation in COMPAS falls in the Chengalpet *taluk*. Chengalpet *taluk* has a population of about 400,000 people distributed in 340 villages. Eighty-five percent of its population are rural dwellers. Forest land in Kancheepuram district accounts for only 5.5% of the area - one of the lowest proportions of any district in the State and well below the State average of 16.6%. Agriculture is the major occupation and about 72% of the total cultivated area is under food crops. A special feature of this district is the extensive network of irrigation pond-like tanks, known locally as *erys*. There are over 2,000 of these tanks. About half of the total irrigated land in the district is under tank irrigation. There are two major seasons for the paddy crop. The first season is when paddy is sown between the months of June and September. The sowing operation peaks in the Tamil month of Adi (mid-July to mid-August). This crop is harvested between December to February. The second season starts with sowing in the period December to January. The crop is harvested between March and June.

The People. The majority of the people in the area are Naikers or Vaniyars. Their main occupation is agriculture and cattle rearing. There is a small population of Irula Tribe people who are well known for their snake catching and hunting abilities. They are also known as Villiyans, which means 'the people with a bow'. They have a very good knowledge of ethnobotany and are well-versed in the medicinal plants found in the area, especially those that are useful in treating poisonous bites. The socio-economic status of these people is very much below the poverty line and they continue to live the life of nomads. The recent ban on snake catching has further exacerbated their position and they now earn their livelihood by labouring on construction sites and the fields. The majority of Naikers live in thatched mud houses. The thatch is usually made up of dry palm leaves over which hay is spread. The leaf is generally of bamboo or the stem of the Casuarina tree tied together with coir threads or any plant fibres.

Both men and women are involved in agricultural practices. Certain types of work such as ploughing are exclusively done by men and works such as sowing and transplanting is normally carried out by women. The young and old also take part in agricultural operations such as harvesting and threshing. The farmers are small land holders and work between a half to one acre. The major crop produced is paddy. Other crops such as groundnut, sugar cane, maize and sesame are also grown. Tamarind is a major agricultural produce and women harvest its seeds. Young children climb the tamarind tree during the season in March and April when the tamarind ripens and shake the branches to make the fruits fall. The fruits are collected and dried in the sun for two or three days after which the outer covering and the seed is removed and stored.

Beliefs and Myths. Before starting any agricultural operation the farmers worship Lord Vignesha, the Lord who removes obstacles. For this they prepare two conical structures made of clay and these are placed at the eastern edge of the field. They burn an oil lamp, offer incense and burn camphor to propitiate the Lord. They also break a coconut symbolising the cracking of all obstacles in the path of agricultural operations. They first start ploughing in the Sani Moolai, or the Saturn corner of the field. They believe that Saturn is the Lord of all agricultural operations and protects the crop from pest attack. The farmers consult the village astrologer or the priest who gives them the exact timing for sowing the seeds. At times the priest goes into a trance or becomes possessed by gods or spirits when deciding the time for sowing. He also describes the reasons for the failures of any of the previous crops and suggests remedial measures, which usually consists of sacrifices and rituals. Before sowing, the gods of the eight corners of the field are worshipped and in most cases a young lamb or fowl is sacrificed. It is believed that, by offering the blood of these animals, the evil spirits are satisfied and will not hinder agricultural practices.

Festivals. The month of Adi, which falls between mid-July and mid-August, is the period of the festivals for the goddesses Mariamman or the Mother Goddess. During this period, especially on Fridays, the temples of the Mother Goddess are well decorated and people offer worship by boiling *ragi* (finger millet) in fresh earthen pots in front of the temples. The fuel used is dried cow dung cakes. The farming community seek the blessings of the Mother Goddess to bring forth timely rains and protect their crops and households. The youngsters of the villages take a dip in the temple tank or sprinkle water from the tank using neem leaves and go through the village streets in procession, carrying decorated pots and accompanied by drums and other musical instruments. Some of them draw small chariots hooked to the skin on their back. Some pierce their cheeks and tongue with a spear (*vel*). In many temples they also indulge in fire-walking in the evening. The festivities in each temple last for three to four days and usually no villager goes beyond the boundary of the village on these days. The beginning of the festivities is marked by hoisting the flag post in front of the temple.

The Pongal festival is celebrated in the Tamil month of Thai (January). This is a harvest festival and lasts for five days. The first day is called Boghi. In the early hours of the morning, people burn their old clothes and other household material. The second day is called Pongal. In the morning people boil freshly harvested rice in earthen pots and when the boiled rice froths up and comes out of the pot all the family members shout "Pongal, O Pongal, Pongal, O Pongal", facing the Sun God. The cooked rice is shown to the Sun God and farmers thank the Sun God for a good harvest. Agricultural implements such as ploughs and tillers are decorated with turmeric and saffron and worshipped. The third day is the Mattu Pongal and it is then that the cattle, who plays an important role in all agricultural activities, are worshipped. They are bathed and their foreheads are smeared with turmeric and saffron, their horns are painted with bright colours and decorated with flowers. The cattle are fed with cooked rice and sugar cane. In the evening they are tied to decorated and painted carts and people go around the village singing and dancing. The fourth day is Kanum Pongal during which the villagers go to their relatives and take lunch together: it is a social time.

Today, although the lives of these farmers has been subject to great change, traditional outlooks and ways of doing things still seem to form the basic substratum of their thinking. Modern practices and inputs appear as a deposit that has been spread over them. For example, traditional seeds may have made way for High Yielding Hybrid varieties, but sowing still begins on an 'auspicious day'. The tractor may have replaced the bullock cart, but ploughing is still commenced at the Sani Moolai. Modern tools are the object of worship alongside the plough and sickle during Pongal.

How important is the analysis of these practices by farmers and the understanding

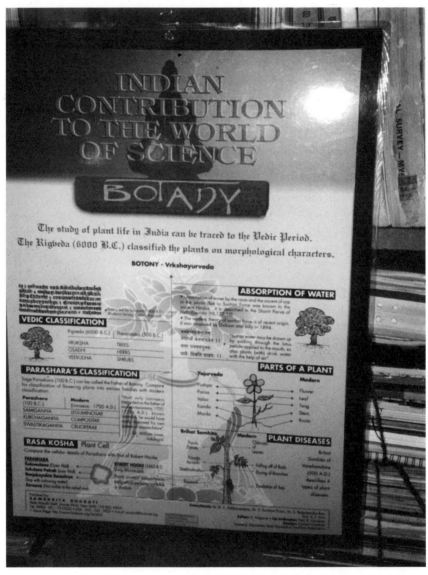

Vrksayurveda is considered the Indian contribution to the world of science.

of their rationale in Ayurvedic terms? From our experience we feel that it has a very important purpose. Such an analysis permits us to extend the scope and application of farmers' practices. For example, once we know that a treatment is effective because it regulates *vaatha* (one of the three bio-logical factors, in this case slender, light and averse to sunlight), it opens up the possibility of modifying, extending or enhancing the efficacy of treatment by trying out other substances or regimens that can regulate *vaatha*. We can also evolve treatments based on the properties of materials known from Vrkshayurveda to new conditions or situations not described or dealt with by Vrkshayurveda. We feel that such an analysis can play a crucial role in the analysis of farmers' practices, validating them and also in enriching and expanding their scope.

Traditional technologies still meet the basic needs of a large section of the Indian population. They are extensively present and are adapted to various circumstances and locations. The cosmovision underlying these technologies and practices is in its very essence, sustainable and eco-friendly. However, it is not generally understood that there is an underlying methodology which is rigorous and dynamic which offers a way of understanding, assessing, strengthening and revitalising traditional knowledge. This we feel is of primary importance and any effort to survey, document, assess or evaluate traditional practices and technologies must have a basis in the fundamental theories and principles underlying these traditions.

Our approach in COMPAS

In the context of COMPAS, CIKS will implement several activities. We will engage in the documentation of the knowledge of plants from the various sources or Vrksayurveda: manuscripts, books and other literature. So far only a fraction of the manuscripts on this subject have been published. There is no proper inventory of manuscripts and books in this area. We will include literature on medicine, food, fodder, agricultural implements, musical instruments, consecration of gardens, grain storage, soul types, conservation practices and biodiversity. A lot of prescriptions of Vrksayurveda appear to be very promising, but they need to be worked on at many levels. In some cases the knowledge is only textual and it needs to be field tested. We need to understand the conditions for their use and standardise them.

We will also make a description of traditional practices in farming such as rituals, ceremonies, the sacrifice of animals, folklore, folk songs, timing for planting, favourable and unfavourable constellations, the locations of star groups (asterism), the concept of boundary spirits and *mantras*. The traditional institutions in the Panchayat system, like village leadership, but also those responsible for water management and market systems will be documented. Through the conventions of farmers in different areas, we will document existing farming practices.

We will conduct introductory workshops to dialogue with farmers on the concepts of Vrksayurveda. During these workshops and other interactions with the farming community, we will discuss and carry out participatory field experiments on the concepts of Vrksayurveda on growth enhancement, disease resistance, pest control, seed storage, and manuring, especially in the region's rice ecosystem. Experiments will be carried out to test, demonstrate, improve or modify the techniques based on local resources and conditions. By means of farmer-to-farmer workshops, we will discuss existing farming techniques, methods to improve them with Vrksayurveda, and find ways to counter obstacles.

Our project staff will be trained and will gain experience in participatory research with a cosmovision perspective. We hope to share our experiences through networking with local institutions and local NGOs and we also intend to organise training programmes for the field staff of other development organisations.

One of the local collaborating institutions is Gramiya Seva Nilayam (GSN), a grass root organisation involved in non-formal education which for the last seven years has focused on organic farming. GSN also has a programme in the conservation and cultivation of traditional grain varieties. The other main organisation is Women's Welfare Development Association (WWDA). This voluntary organisation is involved in training and deals with such subjects as natural farming, the collection of indigenous seed varieties, natural pest control. They also help set up small village level libraries to make books on natural farming available to the villagers. They have had a favourable response to their work. They believe that farming should be based on nature and be economically and environmentally viable if farmers are to achieve self-sustainability.

In India, the Cow is greatly respected, worshipped and is believed to be an abode of all Gods, particularly Laxmi, the goddess of wealth. Its products are invaluable: manure for energy and soil fertility, traction for transport and farm labour, urine, milk. Its products are used for food, medicine, to activate soil and protect plants from disease. ◆

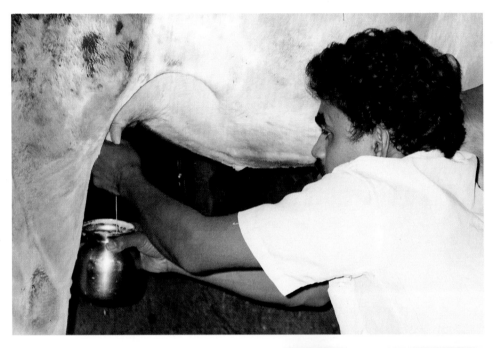

3-1, 3-2 On mr. Purushothama Rao's organic farm, butter milk is added to the compost to enhance bacteriological activities.

3-3 An important ritual for mr. Rao is Agnihotra, *performed twice a day exactly at sunrise and sunset. Cow dung cakes are put to fire, cow ghee and unbroken rice are offered in an inverted copper vessel of pyramid shape whilst a mantra is chanted two times. It is said to heal the environment, encourage healthy crops, animal and human development and elevate human energy.*

3-4 Krishi Prayoga Pariwara (KPP) is a group of 5000 farmers who join forces to experiment with traditional techniques. The activities are to document indigenous knowledge and indigenous institutions, collect and study ancient literature, implement farm experiments, organise sharing workshops and mass meetings, and educate youth.

Traditional agriculture generally ensures food security and preserves genetic diversity. Women play a major role in the selection, conservation and propagation of seeds at the farm level. ◆

3-5 Celebrating seed diversity. Seeds in the Indian tradition are a symbol of life and represent the divinity in life. GREEN Foundation conserves rare traditional varieties of seeds in small and marginal farmer lands.

3-6 During weeding time, women folk perform Karibanta, *a ritual request for a safeguard against pest. A branch of the pacchadi tree is chopped and fixed in crop fields.*

For rural people, the all pervasive influence of good and evil supernatural forces is a reality. Prithvi, Mother Earth is perceived as a powerful goddess sustaining plants. Through ceremonies and festivals, women and the reproduction of biodiversity are linked. ◆

3-7 Women carrying Arathi *during village fair.*

3-8 Arathi *contains sweet balls, is decorated with flowers and neem leaves. Coconut, fruits and betel leaves are also offered.*

Experimenting farmers and biodiversity

KRISHI PRAYOGA PARIWARA:

A GROUP OF EXPERIMENTING FARMERS

Upendra Shenoy, Purushothama Rao, V. K. Aruna Kumara and A. S. Anand

Krishi Prayoga Pariwara (KPP), as the name indicates, is a fraternity of ecological farmers, committed to time-tested principles and human values. KPP was initiated by a farmer peer group in a remote village in Malnad area of Karnataka, India, during early 1990s. The peer group concentrated on the increasing problems facing agriculture. Hence, its major activity is to find solutions to these problems and to collect the information and guidance from experts they need. The group grew informally under the able leadership of Mr. Purushothama Rao, a progressive organic farmer from Thirthahalli on the western Ghats in Karnataka.

In September 1996, this group of experimenting farmers became a registered body. Its vision and objective was broadened. Looking to the future, KPP is trying to develop a practical vision and strategy for alternative development that is not simply economic but which promotes moral, ethical, spiritual and ecological values. There are three broad objectives. Firstly, KPP promotes Swadeshi Swavalambi and Savayava Krishi (SSSK), which means 'indigenous, self-reliant and organic or eco-friendly agriculture, which is thoroughly sustainable'. Secondly, revitalising local health traditions, in which safe, non-chemicalized agriculture and diversified ecosystems play an important role. In other words, the group wishes to promote an ecofriendly life style. Thirdly, KPP provides development education to young people empowering them to play a constructive, non-political, non-partisan, development-oriented leadership role something which is a very important need in India's rural areas.

KPP activities have reached thirteen of Karnataka twenty districts. It intends to work with the COMPAS programme on a specific mini-agroclimatic zone comprising of 7 *talukas*. These are Thirthahalli, Sagara, Soraba, Hosanagara *talukas* of Shimoga district and Sirsi, Siddapura, Yellapura *talukas* of Uttara Kannada district. The major crops grown in this zone are paddy (*Oryza sativa*), arecanut (*Areca catecha*), coconut (*Cocos nucifera)*, banana (*Musa spp)*, pepper (*Piper nigrum)*, cardamum and so on. The area receives an average rainfall of 1800-2000 mm. It has red, lateritic soil that is shallow and which has a low nutritional status.

The area is represented by different ethnic communities including the Havyaka Brahmins, Idigas, Deevas, Siddis, Bovis and Vokkaligas. Each community has its own tradition, values and norms. However, they do not differ much as far as crop cultivation is concerned. They observe all the major Hindu festivals such as Dasherra, Deepavali, Bhoomi Hunnime, Vinayaka Chaturthi and Ugadi.

The Indian society, like societies elsewhere in the world, was formed and developed by agriculture. A lively debate can be generated around the question whether agriculture developed human societies or it is the other way round. Historically speaking, it is agriculture that has sustained human civilisation and culture. In almost all ancient societies, agriculture fostered a life style quite distinct from those found in earlier nomadic societies. Politics, law, social organisation, economics and commerce, religion and culture were all inspired and shaped by agriculture over the millennia.

In India agriculture clearly dates back at least 4,000 to 5,000 years. It was consistently progressive and had developed its own scientific and technological wisdom. It was well advanced in comparison with the status of agriculture in other countries right up to the eighteenth century. A number of Indian texts provide us with information that verifies this. The notes and records scrupulously kept by the British administrators in India during the eighteenth and nineteenth century testifies to the sophistication of Indian agriculture. A report written in 1802 notes: *'In passing through Rampore territory [Rampur in present Uttar Pradesh], we could not fail to notice the high state of cultivation which it had attained. If a comparison be made between it and our own, it is painful to think that the balance of advantage is clearly in favour of the former.'*

Luke Scrafton, a member of Robert Clives Council, in his book 'Reflections of the Government of Hindustan' (1770) had this to say: *'The manufactures, commerce and agriculture flourished exceedingly [...] nor is there a part of the world where arts and agriculture have been more cultivated of which the vast, plenty and variety of manufactures and the merchants were proofs sufficient.'*

But the situation has vastly changed in recent decades. Traditional agriculture has increasingly given way to modern (westernised, mechanised and chemicalised) agriculture, the norms and methods of which are antithetical to our traditions and values, both cultural and agricultural. A tremendous and sustained propaganda through the media, the policies of the government and agricultural universities, and pressure from the national and international economies - have all contributed to the present situation. Hence, time honoured principles and policies have dwindled and are on the verge of extinction. No critical evaluation of this situation has been attempted, although it is clear that the losses in terms of civilisation and ecology are immense.

Indian agricultural experiences - the old and the new - when compared reveal certain interesting contra-distinctions. The pre-modern practices were never eco-destructive like many of their modern equivalents are. The old system was based on a spiritual view of nature whilst the contemporary view is totally mechanist and materialist. Cooperation with natural forces was the hall-mark of the traditional agriculture. Modern agriculture wants to compel, direct and dominate them. Devotion was the human feeling that used to link humans to the nature. Now this has been replaced by an insatiable greed. As a result, far-sightedness has given way to short- sightedness and chaos is gradually taking over. Because of this basic change, it is little wonder that mankind's tensions both within himself, his surroundings and the animate and inanimate creatures that share his world, have increased. These tensions lead to the signs and symptoms of wholesale degradation in the quality, the motives and the management of human life. Clearly this is a situation that requires urgent attention.

Obviously, we will have to understand and revive the old mental framework and the life pattern that evolved from it. This is difficult because the values involved have become dim and discordant. They will have to be reasserted and assiduously promoted. This should not and will not mean that all that the modern mind has created should be rejected. It means, however, that those values and methods that come into conflict with the sustaining ideals of the earlier regime and those that promote disharmony at any level should be disgarded. Also, new ideals and practices that clarify and qualitatively improve the traditional ones should be adopted as being benifical.

For this, we will have to overcome the vain glorious myth that all that is modern is good and has to be accepted and all that is old is worthless and should be disgarded. We should remember that the world works on the basis of *satya*, an Indian word for reality, which is constantly being revealed to human beings all the time. For example, it was discovered a long time ago that one plus one is two and no new invention has altered this mathematical truth. The higher and newer mathematics can never be true if they reject this basic but ancient truth revealed to man thousands of years ago. Similar analogies apply to the cultural and agricultural realms as well.

India's cosmovision and Indian agriculture

India's approach to life in all its dimensions before the present era was based on the Vedic cosmogony which was totally spiritual. Vedas have preached that the world as a creation has a divine substratum. All kinds of created things, animate and inanimate, are mutual and bound together by divine love. The universe has a purpose and all that has been created has to work to fulfil this purpose. Humans have a particular responsibility because they have been endowed with unique powers of discrimination, knowledge and wisdom and should understand these principles of creation, apply them to all the situations and live a happy and contented life. All human activities whether political, economic or artistic should be kept within the bounds of the moral law.

It is interesting to note that Vedas see agriculture as the most honourable of human activities. Agriculture is the one area where humans and the divine cooperate with each other to sustain creation and work out a plan for the improvisation of the created ones. A hymn in Rig Veda says: *'Don't play the game of dice. Get involved in agriculture. You will acquire plenty and prosperity. This will bring you fame and recognition. Thereby you lead a happy life.'* The Bhagavad Githa, another honoured script based on Vedas says: *'If you respect and cooperate with the Gods, they will also respect and cooperate with you. By this mutual respect and cooperation, you derive prosperity - both material and spiritual.'*

There are two famous *suktas* (collections of hymns) in the Vedas. One is Bhoomi Sukta or Earth hymns, the other is Anna Sukta or Food hymns. In the Bhoomi Sukta, the Mother Earth has been extolled and the human relationship with her has been equated to that of a son with his mother. She expects that we worship her devoutly because she is the bestower of our food, water and air, the three essential requisites for our life. The Anna Sukta equates food to God. It gives us vigour and valour and through it we achieve our ends - both material and spiritual. Thus, throughout Indian thought, not only the earth, but also her constituents and products, the mountains, rivers, lakes, oceans, forests, birds and animals have been deitified and worshipped. The earth was seen as a sacred environment and people were warned to live frugally, to adopt a 'live and let live' attitude, not only with other humans but with all life, mobile and immobile. Because humans had the power of a superior mind, they had to behave like trustees and care for the wealth called nature.

The saints and sages, the wisest and well-informed leaders in Indian social life, devised a balanced way of life that was rich both materially and spiritually. Agriculture and agro-based activities of various types had been designed well within the framework of moral law that also ensured ecological sustainability. Human needs could be met but human greeds were condemned. A culture based on these ideas had evolved a society that was as ideal as possible. This culture used rituals, rites, festivals, arts and architectural designs as tools to achieve specific ends. Nature's evolutionary process and human development policies never were intended to be adversaries. The modern world has taken a very different road, one that is sure to prove suicidal in the ultimate analysis. Krishi Prayoga Pariwara wants to recreate this ancient vision and update the techniques and strategies towards that end by utilising both traditional and modern experiences and wisdom.

Cow - the sacred animal

In India, the Cow is greatly respected, worshipped and is believed to be the abode of all the Gods, particularly of Laxmi, the goddess of Wealth. In farmers' families, food is offered to the Cow every morning before the days activities begin. The Cow is an inseparable part of the farming community. It is worshipped in particular during the festival of lights, Deepavali, in the month of October, when the Cow is referred to as 'Kamadhenu' which means an animal with the power to provide whatever the person may asks for. All the products of Cow are used in agriculture. Sage Parashara (500 AD) notes on the importance of using of animal and cow manure in agriculture. Vrkshayurveda of Chavundaraya (1025 AD) deals with agriculture and botany, and describes the use of milk in changing the flowercolour and in enhancing fruit taste. Panchagavya, a mixture of five Cow products namely, dung, urine, milk, curd and ghee is used in human medicine, to activate soil and to protect plants from diseases.

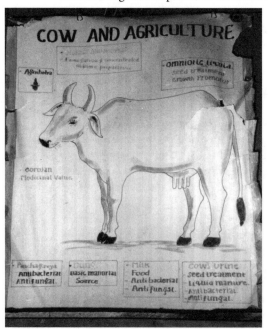

Poster used extensively by Krishi Prayoga Pariwara (KPP)

KPP experimented with the ideas furnished in the above texts and got good results by using the products of the Cow. KPP advocates the use of Cow's urine (both pregnant and non-pregnant), Cow's dung, milk, curd, buttermilk, ghee and whey in agriculture. It advocates the use of amniotic fluid as a growth promoter and flower inducer. Cow's urine is used as a foliar spray, the dung is used in composting, milk used as an antiviral spray, curd and buttermilk in increasing the microbial activity in soil, ghee in seed treatment and so on.

Strategy

At present, Krishi Prayoga Pariwara, along with the Sanjeevana agro-research foundation, is developing an agricultural research wing, a health research and service wing and a development education wing. All these are to be housed in a 15 acre plot at Jambane, Sagar Taluk, in Karnataka.

The agricultural research wing has already started IKST (Indigenous Knowledge Systems and Technologies) in agriculture which are the mainstays of alternative development plans. The process will be hastened through active cooperation with the COMPAS programme. KPP has developed a questionnaire that gives ample opportunity for the collectors to acquire information from the villagers. Already a quantity of ancient and medieval agricultural literature on agriculture and related subjects has been collected and this search will continue. KPP is designing on-farm research and the scientific validation of ancient practices obtained from these texts. Proven technologies will be disseminated through seminars, workshops and training. KPP has already organised more than 300 seminars and workshops with this goal in mind over the past 4-5 years. More than 25,000 farmers have participated in these programmes. They have influenced quite a large number of farmers to move into organic farming. KPP keeps the public informed about activities through periodic newsletters and books published in the local language, Kannada. KPP has developed linkages with many like-minded individuals and institutions within the state, in the country and also abroad to help strengthen its efforts to develop a holistic agricultural philosophy and safe techniques.

A health research wing has started documenting local health traditions. It has plans to develop mini-herbal gardens for research purposes in various parts of the operational area and is planning to provide services to the sick through a combination of herbal medicines, naturopathy, yoga, magnetotherapy and meditation.

The development education wing has plans to selectively draw young people from different village units organised by KPP and train them. The training will be aimed at promoting the right philosophy for development, an eco-friendly life style and at promoting desirable socio-economic changes based on the time-tested and positive cultural values of our country. Training would be non-formal and participatory.

Research approach

Goals. An experiment could have various goals as far as Indigenous Knowledge Systems and Technologies (IKST) are concerned. Testing can be carried out to measure the efficacy of technology in solving the present problem; or to understand cause and effect relationships and the values, inter-relationships or interdependencies of the different factors involved in the IKST. We can also embark on experimentation to make the necessary modifications and improvements to IKST which will make it more suitable for present problems and local conditions. Finally, we can validate a technology from the ecological, environmental, economic or psychological point of view.

Entering the community.

Usually KPP is approached by the members or representatives of the village who are in search of help. The KPP team then studies the group or the village or a bench mark survey will be conducted to provide all the information needed with regards to infrastructures, cropping pattern, status, cropping methods, socio-economic conditions, community or village institutions, festivals, rituals, beliefs, customs, norms and values. The participatory method of study encompasses both the individual and the community. However, there are also occasions when KPP enters a community to help certain individuals who have been in contact with them or it may follow-up previous dialogues and visits. KPP staff may also be involved in fairs, festivals, ceremonies and rituals organised by the community. KPP itself may also organise meetings to which community leaders, healers, physicians, priests, spiritualists or other members of community are invited. The process of entering the community is often guided by the intuitive, spiritual and logical capacities of KPP team.

Prerequisites for experimentation.

The KPP team has to consider certain prerequisites for engaging in an experimentation process with farmers or villages. First, the local institutions, tradition, culture, beliefs, customs, values and norms have to be respected and understood. It is also important to consider the resource position of the community and the location specific customs that must be respected when dealing with the community. If there are any differences in gender, generation or similar differences, these have to be considered together with the communities' time frame. Both KPP and the community has to be ready to accept the results of experiments.

Identifying a problem.

KPP gives priority to the present day problems faced by the community. Hence there is a need to identify these problems and the village survey is an important basis for this. The KPP team together with community leaders and other essential members of the community will analyse the survey and identify the problems. Then the problems are categorised on priorities set by the community, after a dialogue with the KPP team. Now the task is to tackle or solve the problem. First, the roots of the problem will be studied and understood. This information will then be related to the appropriate IKST of the community and an experiment will be conducted to test the efficacy of the appropriate IKST selected to solve the problem. Besides this, KPP also conducts experiments to achieve the goals stated earlier.

How to select parameters?

KPP selects the parameters on the basis of the goals appropriate for the experiments. The parameters will be selected from technical, spiritual, social and economic perspectives. The selection process is supported by the literature, whether contemporary or ancient, dialogue with the experts, scholars, scientists, spiritual leaders, spiritual mediums and the experiences of individuals. Apart from these, parameters are also selected through intuitive, heuristic and/or a logical approach.

Design of experiments.

Experiments are designed with the help of community representatives, scientists and the KPP team. The process considers conventional design and also traditional or local designs if any. Based on the goals and the parameters selected, spiritualists, healers, priests, astrologers will be involved in designing the experiment.

Monitoring. The experimental process will be observed and recorded by the persons involved in the experiment. The necessary training, inputs, logistics, information, guidance and suggestions will be provided by the KPP team.

Analysis and evaluation. The observations are analysed and evaluated with respect to the parameters set for the experiment. There will be a statistical analysis, a logical analysis and an analysis which takes account of the cosmovision aspects of the IKST. Economic analysis of the whole process will also be conducted to assess the economic feasibility of the IKST. The results will then be discussed in relation to the objectives of the experiment and a bias free conclusion will be reached. This approach can be summarised by the following diagram.

CHART OF KPP'S PROGRAMMA

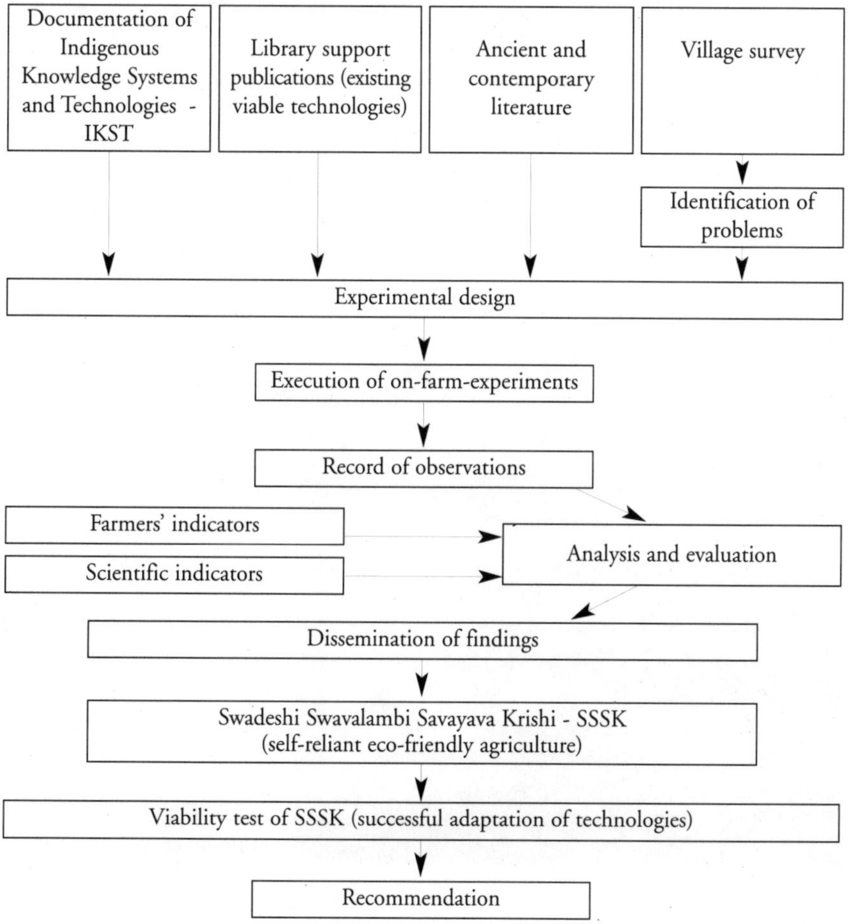

Positive conclusions that proves that IKST is efficient and able to solve a particular problem will then be disseminated to community members or other interested individuals. Major acceptance and successful adaptations by the community will motivate KPP to formulate necessary recommendations in its SSSK philosophy and package.

Achievements

KPP advocates Swadeshi Swavalambi and Savayava Krishi (SSSK). The philosophy is to use local resources efficiently and optimally to achieve self reliance and eco-friendly agricultural production. The package includes Agnihotra, a cow and a *tulasi* (*Basil - Oscimum sanctum*). Agnihotra symbolises the individuals' contribution to the environment and society. It is a ritual performed twice daily exactly at sunrise and sunset. It requires a copper or mud vessel of pyramid shape, a cow dung cake, cow ghee, and unbroken rice, *akshatha*. Cow dung cakes arranged inside the vessel are lightened. *Akshatha* smeared with cow ghee will be offered to *agni* (fire) during two *mantras* which are chanted exactly at sunrise and sunset. The process is said to heal the environment. It purifies the atmosphere and devours noxious gasses. It also elevates human energy. The ritual is meant to be a reciprocation for what the individual has received from the environment. Agnihotra has multiple uses in agriculture. Quite a few pests and diseases are said to be unable to thrive in this atmosphere. Agnihotra ash is used in seed treatment. Ash water is applied to the field. In addition, the ash is used in curing several human diseases and ailments. Agnihotra is a simple ritual that can be done by any person: there is no barrier of caste, sex, religion or age.

KPP, prima facie, advocates cow-based agriculture. One cow is necessary to manure an acre. There are different methods of preparing manure such as Nadep composting, the Pradeep Tapas method of composting, the Krishi Nivasa methods and Vermi-composting. A farmer can assess field conditions and crop requirements and can opt for any of these methods. The manure enriches soil health and fertility. Composts, full of helpful microbes, provide necessary nutrients to the plants. Cow dung is a necessary input in composting. Apart from cow dung, cow urine is also used in crop production. Cow's urine, especially that from pregnant cows is rich in growth hormones and helps crop growth. Cow urine is sprayed on the crop at a dilution of 1:10. It also helps keep pests away. It can be mixed with various plant recipes for different functions. Cow milk is known to be antiviral and viral disease in many crops can be controlled when 1:10 of diluted cow milk is sprayed. It

Purushothama Rao shows a compost heap

68

is also used in seed treatment. Lokopakarum (Chavundaraya) a text that dates from 1025 AD states that diluted cow milk poured at the base of the red hibiscus plant regularly results in yields of white flowers. Bullock urine is used in seed treatments. Cow horn is the in-strument used to absorb astral and cosmic energy and is used in biodynamic agriculture. The horn, filled with cow dung or silica, is instrumental in so-called 500 and 501 preparations.

Apart from these ideas, KPP suggests many environmentally-friendly agricultural techniques. Parthenium, Eupatorium, Glyricidia are used in liquid manure preparation. The manure is applied through foliar spray. Sometimes it is also applied to the base. Amniotic fluid is used as a growth promoter and flower inducer. It is rich in auxins growth hormones. Diluted amniotic fluid promotes growth and quick bearing. We have developed recipes that help in fruit setting and prevent flower dropping. As far as biocides are concerned, KPPs major work is to help in plant protection. Decoctions of Neem, Adathoda, Calotropis, Agave, Pongamia, Lasiosiphon, Sweet-flag, Amosphophallus, Bouganvilla, Cleodendran, and Embelia are used to prevent pests and diseases.

Within COMPAS, KPP wants to undertake the following activities:

□ **Documentation of indigenous knowledge and indigenous institutions.** Documentation will be done in a participatory way. First, the population or community concerned will be identified. The population will be studied with respect to its socio-economic condition, location and specialities. The elders will be consulted in documenting indigenous knowledge and indigenous institutions. Collectors of information will listen to the farmers and will provoke them through questioning to come up with more information. Information will also be collected through school children. They will be motivated by special prizes. The collected information will then be systematically compiled according to crops, season, locality, agricultural operations, ethno-communities, beliefs, faiths and worship.

□ **Collection of ancient literature.** To support the documented indigenous knowledge, and also to get new information, classical texts like Vedas, Puranas, Shastras and other ancient literature as well as contemporary literature will be collected and studied. Persons that posses ancient literature will be identified. We will also contact oriental research institutes, major libraries and institutions that have similar interests. If necessary, classical texts will be translated into local languages.

□ **Identifying farmers who are research minded.** KPP believes in this statement: 'Necessity is the mother of invention'. Farmers face a lot of problems in the field. The problems may be technical, financial, administrative or of another nature. KPP concentrates on technical problems. To maximise profits, the farmer tries to find a solution to his problems. In this process he becomes a scientist. He has to get all the information he can on crops, soil and environmental conditions. For this information he contacts the veterinarian, agriculturists, research stations, universities, other institutions or individuals and may refer to the literature on the subject. The process is purely explorative in nature. KPP now has more that 50 scientists of this kind whom farmers can consult. Their interests vary and include seed selection, seed treatment, soil reclamation, soil enrichers, plant protection, liquid manures, growth harmonisers and regulators, quick or delayed ripening, processing, value addition, harvesting and storage. KPP admires the achievements of the farmers and provides them with the necessary information and resource persons to facilitate their experimental process.

☐ **Organising experience sharing workshops and exchange workshops.** For the last six to seven years, KPP has organised meetings of farmers and scientists twice a year. Farmers from different parts of Karnataka gather together on this occasion. Sessions highlight the successful techniques experienced by the farmers followed by their more bitter experiences with experimentation. The programme is a two-way interaction programme. A few problems that have not been solved will come up for discussion. Different treatments will be suggested to the farmers conducting the experiments.

☐ **Organising mass meetings of farmers.** Since 1992, mass meetings of farmers have been organised every now and then to keep them in touch with Swadeshi Swavalambi Savayava Krishi (SSSK), the Philosophy of Agriculture. The accepted, successful techniques of experienced farmers are advocated to these farmers. Farmers will be educated in all aspects of agriculture including marketing. Farmers' questions will be answered during these meetings. Usually these programmes are organised in the villages for the benefit of individual farmers, farmer groups, the village, and the nation. The programme is followed by the formation of KPP units.

☐ **Organising KPP units at village level.** Village level units will consist of a minimum five farmers who practice indigenous, self-reliant eco-friendly agriculture. The KPP headquarters team will assist them develop cosmovision, skills and capabilities for the alternative approach. KPP will attend to the individual needs and promotion of group interests for the benefit of the village as a whole. The unit will become the production centre for organic foods. The group will be educated in understanding their village, its resources and knowledge and ways of optimally making use of these resources. The approach is holistic and eco-friendly. The unit members will be involved in the 'Grama vikasa', the endogenous development process that aims at achieving self-reliance for the village. The necessary visions for this development will be provided.

Clearly the acceptance and down-to-earth actions by large groups of farmers serves as the test of viability of indigenous, self-reliant eco-friendly agriculture.

On 18th September 1998, Mr. Purushothama Rao suddenly died. He has been the iniator of KPP and was a men with great vision, charisma and dedication. He has been a pioneer in developing farming practices that are in line with the laws of the natural and spiritual world. His ideas and example will remain a source of inspiration for COMPAS.

THE SYNERGY OF CULTURE
AND SPIRITUALITY ENHANCES BIODIVERSITY

Vanaja Ramprasad, Krishna Prasad and Gowri Gopinath

A village remote, yet not far away from a metropolis, is waking up to the call of birds and animals as morning dawned. Yellamma, mother of three children (ten, eight and six) remembers it is Sankranthi, a harvest festival to be celebrated in the village. It is a day of gratitude and thanksgiving. Yellamma busies herself decorating the house and cleaning the floor with a paste of cowdung. Flowers and ears of grains representing a bountiful harvest are pasted on the walls of entrance. Yellamma goes into the house and starts cleaning the shed and decorating the animals. The family gets ready for the *pooja*, an offering or prayer performed in the field where the harvested grains are stacked. In the open field, in the midst of everything that is part of their livelihood - the animals and the implements - a small fire that symbolises the all powerful Sun is invoked. A dish of rice, lentils (*dhal*) and *jaggery* (unrefined sugar) is offered as thanksgiving. Her cattle is washed and carefully decorated with flowers and vermilion. That evening the animals will jump the sacred fire in front of the temple. Jumping the sacred flame signifies a prayer for cattle health.

South of Bangalore, India and close to this electronic and computer city, a cluster of villages nestles between the mountains. They are well-shielded from the urban population and technological developments of the city and are populated mainly by farming communities and tribal people such as the Irulas. The traditional practices and perceptions of these rural people and the main spring of their daily life are outside the domain and interpretation of modern science.

An important and integral component of natural resources is the biodiversity of all forms of life. From the tiniest organism to the wide variety of flora and fauna found. The notion of all life forms coming together and sustaining the earth used to be a familiar concept. The lives of indigenous people, the 'tribals', were intricately intertwined with the ecosystem. Ancient civilisations, indigenous and folk people thrived on the art of conservation. With the increasing urbanisation, automation and chemicalisation of life, the burden being placed on life-supporting systems such as air, water, plant and animal life grow. The pressure on shrinking resources has brought many life forms to the brink of extinction.

GREEN Foundation is a NGO working with small farmers in the dryland regions of South India. Its key objective is biodiversity conservation for sustainable agriculture. Its major concerns are the restoration of lost genetic resources in food crops (millet, paddy and other crops) and vegetables. GREEN Foundation seeks to unravel some of many untold facts of biodiversity as they relate to the conservation of wild flora, agricultural crops, trees and livestock. This approach to conserving the different forms of diversity meant building on people's ways of cultivating, propagating, utilising and conserving various life forms. Within COMPAS the thrust of the present project will be to focus on the conservation of life forms which include agricultural crops, medicinal plants, livestock, agroforestry and soil micro flora.

Around fifty villages will be covered, twenty-five in Denkanikottai, Tamil Nadu and twenty-five in Kanakapura Taluks, Karnataka. The villages are closely intertwined and have much in common. They live either inside or adjacent to the forest. We are particularly conscious of the fact that, because of their remoteness, their culture and lifestyles are intact. Thalli is one of the biggest blocks with 50 Panchayats and nearly 370 villages and small hamlets. Out of the total population of 148,000 nearly 46,966 are from the villages in the forest area. It is a beautiful landscape with hills and undulating terrains. Night temperatures, however, are low and can reach 10°C in winter; summers are pleasant. The soil in the project area was identified as red laterite and the most common type in the area is the red sandy loam. The average annual rainfall is around 800 mm. These villages have been neglected as far as infrastructural facilities such as approach roads, education, health centers, transport and communication are concerned.

The area is a continuation of Madumalai forest range of the western Ghats: a deciduous forest with rich flora and fauna. Lantana camera spreads everywhere along with other thorny bushes. Rare forest species like Semicarpus, Anacardium, Glorylily, Orchids are rich and ornamental. Commercial species include Sandalwood, Rosewood, Tamarind, Honge and Bamboo. Bamboo has been disappearing fast in recent years, not only because it is food for elephants but also because of auctions held by the government. Replantation is now underway. Elephants, deer, jackals, rabbits, wild bores, foxes, monkeys and bears live in these forests. Elephants give the farming community a lot of trouble and crops have to be protected against them.

Crop diversity has been maintained by the farmers. A basic mixed cropping system has remained intact over time. To some extent indigenous seeds have been replaced by High Yielding Varieties. *Ragi* (finger millet), minor millets, pulse varieties and oil seeds are the main crops. North of Thalli, where there are sandy loam soils and slightly warmer temperatures, groundnuts are grown on a large scale and the area is famous for them. Here, farmers buy their food and straw for their cattle. Water is drawn from perennial streams and small tanks. However, the streams flow in the forest to join the River Cauvery and are not used for irrigation. Instead, tanks and private wells supply irrigation needs. Rainfed irrigation is the most common and around 90% of the farmers depend on rain. Due to increasing population and migration, deforestation is a common feature and is caused by extending the area cultivated and by need for firewood.

Caste groups like Lingayat and Vokkaligas dominate the area. Other caste such as Vanniyar, Gounder, Vadda, Kumbai, Golla, Besta, Harijans and also Muslims are also found to some extent in the villages. Lambanis and Irulas form a negligible percentage of the village population. The Muslim population is concentrated north of Thalli, because this is a potential area for business. Though diverse in castes, people normally follow the common values, rules, customs and beliefs of their community. Along with the major festivals they also celebrate local festivals associated with the village deities for thanksgiving, to evoke blessings for good harvests, and to secure the welfare of the entire village community. Despite considerable advances in many aspects of life, transport is still very poor and people have to walk miles to their villages. Invalids have to be carried in baskets for many miles if they need treatment at a medical centre. Although the tribals are shy about their costume, which is heavily embroidered, the elderly still continue to use it. The younger generation dress in this way too or choose more modern styles.

The people still resort to the forest for their food crops and income-generating resources off-season or in summer. Bamboo shoots, tubers, gooseberry and special tender leaves are the most preferred food supplements. Collection of Pongamea seeds and Tamarind processing are the main summer-income activities. The village community's contacts with towns and cities, their exposure to the mass media as well as outsiders' intrusion has had an impact on the younger population. The older members of the community are self-reliant, independent and tough in their attitude and are rich in human skills and knowledge. Young people and children are at the cross roads, still finding their values.

Sacred seeds, gender and cultural sanctity

Traditional agriculture in India is one of the oldest, yet one of the most advanced forms of food production. Traditional practices did not simply come into being because of an understanding of the mechanism of nature, but as a result of a science that was accessible to people as they went about their everyday work. It was not the science of the laboratory. Farmers choose crop types or varieties depending on soil depths, water-holding capacity, slope and drainage and by observing their interactions with each other. The combinations of different agroclimatic conditions such as low rainfall and high temperatures coupled with different soil conditions gave rise to various crop combinations and crop rotations. The limitation of household labour further determined the type of crops and cropping pattern. Traditional agriculture generally ensured food security and preserved genetic diversity.

Gender and biodiversity are linked not only symbolically but also in the material domain. Women play a major role in conserving seed at the farm level. It are women who decide the amount of seeds that has to be preserved, the variety, and the preservations methods necessary. Women are the ones who decide when change is required and that seed has to be borrowed or exchanged. Because women share the sacred power of Shakti (female power of reproduction), with the seed, it is women who are vested with the responsibility of selection, conservation and propagation. These processes are intimate aspects of the reproduction of biodiversity through ceremonies and festivals.

The role of women in the selection of seeds begins when the crops come into flower. In the *ragi* (finger millet) growing areas of South India, the first flower to bloom in the field is mustard. Coinciding with the appearance of that flower, a festival called Gowri Pooja is celebrated in which the many relationships of the plant with the soil, water and other crops are recognised and maintained. The Goddess Gowri is identified both as a Goddess of water, which is essential for the growth of the crop, and with the fertility of the flower so that good grain is formed. As part of the festival, the flowers are brought home and worshipped. In parts of the sorghum growing regions of Karnataka, young unmarried girls collect contributions from the public, singing songs praising the power of Goddess Gowri. The girls also bring in fresh soil from the village pond symbolising fertile soil, and make an idol out of it. After the ceremony, the idol is immersed in water. The ceremony thus rejuvenates the connections between soil, water and biodiversity. Seed selection is a continuous process and, because women are involved in weeding, harvesting crops and collecting grains, they watch plants grow through their whole life cycle and select seed at all stages.

Identifying fruits which will produce good seeds begins with the collection of green vegetables in the case of the pulses that are associated with *ragi* or finger millet. While collecting the green beans, women identify which plant will be allowed to mature into seed of good quality on the basis of size, grain formation, pest and insects attack, for example. While collecting beans, women keep a watch on the ears of the main cereal crops, especially in the case of sorghum and *bajra* (pearl millet). The ears that are largest with plenty of grains are selected for reproduction. While selecting and storing seeds, women determine the quantity needed for two planting seasons. This is to avoid the risk of drought and the possibility of going without seed. In addition, a certain amount of seed is kept aside to offer as gifts to the poor and to Goddesses and Gods.

Honneru germination test performed on Ugadi day

When the selected cereal ears are brought to the threshing yard, the first head load or cart is welcomed into the threshing yard by women making a *pooja* or offering. On the last threshing day the heaps of grain including the seeds, are worshipped by women. Before transporting the grains home, some grain from each heap is given as a gift to the poor. Families who have provided help are also given a gift of grain. In the ceremony performed by women before the seeds of cereals are carried away for storage purposes, forces are evoked that are essential for a good crop. Water is symbolised in the form of the winnowing pan, pest protection is symbolised in the form of leaves or the branch of a tree or bush. Soil fertility is symbolised in the form of cowdung and weeds in the form of grass. The ritual thus locates biodiversity conservation in the complex web of the life that maintains and rejuvenates plant productivity. The ritual also forms the basis of seed preservation. Thus, the leaf used in the ceremony for pest control will be used for seed storage. The *lakkli* (*Vitex negundo*) leaf is used for preserving paddy. Wherever *lakkli* is not found in abundance, neem is used as a preservative. In a few cases, seeds are mixed with other seeds for preservation. For example, *Dolichus lab lab* or field beans are mixed with mustard or finger millet for preservation. *Tur* (pigeon pea) is mixed with sand for preservation. In other instances, seeds are stored above the kitchen, so that the smoke keeps the pests away.

Seed quality is tested through ceremonial ritual in a variety of ways. The stored seeds are tested for germination during a selected festival. It can be Ugadi or the Kamanna Festival, or Holi or the feast of the village gods. In the sorghum region, immediately after the threshing operations, farmers celebrate a festival called Kammanna Habba which is also called Holi. In this festival, all the planetary forces are thanked for helping produce a good crop.

On all three days women draw various symbols representing various planets and worship them as part of expressing thanks to the planet. Before the conclusion of the ceremony, women will make small heaps of all the seeds they have collected for that year. On each heap, women will pour sanctified water. If the water carries the seeds a little way off, they are considered to be of good quality. If they are not, the women of the household have to try to exchange them or borrow seed from others. On the last day of the Holi festival, after conducting the quality test, a germination test will be carried out. In this test, all the seeds screened for good quality, will be placed in a coconut shell with a medium of good manure selected from the manure pit. All the grains including cereals, pulses, and oilseeds are placed in the shell for a test. There will normally be nine seeds, the Navdanya. These seeds will be worshipped, and on the seventh day when the seeds have sprouted, they will be examined. Women will look for replacements for seeds that have not sprouted well. Thus, by repeated testing, the quality of seed at the level of the individual farming household is maintained.

In the finger millet growing area, the test for quality will not be conducted immediately after the threshing ceremony, but the test for germination will be carried out on the day of Ugadi i.e. New Year's day in the Hindu Calendar based on the lunar cycle. After an offering has been made to the household deity, both the couple place all the seeds selected for reproduction in the coming agricultural season in a medium of manure brought from their own manure pit. This manure has been dried before hand. After sowing all the pulses, cereals and oilseeds which number about nine, are worshipped. On the seventh day, the plank is carried to the nearest source of water, where a sacrifice (*pooja*) is made and the seeds are examined for sprouting. If the sprouts are not good or are low in number, or the growth is not of the level expected (about three inches in length), the seeds of that particular variety will not be considered good enough for sowing in the coming agricultural season and farmer will look for replacements. Within the space of the three months available between the tests embedded in ceremonies and the sowing season, replacement seeds are looked for through exchange or borrowing. Normally, buying seeds is avoided because trading in seeds is considered bad behaviour. Reciprocal exchange is the basis of seed exchange in traditional agriculture.

A few days prior to sowing, the seeds are taken out from storage for drying and cleaning. If, due to improper storage, seeds have been affected by worms or insects, then these seeds are weeded out and the good seeds are identified. On the day of sowing, women keep all the seeds meant for sowing before the house deity and worship them. On their way to the field each woman who carries seeds will visit all the seven sisters (seven village Goddesses) and make an offering. Before sowing begins, women worship the draft animals, the plough, the seed drill and other equipment to be used in sowing. In the sorghum-growing region, it are the women who carry out all the sowing whereas in the finger millet growing region women will give the seeds to men to sow them. The seeds offered to the village Gods and Goddesses are collected by the poor.

None of the above procedures are followed for the so-called High Yielding Variety (HYV) seeds purchased in the market. While the farmer-reproduced varieties are considered sacred, the HYV varieties are considered impure. They are sent directly to the field, and the men are responsible for sowing them.

Navagrahas: symbol of macrocosm

The Sun is addressed in the Vedas as soul of the Universe. Varahamihira the author of BrahatSamhita, calls the Sun 'Kalatma' or the soul of time. The planets referred to in the literature, however, were merely reflectors or transmitters of light and solar energy. These planetary rays affect biological and psychological processes in human beings, influencing their destinies as malevolent or benevolent experience. The texts describe Navagrahas: the planets Mars (Mangala), Mercury (Budha), Jupiter (Brahaspati), Venus (Shukra), Saturn (Sani), Sun (Ravi) and Moon (Soma) and the two ascending and descending nodes as Rahu and Kethu. Usually all nine are worshipped together. It has been described that the planetary positions of the sun and moon affect the sea water causing tides. They also affect the stores of fluid on the surface of the earth and its vegetation. Recent studies of scientists in the west have revealed that the sun spots and solar radiation do influence biological behaviour. Sunspots have been observed over many years and they are found to vary in number over time.

Some of the traditional beliefs about farming have been linked to planetary rays. It is an old belief that trees should not be cut near the time of the new moon for then the sap will dry quickly. It has been shown through experiments conducted for over nine years that the maximum growth of wheat corresponded with the period of the increasing moon and that maize was found to grow best when planted two days before the full moon.

Rituals and worship of nature

For village folk, living in close proximity to nature, there exists the all pervasive influence of the supernatural forces of good versus evil and the glorification of nature

Tribal cosmovision and powers in agriculture

The eastern hills and forests of India are the homeland of sixty indigenous peoples or 'tribal communities'. Tribals believe in divine beings which are closely connected to their agro-ecological practices and socio-economic life. ◆

4-1 Tribal women threshing crops by hand.

4-2 Whilst the majority of the divine beings are female, women are a minority among ritual functionaries. The most important one is the gurumayi, *the community priestess or shaman.*

4-3 Tribal people have various traditional functionaries. The poojari *is the village priest and performs rituals.*

4-4 The disari *is the magico-religious and medical man.*

Tribal knowledge on cosmovision is preserved in *mutte* (ola scripts), *gondas* (chalk marks), folk songs and dances. IDEA, Integrated Development through Environmental Awakening, is an NGO which builds on tribal knowledge to develop sustainable agro-ecological practices. ◆

4-5 Some customary practices are limiting women's participation. As some traditional functionaries realise this, women in their villages nowadays are allowed to fully participate in the ceremonies.

4-6 Touching, eating or selling food and fruits is prohibited unless specific 'first eating ceremonies' are held by the Disari *and the* Poojari.

4-7 Prosperity depends on the proper functioning of the traditional functionaries. In order to communicate with supernatural beings, the Disari *is using* gondas.

Tribal cosmovision and powers in agriculture

Traditional Sri Lankan agriculture is based on spiritual practices, astrology and eco-friendly techniques. Together they activate the multitude of powers: the power of the moment, of location and place, the power of sound and symbols, mental powers, powers of plants and supernatural powers. ◆

4-8 After the kem is performed, the chanted and energised water is sprinkled over the rice field. Rats, mice, elephants, wild boars and insects are asked to leave or only take a fair portion of the crop.

4-9, 4-10 After a training given by the Ecological Conservation Organisation (ECO), the farmer (centre) recalled that his father used to keep an old booklet on his attic. He traced it and found the remaining pages showing some twenty symbols and yantras for crop protection.

Buddhist Monks possess invaluable knowledge about indigenous techniques like charming water and sand. Beyond the reach of outsiders' eyes and ears, village priests perform a great variety of rituals in the domains of construction, farming and health. ◆

4-11 The Buddhist monk Mabima Pangananda is knowledgeable about rituals in agriculture such as seed selection, land preparation for sowing, and determining the right moments for sowing and harvesting.

4-12 With the help of self-made posters, a farmer and spiritual leader explains traditional rituals to other farmers and encourages them to experiment.

Tribal cosomovision and powers in agriculture

in its various forms in maintaining cosmic order. Prithvi, Mother Earth is perceived as a powerful Goddess sustaining plants. Trees, animals, mountains, lakes, stones and weeds are deified and worshipped with great reverence.

How indigenous knowledge is linked to traditional healing and cosmovision can be illustrated with a glimpse at the life of 70 year old Chikanna. He is the village headman, a farmer and well-known local healer in the Irula Tribal Community of Masthappana Doddi. His daily life is governed by a series of rituals (largely spiritual), which shape his mental well being in general. Awakening from the right side of his bed, he looks at the picture of his family deity hanging against the wall. He believes that all will go well that day after this act of observation and prayer, which has a therapeutic effect on him mentally and emotionally. After washing his face, he stands and prays towards the east. He believes that the sun is a powerful and divine force which gives brightness and energy. He then offers *pooja* to the household deity. Before eating, he throws a handful of food upwards to the roof because he believes that food comes from nature and this rite is a mark of respect. He collects herbs from the forests only during Shoonya masa, from mid-December to January. The herbs are dried and medicines are prepared and stored in the gods room. They are offered in worship on Ayoodha Pooja festival. Before administering these medicines to his patients, a salutation is offered to his family deity and *guru* (his teacher). Medicines are not administered on Mondays and Saturdays as they will have no effect. The new moon day is ideal for administering medicines, especially for old and chronic diseases. It is also his belief that evil spirits will be destroyed on this day. He will not allow women to learn this knowledge, but he teaches it to his sons. As a head of the joint family (16 male and 6 female) all major festivals and rituals are celebrated. They also participate in village fairs. Some other forms of ritual worship and significance of various natural objects are indicated in the tables below.

Arathi is offered during a village fair and contains coconut and sweet balls.
It is further decorated with flowers and neem leaves.

81

RITUAL/FESTIVAL	SIGNIFICANCE	NATURE OF CELEBRATION	MONTH/PERIOD WHEN PERFORMED
Hiricara Habba festival	Ancestral worship for appeasing the spirits of ancestors in the event of calamities. The ancestral spirit will appear in dreams of the eldest in the family indicating how to solve the problem.	Varieties of food and clothing are prepared to appease ancestral spirits.	Celebrated in Ashwa-yuja masa (the seventh month of Hindu Calendar (mid Sept-Oct)
Holada Mune	A farm deity constructed with three natural stones. The deity is worshipped at periodic in--tervals during the agricultural season: ploughing, sowing and harvesting. The ritual signifies protection of crops from cattle grazing, wild animals and thieves.	Offerings made to deity.	Different stages in the agricultural calendar year. Varies from one location to the other.
Yanagi Paravu	Protection against elephant grazing.	The south east corner of the field is cleared and a picture of the elephant drawn on the ground. Flowers, food, incense and coconuts are given in offering to the elephant (God of protection).	Carried out before harvesting.
Worship of anthills 'Naga pan-chami' (Snakes)	A prayer made for fertility and procreation.	Milk, coconut and fruits are offered to the snake goddess who is perceived as a symbol of fertility. Women mainly perform this pooja.	End July every year.
Worship of Prithvi (Mother Earth) e.g. amongst the Irula tribals	A prayer for blessings of Mother Earth.	Performance of pooja during which offerings are made.	Carried out before the first ploughing. Wednesday is believed to be the day of birth of Mother Earth. Ploughing, digging and sowing on that day would signify woun-ding Mother Earth.

Hill worship	Sanctity of the hill.	Surrounded by sacred trees and water. A temple is constructed on top. Pooja and offering are made. Collection of firewood, stones and timber from this hill is tabooed.	Varies (Local specific)
Harvest rituals Rashi Pooje Kanada Pooje	A prayer for continuity in good yields of ragi (finger millet, staple crop in several communities).	This festival has particular reference to ragi. After threshing grains are heaped and worshipped.	After threshing of grains - February every year.
Karibanta	The ritual is a request against pest attack of crops.	The trunk of Pacchadi tree turns black is cut due to its 'infestation' by pests.	Weeding time (Sept-Oct)
Honeru	A community festival (18 villages) signifying different agricultural operations, like ploughing (Negalu).	Pooja and offerings to agricultural implements.	Carried out before ploughing.
Tepothsava	A worship of tanks and water sources for plentiful water.	Offerings are made in the site.	Once a year.
Sathyhabba and Yedagujathre	A community festival for better rains and bountiful harvest.		
Worship of female deities: Maramma, Pat talamma, Karagadamma	Village fairs and deity worships are at times collectively celebrated and animals are sacrificed for the good cause of the village (goat, buffaloes, chicken).		

THE RELATIONSHIP BETWEEN SACRED PLANTS AND ANIMALS WITH THE DIVINE IN KARNATAKA, INDIA

SACRED PLANTS AND ANIMALS	RELATED DIVINE BEING OR SPIRITUAL FORCE	SIGNIFICANCE OF THE DIVINE BEING
Tare (Terminalia belrica)	Shaneshwara	Creates problems and only by worshipping him problems may solve
Bevu (Melia Azadriach)	Maramma	Village deity protects the village
Ala (Ficus Bengalensis)	Muneswara	Farm deity protects the crop
Ekka (Calotropis gigantea)	Ekkada Benaka	Solves problems
Hale	Madduramma	Village deity
Banni (Acacia ferruginea)	Pandavaru	Symbol of protection. The tree is worshipped on Ayudha pooja dya during which agricultural implements are worshipped.
Beli Kanagile (Plumeria Bilwa)	Grows around temple for the sake of flowers	
Bilwa (Aegle marmelos)	Grows around temple for leaves to worship	
Elephant	Ganesha	God of Knowledge
Horse	Madduramma	Village deity
Tiger	Muneswara	Farm deity
Tiger	Mahadeshwara	Great tradition God
Cobra	Nagaraja	Fertility Symbol
Cow	Shiva	Destroyer of Universe

Ashwatha Katte (sacred trees).

The GREEN approach

The GREEN approach will start with the documentation of indigenous knowledge and practices: rituals related to fertility and seed testing, the role of women, practices related to weather, pest control, varied combinations, nutritional management, conservation of sacred plants and groves; folk stories, proverbs and poetry; basic health care systems and traditional resource management systems. Then field experiments will be carried out based on traditional concepts and in cooperation with traditional leaders. The different activities and methods are summarised in the following diagram.

CHART OF GREEN'S PROGRAMME

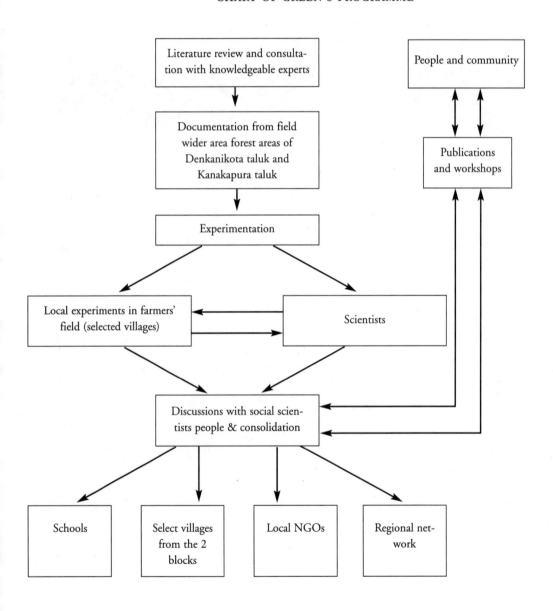

TRIBAL AGRO-ECOLOGY AND COSMOVISION

K. J. N. Gowtham Shankar

The Eastern Ghats is one of India's major natural resource bases. This 20 million year old mountain range lies between the Phulbani of southern Orissa and Nilgiris of Tamil Nadu covering Andhra Pradesh and a some of Madhya Pradesh. The coastal area in the east defines the eastern boundary. The Eastern Ghats is the homeland of about 60 indigenous tribal communities and the local population numbers some 10 million people. The majority live in hilly forested areas. The tribes of the Eastern Ghats are commonly known as the Adivasi, Girijan and Vanya Jati. Each tribal group has a distinct lifestyle based on the belief that nature, mankind and the spiritual world are interrelated.

In the first phase of COMPAS, IDEA (Integrated Development through Environmental Awakening) documented the agro-ecological practices and cosmovisions of the 10 tribal communities with whom we are working in the hills, valleys and plains of the Eastern Ghats. An attempt was made to understand the linkage between tribal and modern knowledge, and specifically the role of gender. Several resource persons and agencies were consulted in order to ensure conceptual clarity. Oral and written literature was verified to allow a better understanding of the concepts. Our study thus provides an overview of the varied traditional practices that exist in the region and their present status.

The tribes of Eastern Ghats practice three main types of agriculture, depending on the location of the land. First, shifting cultivation is practised in the hills. It is the major component of the subsistence economy in all 10 communities. It involves a mixed agriculture with a variety of cereals and millets, pulses, beans, tubers, medicinal plants, fuel, fodder and roofing material. Patches are community property, controlled and regulated by traditional village institutions. Each clan is allotted a particular corner of the hillside for cultivation and the selection process is normally carried out during the Pushya festival in December and January. Different types of shifting cultivation are practised, based on the nature of the land. Short duration crops produce a harvest in a relatively brief period of time and thus maintain economic stability and food security in times of drought and floods. Mixed cultivation has many advantages from an economic point of view. The harvest is sequential, which enables the farmer to use some of the crop for food grain, some for investment and festivals and some to clear off debts. They provide some buffer against hunger and from financial commitments such as those with money lenders.

A second type of agriculture is terrace cultivation, which is generally found in the valleys where there is adequate water and the land can be managed in a way that allows for the cultivation of wetland crops. The ownership of terrace cultivation and the selection process of such plots is in the hands of individuals or clan members. Cultivation involves terrace bunding to control soil erosion and the application of farmyard manure and bio-fertilisers. A third type is plain land cultivation, consisting of wetland and dryland agriculture. Normally the plain lands belong to individual families and varieties such as dry land paddy, finger millet, barren yard millet, Italian millet and sorghum as well as varieties of vegetables, tubers and beans are grown.

Tribal cosmovision

The tribal people believe in the existence of natural and supernatural divine beings and spiritual forces. They recognise the diversity of these forces and believe they are able to exert an influence that can help or harm nature and human beings. They believe that their work and everything in life is controlled by divine beings who inhabit their houses, villages, agricultural fields outside the village, mountains, forests, rivers and burial grounds. These gods, goddesses and spiritual beings differ from one another in nature, composition, function and character (see table page 92). The tribal people believe that some of these beings are benevolent and some are malevolent. The supernatural beings are beyond human control; hence submission, devotion and reverence is accorded to these powers. The tribal people also believe in good and bad ancestral spirits. These ancestral spirits watch over them always and help them when they are in danger and distress. They perform appropriate rites and rituals to appease the divine being and ancestral spirits in order to protect themselves and get rid of evil influences. They do not construct their houses, distribute land, start felling trees for shifting cultivation, eat fruits and cereals, perform marriages or go hunting until they have performed these rites.

Almost all these communities have many divine and spiritual beings. For example, the Kondh priest Korra Gasi describes how the Pulikonda have more than 100 gods, goddesses and spirits some of whom are good natured and some of whom have evil intentions. It is interesting to note that the majority of cosmovisions in this region contain beliefs that pertain only to their agro-ecological practices. The tribal people from villages such as Konda Reddy, Koya and the Konda Dora believe that the major millets, hill paddy and *chodi* (finger millet) are not only an important food crop, but

Most of the ceremonies and rituals are related to agriculture, the environment and health.

are also sacred. Similarly the other communities consider the minor millet *korra* (Italian millet) and *saama* (little millet) as sacred crops and gifts from their ancestors. The red gram, especially the hill red gram, is the gift of the Goddess of Earth to the tribal people. Hence any ritual connected to their festivals would not be complete without offering these grains to the divine beings and ancestral spirits both good and bad. Festivals such as Chaitra Porob, Pushya

Porob, and Magh Porob, for example, are all related to seeds and crops. Other festivals are related to food conservation.

The tribal people believe they are the children of Mother Nature and that she protects and guides them. Some trees such as *mahua*, tamarind and mango; wild animals such as the Indian bison, tiger and common *langur* (monkey), birds like peacock and dove; and streams, mountains and caves are all holy and contain sacred elements. Because of this they are worshipped. In addition to these sacred objects, the people also have sacred hills where they perform annual rituals, ceremonies and Jatras or fairs. These special occasions are attended by other members of the tribe. The sacred forests called *onum* are inhabited by divine beings. Such places can be found on the plains in particular. For most communities, the mountains come first in the hierarchy of things and streams occupy second place. Trees and animal species come third.

Traditional institutions

The physical and material well-being of the tribal people is well organised and controlled by traditional institutions and functionaries. The *naik* is the village headman and is responsible for village administration. He maintains law and order and controls or settles inter-village land disputes. He also mobilises financial resources when necessary by collecting contributions in cash and kind from the community to celebrate community-based agriculture-related feasts, festivals and rituals. The *kotpaik* is the sacerdotal head and works to ensure the smooth functioning of various social, cultural, religious and agricultural norms. The *disari* is responsible for magico-religious matters and he is the medical man of the village. He has considerable knowledge of agro-ecological matters and land management practices. The *poojari* is the priest who controls the religious protocols of the village and performs rituals associated with agriculture. Further, there is the communal woman priest or shaman called *gurumayi* and the *guniya* and *sutrani* who are the traditional birth attendants. *Kattela disaries* and sirla disaries are the religious and medical men of the region and the communities consider them to be supreme and sacred saints. A group of eight to ten villages constitute a *muta* and this is headed by a *mutadar.* This person plays a vital role in maintaining the cohesion, integrity, stability and social identity of the communities in their specific geographical habitat. The community has a clearly visible knowledge

Gondas (chalk marks) are used by disaries and guniyas to communicate with divine beings.

of soil conservation and land management. Soil testing and the selection of land for different crops requires the skilled knowledge of *disari*, *kattela* and *sirla disaries* who are able to test soils by colour, weight, and taste and assess the gradation of the land. They know about specific floral species for controlling soil erosion, improving soil fertility and understand how to use green manure and growth hormones for the benefit of the plants. They celebrate the festivals related to grain conservation and ensure that individual members follow the principle of conserving food grains. Touching, eating or selling grains and vegetables without celebrating the necessary festivals such as Korra Kottalu is taboo.

The information storage systems and mechanisms related to cosmovision are mainly vested in the four important functionaries of the village: the *disari*, *poojari*, *guniya* and *gurumayi*. Though the traditional dormitories have disappeared physically in all the villages studied, we still found that tribal people have retained their knowledge systems in different forms.

Mutte is the name given to the body of agricultural science. It contains a wide range of traditional agricultural practices written on palm leaves: Thalapatra Grandha. Only *disari*, *poojari* and *guniya* can possess *mutte*. Some villages have lost their tradition of keeping *mutte*, other communities, however, still maintain it. The Thalapatra Grandhas cover three main subjects: calculations in astronomy; herbal medicines; and information on natural and supernatural beings and evils and ways of influencing them.

Knowledge is also preserved in the form of folk songs, mostly retained by the tribal women. These songs contain the mythological histories of the communities and their worldviews. Knowledge relating to the agricultural activities of the men are generally preserved in the form of dance and music. For example, the Kandul Baza is a combination of music and song that explains the origin of red gram and its cultivation practices as well as the need to protect its germ plasm. The *karkota* is a musical instrument made of wood that is used to create different sounds with different pitches. It is employed to threaten or drive away different types of wild animals and birds and prevent them from damaging the crops.

The *onum* or sacred forests physically show traces of their mythological histories and the times of origin of various natural and supernatural beings and their dwelling of abodes. *Gondas* or chalk marks are used by *disaries* and *guniyas* to propitiate or to appease evils spirits and to protect the crops from humans, animals and witch craft. For example, Chitti Ban Gonda can undo black magic and witchcraft, and Thaas Gonda can

TAAS GONDA
(to treat pest in crops)

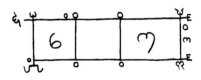

UPAI GONDA
(to protect cattle, crops and animals from black magic)

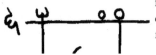

90

control pests in nurseries. Some of the chalk marks observed on the walls of houses also contain information that concerns agriculture, but the village heads, including the *disari*, find it difficult to explain the purpose and the meaning of these marks. *Gondas* are the symbol of communication with supernatural beings. They have the power to absorb and release the most sensitive information and knowledge systems as well as supernatural powers. Though these knowledge systems look complicated to outsiders, it is easy for a tribal person to grasp the knowledge they contain and their meaning and to learn the art and project it without difficulty.

DONGOR POOJA GONDA
(to pray/please mother nature)

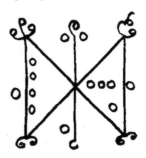

To appease the benevolent divine beings, the tribal people carry out acts of propitiation with a number of rituals and ceremonies that ranges from simple to complex depending upon the hierarchical position of the divine being and the nature of benefits they get from them. The *disari* fixes the auspicious dates for festivals or rituals on the basis of his astrological calculations and the lunar month calendar. The *poojari* performs the ritual for the community. There are different costs for performing the major festivals. For example, the Nandi Panduga festival in honour of the god Nandi Demudu costs Rs. 4,000. Generally these costs include such items as turmeric, rice or *ragi* powder, vermilion debs, milk, liquor, incense, camphor wicks, paddy, husk animals for sacrifices and grains for the communal feast. The village *naik* will collect contributions of between Rs.1 to Rs.10 and at least a kilogram of rice or millets from the villages for these ceremonies and rituals. The individual families also celebrate the same festivals in their homes with the head of the family as family priest. The cost involved range from a minimum of Rs.150 to maximum of Rs.1,000 depending on the festival.

Prosperity always depends on the proper functioning of the *disari*. Their lunar month-based agricultural calendar and the festivals for supernatural powers are worked out according to astrological calculations. Hence, it is the responsibility of the *disari* to maintain the order. If he miscalculates the dates of festivals relating to specific religious, cultural, agricultural and environmental events, it would disturb all agricultural practices, upset the benevolent divine beings and spirits, and result in serious consequences for the community. There is also the risk that benevolent or divine spirits may become malevolent.

The position of *poojari* is also very important, critical and sensitive in village life. If he fails to perform rituals properly the divine beings will curse the village and the result will be crop failure, cattle death and humans themselves may fall sick and die. If something goes wrong in the village, if crops fail for example, or epidemics break out, the community attributes this to the fact that the god or goddess have not been properly propitiated by *disari* and *poojari*. They must offer an explanation and perform the necessary rituals. If the problem is related to an individual family, then the *disari* will perform the necessary rituals in that family's house.

MAJOR DIVINE BEINGS OF THE KONDA DORA COMMUNITY, EASTERN GHATS, INDIA

NAME OF GOD (G), DEITY (D), SPIRIT (S)	HABITAT	SIGNIFICANCE OF RELATED FESTIVAL OR RITUAL	METHODS TO INFLUENCE	MONTH
Sanku Demudu (G)	Outside the village	Seed testing, fertility of crops; protection from their totems.	Sacrifice goat, chicken and offer grains	March-April
Kora Gangamma (D)	Forest	Harvest of finger millet	Sacrifice chicken	July-August
Sama Gangamma (D)	In forest between two stones	Harvest of little millet	Offer food and chicken	December
Gowramma (D)	Forest	For better crop production	Offer food, incense stick and coconut	April
Adavi Thalli, Mother Nature (D)	Forest	Initiation of all agricultural operations as well as pest control	Offer bananas, food and chicken	July
Dhara Gangamma (D)	Forest	To protect humans and cattle from wild animals in forest	Sacrifice goat or chicken	December
Inti Demudu, Ancestors (S)	Inside the house	First eating of mango	Sacrifice chicken and offer cooked food and food grains	May
Tenki Demudu (D)	Mango stone	First eating of mango stone	Sacrifice chicken	May
Pedda Rai, Goddess of stone (G)	Stone	To protect their village from stone sliding	Sacrifice goat and pig	July
Gali Demudu, God of wind (G)	Wind	To protect their crops from heavy winds	Sacrifice chicken	June/July
Nandi Demudu (G)	On hills between the stones	For cattle health	Sacrifice chicken and pig	February
Amma Thalli (D)	Inside the house	Family wealth and health	Sacrifice chicken and pig	Any time
Peeda (S)	In the wind	Family health	Treat with mantras, bethu and offer chicken	Any time
Pandavulu (G)	Outside the village	To get rain	Sacrifice goat	April

Gender aspects

During community rituals and ceremonies pertaining to the gods and goddesses, the poojaries, disaries and guniyas play a major role. However, the female gurumayi (the shaman) and spiritual leader is only allowed to attend and officiate at rituals and ceremonies relating to the family goddesses or spirits in which she is specialised. It was interesting to find that in some villages the gurumayi did not even play this role and was in fact confined to attending to the spiritual healing of diseases especially those that affected women. Their ritual status is not equivalent to that of men, hence they are subject to several taboos including those associated with menstruation. This period is seen as objectionable to both divine beings and bad spirits.

The majority of divine beings are goddesses and priest are men. On the positive side, this shows the communities attitude towards gender at the cosmovision level. However, on the negative side communities do not allow women priests directly or indirectly to serve or to communicate with the goddesses during communal ceremonies. For example, women are not allowed to attend 'Mokka Panduga jatra', a fair for pest control to the goddess Maatha Thakrani.

Women are confined to their houses and required to prepare food and offerings for the divine beings and ancestral spirits during most major festivals. Women take part in the merry making, dancing and singing after a ceremony has been completed. Women are allowed to celebrate and worship the god or goddess on two occasions. During Chaitra Porob (mango first eating ceremony) they worship Bondurga, the goddess of forest. In Sirlamamidi village during Kumdanua, the festival for newly harvested pumpkin and little millet, women worship and extend offerings to the deities and ancestral spirits. It is clearly pointed out that no woman is allowed to touch the sacred sword, axe or spear belonging to the divine beings, but they are allowed to worship them.

External influences

It is clearly observed in almost all the communities studied that rapid changes are occurring in religious practices, cultural ethos and ceremonial rituals. This acculturation process is due to frequent contacts with neighbouring non-tribal communities, settled landlords, merchants and the coming of Christians. The adoption of alien religions and practices can create disharmony. This is generally seen in Christian influenced villages. In such villages we have observed, and the traditional leaders have also reported, that their own kinsmen who have been converted do not participate in the religious ceremonies connected with the agricultural and environmental welfare of the village. They also do not cooperate and participate in the administration of the village, or in development works relating to traditional norms and practices. They also do not obey the traditional leaders. This causes friction. Many of the Christian missions openly advise people to change religion and rid themselves of the wrath of deities whom they cannot please because the cost of performing the necessary rites are too expensive for poor people.

The adoption of new religious practices and festival calendars also affect crop calendars. This leads to the disruption of the entire agro-economic base and productivity and affect food security. Their traditional musical instruments such as the *dompu*, *kiridi, tomuku, bousi* have been replaced by the harmonium, clarinet, guitar, and Khanjara and their Oili and Sankidi songs are now dominated by songs from the film world and Christianity.

Traditional communal institutions that were formerly empowered to take decision on land, crop management and traditional agricultural practices have been eroded under the influence and impact of modern agricultural policies such as watershed development, water harvesting technologies, hybrid seed and cash cropping. The functions of *disari* and *naiks, kattela disari* and *sirla disari* in relation to agriculture have weakened. This change in agricultural practices under the influence of a high-tech approach to agriculture has not taken into consideration the possibility of judiciously combining traditional tribal agricultural and land management practices with modern agricultural development technologies. This further erodes and upsets tribal agriculture and related cosmovision beliefs, festivals, crop calendars and crop and pest management practices.

We found that the communities are trying to maintain their identity and their traditional systems and practices. Some have been successful. For example, the institutions and functionaries headed by the sacerdotal head, the *kotpaik*, are gaining in importance especially in agriculture. The *poojari* celebrates festivals related to agriculture and is increasingly consulted on crop management practices as is the *disari* for biological pest control. The *disari* is gaining in importance nowadays. In the hill-top villages, the traditional leaders still secure the generation of new agricultural technologies and knowledge, while in plain and valley villages, farmer-to-farmer exchange systems through participation and demonstration is prevalent.

Though changing trends are affecting tribal life, the well-knit social systems still control and resist the influx of alien cultures. It was also observed that in many villages

The influx of alien religions is affecting tribal cosmovision and agro-ecological practices.

the traditional functionaries themselves realised that there were negative elements in their practices and slowly began to change their attitudes. They seem to be strengthening their positive practices. For example, the villages of Konda Reddies have never allowed women to participate in religious ceremonies or worship the goddess in the communal ceremonies. Now women are allowed to participate in these ceremonies. In Sirlamamidi, the *disari* now teaches women about his functions including *mantras* and *gondas*. In some villages, *guniya* and *sutrani* - the traditional birth attendants - are interacting with governmental health workers. These trends indicate the attitude of the functionaries and their intention to interact with modern development approaches while keeping their identity intact and continuing to serve their community. These functionaries can be strengthened with the introduction of a workable combination of modern and traditional methods that suit their needs.

Emotional integration

IDEA is concerned with the sustainable development of the tribal people on par with the development of other non-tribal communities. We have been working with tribal communities for twelve years and our main objective is to enhance endogenous eco-agricultural diversity as well as revive tribal traditional institutions for sustainable development.

Central to our approach is the concept of Emotional Integration and Awakening (EIA). We see working in this way as an alternative to mainstream development models that only take tribal and rural livelihoods into account. Mainstream develop-ment models are based on the organisation of the target group along physical lines, and project leaders and staff are bound to be controlled by certain authoritarian disciplines that thrive on dependency, top-down approaches and external support. Sustainable development has to go beyond the physical integration and organisation of the target group to promoting empowerment and a culture of identity. If there is no emotional attachment and concept as far as the issues are concerned, the development model will collapse.

The concept of emotional integration is a complex and sensitive new development model. It refers to the tribal peoples' perceptions and life styles that in turn are based on an emotional attachment to their history as a group (the roots), their culture and cosmovisions, the way they organise social and economic life and how this is linked to the ecosystem. It refers to their identity and self-respect: their human values, psychology and social ethics. Emotional integration and awakening consists of four elements. First, emotional content: the amount of specific information, perception and knowledge of identity in the mind of an individual or group. Second, an emotional realisation or awareness of the mind (which often follows a change of mental attitude) leading to the choice of proper action based on proper perceptions. Third, emotional involvement indicates the need to participate not only with the mind, but also with the heart, and this applies both to tribal people and to outside support organisations. The last element, an emotional edge over rationality, integrates the last three: it is the realisation of set objectives with emotional content, involvement and realisation.

The staff of support organisations have to use different social techniques to build up this process of EIA. For example, when organising tribal communities each with its own habits, habitats, customs, cosmovisions, anthropological, linguistic and agro-ecological characteristics, one has to talk with them about the human, cultural, tribal and socio-political issues in a language that they can understand. This will give the tribal people a feeling that they belong to a single race that is divided into heterogeneous groups and this will set them thinking about tribal solidarity. Another example might be that when an eco-restoration programme needs emotional commitment and participation, considerable sensitivity is required in dealing with cultural norms, customary practices and social controls that are based on the animistic beliefs of the tribal people.

It must be fully recognised that these are ideas that not only guide religious practice and other aspects of their life. Their traditional, animistic religious belief is acquired by tribal people through their reciprocal respect, and psychological and emotional attachment to the entire race. This respect and attachment is not imposed on the tribal, but is culturally preserved, ecologically respected and emotionally transferred from generation to generation. This respect and attachment always remains with the tribal person in some way. He or she never tries to loose the identity of totemic clan ethics, through which he or she respects, protects and conserves the species of his or her clan totem. They are bound to observe the social and ecological controls of the community when using agro-ecological and natural resources. We, at IDEA, have several examples of reviving traditional, natural resource conservation practices, sustainable agriculture programmes, herbal medical practices and women development activities through the concept of EIA.

We can distinguish four main stages in our approach. When entering a new community, we start by building up a rapport with individuals. Case studies, group discussions, and building up relationships with traditional institutions and heads follow. We encourage cultural programmes with songs related to the people's history, culture and festivals, their lives, their ancestors, clan totems, beliefs, customs, norms and interrelations with the forests and the environment. This attracts immediate attention and creates emotional participation and physical integration. Usually this is our entry point.

Then the formal process begins. In a simple and analytical way, short lectures are given during group and village meetings. Living examples and evidence from the community are cited and further explanations of the meaning of songs are given. We try to establish interrelations between customs, norms, festivals, forests, environment and animistic religious practices. This gives them the confidence in their life and practices and to further build up emotional strength. The 'we' feeling develops in their minds and hearts. All people, including the traditional institutional heads participate in the programme.

The third stage of our approach begins at this point: the process of formalising the group with more elements of building emotional integration and awakening. For example, CODE centres - COmmunity Development Education - are established for the young people of the tribe. These centres cater for the needs of individuals, groups, and traditional institutional heads as far as those subjects relating to particular village or community practices are concerned. Care will be taken to avoid commenting on their superstitions. These are normally discussed at a later stage and people sort them out with full emotional consciousness. This stage further develops their confidence. The questions raised for further clarification, the intensity of group discussions, but also the learning and singing of their songs in their houses, fields and during meetings indicate to us the quality and degree of participation.

The fourth stage starts with leadership building, the introduction of modern development technologies and inputs, the revival of traditional conservation and cultural practices. Meetings with other villages are also organised. Further analyses of present problems are made and responsibilities shared. Our approach now shifts to crystallising the EIA concept. The informal nature survey is formalised with scientific support and people with training, organisational and leadership skills are identified. Status reports are prepared and analysed; the community is helped to prepare their own plans, evaluations and assessments. Traditional herbalists receive training in allopathic first aid. Traditional birth attendants receive training in modern mother and childcare, immunisation and nutritional improvement. Village-based women's development groups are organised and the traditional heads are involved in these groups. Environment Protection and Development Groups (EPDG's) are also established to work out plans for the integrated sustainable development of the village and for the integration of their ecology-related cultural festivals, ceremonies, hunting and revived totemic clan concepts with natural resources surveys and analysis.

The experience of IDEA proved the feasibility and viability for this new type of development approach. We have reached the goals of building up alternative sustainable eco-development processes in about 200 villages in Andra Pradesh and Orissa.

Tribal women possess a good knowledge on wild leafy vegetables.

Need for further activities

IDEA has initiated the revival of indigenous, tribal eco-agricultural practices that combine indigenous and modern knowledge systems. Tribal indigenous knowledge systems are in a process of rapid transition in the North Eastern Ghats. Hence there is a need for continuous action research programmes and farmers' experimentation to help document and revive indigenous knowledge. There is a great need to promote and strengthen these activities and to strengthen cultural identity and endogenous development at different levels in close cooperation with interested NGOs.

During the second phase of COMPAS, we therefore want to further document, establish and crystallise tribal indigenous eco-development processes, practices and knowledge systems and extend them our support. It will be important to further strengthen and promote tribal traditional institutions and the tasks of functionaries and we also hope to promote people-based platforms for cross-cultural dialogues and the exchange of information on agri-eco-cultural practices and cosmovision beliefs. It is essential to conduct comparative studies, demonstrations and local experimentation on the different knowledge systems and practices of the indigenous (tribal) villages.

In order to promote and strengthen these activities small NGOs such as CERT, STAR, TYO and GRASS and a few selected youth groups from the tribal and rural areas will also take part in the programme. Each selected NGO will implement the programme independently in order to achieve the overall objective. Their work will be coordinated and supervised by IDEA with specific monitoring mechanisms.

As for exchange with other COMPAS partners, we hope to participate in studies on different forms of indigenous (including tribal) agricultural knowledge systems, and the way these are expressed in agriculture-related songs, dances, music, and *gondas*. We suggest comparing cosmovision-related practices on herbal fertilisers, bio-fertilisers and bio-pesticides. We are also interested in participating in comparative studies of knowledge systems and cosmovision related to natural resources conservation, not only within India, but also in African and Latin American countries.

COMPARING COSMOVISIONS IN NEPAL

Maheswar Ghimire

Nepal is a small Himalayan kingdom with tremendous diversity in topography, natural resources and cultural heritage. It has more than 36 different ethnic groups, each with its own culture, traditional beliefs, festivals and rituals who have lived together for centuries and understand each other well. Spiritually, their roots are either in the Hindu or Buddhist traditions. People celebrate different types of colourful festivals according to the season and their spiritual belief. A festival with its ancient processions and rituals has mythological, religious and historical significance. From these festivals and ceremonies one can derive a wealth of delightful legends and folk stories, but one can also come to a deeper understanding of indigenous concepts of life, agriculture and health. Unfortunately, cultural and natural diversity is gradually being eroded in the name of political stability and under the influence of economic development and western culture. Modernisation has made the younger generation in Nepal less interested in discovering the meaning of these ancient festivals and rituals.

In this article we describe the history and the environment of the Chitwan Valley and Dibya Nagar, the area and village where we will work in the context of COMPAS. We will go on to describe one festival, Holi Purnima and offer it as an example of our initial attempt to understand the intricate relationship between festivals, cosmovision and agriculture. In our conclusion, we discuss the activities we plan to carry out within COMPAS.

Chitwan: a source of ancient civilisation

The high mountains, hills and plains, the different types of farmland, the temples, and the way in which the houses and the countryside have been patterned, reflect Nepal's natural diversity and cultural heritage. In the Chitwan Valley, which in ancient time was known as the kingdom of King Chitraban, we can find the places of devotion and meditation of such ancient scholars as Balmiki who wrote the great epic Ramayana. Archaeological sites have also been discovered in the area which reveal information about the period of Lord Krishna, one of the heroes of Mahabharata.

The Chitwan Valley is situated in the foothills of Mahabharata and covers the catchment of the River Ganges, a region regarded as the source of ancient Indian and Nepalese cultures. Lumbini on the south-western Chitwan Plains is the birthplace of Lord Buddha. Janakpurdham is also famous and considered to be the Kingdom of King Janak of the Great Hindu epic Ramayana. The ancient and historical relationship between the people of Chitwan and these two important sites has been recorded in different epics, scriptures and traditional literature. In the north-western region of the Chitwan valley, Devghatdham is a place of special religious and holy significance for the majority of Hindu people.

In Hinduism, Mother Earth and specific plant and animal species are considered sacred. Nature is considered the source of life, a life which came from a divine source. Humanity is intimately related to nature and people have a strong belief in the Wheel of Life and the way the different stages of life and death are related. Living beings can utilise products from nature to complete a cycle. As in India, the concept of 'Panchamahabhoota' or the five primordial elements earth, water, air, fire and sky, is strong. Religion is the main source of cultural development and social organisation. In Dibya Nagar, more than 36 Hindu festivals are celebrated each year. The majority of these festivals have a meaning and sacrifices and offerings are made to please the gods and goddesses in the homestead, village and region. The festivals are related to the seasons, natural resource management, weather prediction and farming. For older people such festivals and their rituals are an intimate part of their day to day life and spiritual practices. Rituals have an educational purpose: they encourage the new generation to understand the intrinsic relationship between people and other living creatures in the area. Thus, rituals are the medium for understanding and developing an awareness of nature.

As modernisation enters the Chitwan Valley, however, a younger generation is growing up with less interest in the true meaning of these festivals. They see them simply as a source of entertainment and recreation.

Holi Purnima: the Spring festival

Holi Purnima, is one such festival, and we will describe it here. It is the Nepalese Spring Festival. Local innovation is related to the many festivals celebrated in the area and has a direct relationship with farming, livestock and natural resource management. Holi Purnima comes in the month of March. The major characteristics of this festival are red powder, romance and haunting demons, Holika. The ancient scriptures tell the story of the role of Lord Krishna during this festival. Holika begins on the eighth day of the waxing moon in the month of March and ends after 7 days on the day of the full moon. Farmers in the hill region of Nepal see it as the signal to get ready for planting new crops. This indicates the way in which the festival is related to farming practices.

During this festival, cereal grain (especially rice) is fed to pigeons and it is hoped that the pigeons will return an enormous quantity of wealth to the family performing the rite. According to an ancient legend, a boy spread his paddy rice over the farmyard and went to sleep in his house. The pigeons came and ate all his rice. When the boy woke up there was not a single grain of paddy rice left. He started to cry and prayed to the God and Goddess. The God and Goddess saw what had happened and asked the pigeons to bring back the rice or give wealth or gold of equivalent value. The pigeons left their dropping as gold pebbles. Because of the gold the boy was able to live a happy life. The story is interesting when seen in the context of the importance of the droppings of different types of birds in providing manure for the fields. According to traditional agriculture practitioners in the mid-hill regions of Nepal, pigeon droppings are good when planting new crops because they contain the nutrients the plants need. Another belief close to the heart of the Nepalese is that feeding pigeons will bring peace and prosperity to the family, village and area and custom advises that pigeons should be feed every day.

It is also interesting to observe that when Holi Purnima begins, the majority of farmers in this part of Nepal start spreading compost from their compost pits over their fields. Why do farmers normally select this time of year? One farmer in the Chitwan District put it this way: *'Holi Purnima falls at the turning point between two different seasons: winter is going and spring is coming. There is also abundant sunlight and the phase of the full moon brings more energy (from sun). In addition, the quality of the water in plants, soil and other living beings is good which helps the new seeds to germinate and the young plants to grow.'* This festival takes place in the early spring according to the lunar calendar. The weather is neither cold or hot and it is the time of the year when major agricultural tasks such as preparing the land and applying manure in readiness for the new crops are carried out. Insects and other pathogens in the soil will be turned up and exposed to sunlight, a process that will help decrease the chances of pest resurgence. The last day of Holi Purnima falls on the day of the full moon, and this is when planting should start. There may be some relation between agriculture and the cosmic influences affecting water. Holi Purnima has a special significance within the Tharu society of Chitwan Valley. It is one of their most important festivals and one that is greatly enjoyed. During the festival the 'Imta dance' is performed. In the indigenous wisdom of the people we see how farming is related to festivals. This gives a special relevance to the task of revalorising these festivals so the teaching contained in the legends associated with them can be better understood. Our aim within COMPAS is to come to a fuller understanding of the intricate relationships between indigenous knowledge, cosmovision and farming practices.

Another important aspect of celebrating festivals in the family or the community is that they fulfil particular needs. They provide the physical body with a change of food and drink. People like to prepare and eat food which is more tasty, diverse and nutritious than their everyday diet and which gives them more vitality. Festivals also contain elements of security. They confirm the people's belief in the power of the God and Goddess and their ability to protect and treat the physical ailments of the farm family and those living nearby from evil spirits. Rituals are also performed to bring favourable weather.

Like all festivals, Holi Purnima also has a social significance. Festivals enable interaction between people in the spirit of friendship, love and happiness. Festivals and rituals are special occasions that bring family members, friends and relatives together and create an atmosphere of

On a small altar, each day fresh flowers are dedicated to the gods and goddesses.

cooperation and mutual understanding in which strong relationships can be built up. For some people, festivals are times when they feel free and able to express their feeling without hindrance. In Nepal, the majority of people live below the poverty line and face many different types of problem. Even though people are extremely poor and live at subsistence level, it does not mean that they are always concerned about their material well being. Of course, material improvement is important, but they always seek to fulfil their spiritual needs and to develop their inner consciousness.

Festivals and rituals play an important role in Nepalese society and they answer many different needs. Today, farmers are thinking more constructively about this festival. They feel that the way that festivals should be celebrated should be creative and related to the various seasons. This means that they should have some creative significance which can help the new generation in their moral and ethical development and support their interests in the perspective of their future as farmers.

Our plans within COMPAS

Dibya Nagar is a village of some 6000 inhabitants in Chitwan District. The Hindu population consists of Brahmin, Chhetry and Tharu, and the Buddhist population is made up of Gurung and Tamang. There are also other minor ethnic groups. The Gurung are mainly followers of Hinayana Buddhism that has a close relationship with Lamaism. We still need to gather more information about their religion. Because the Hindu community is larger than the Buddhist community, the later follow the Hindu as well as the Hinayana culture, ritual and festival. The Tharu can be considered indigenous to the area. Most other ethnic groups have migrated from other parts of the mid-hill region following the implementation of the Rapti Dun Development and Resettlement Programme, initiated by the Government of Nepal in 1956. Before that time the area around the village of Dibya Nagar was dense natural forest and only a small part of it was occupied by the Tharu. After 1956, a large number of immigrants transformed this forest area into cultivated land. It is well known that the Tharu are rich in traditional agricultural knowledge but their livelihood has been affected by the migrants. Within COMPAS, we hope to assess and possibly revalorise Tharu indigenous agricultural knowledge and compare it with that of migrant Hindus and Buddhists from the hills. We want to explore the positive and negative aspects of the acculturation process that has taken place.

The Tharu are simple, gentle and friendly people. They speak a mixture of tribal languages whose vocabulary has some similarity to Bhojpuri and Magadhi. Sanskrit is its most likely source. In the past they did not measure what their crops yielded. If somebody asked about their grain stock they would say: '*Whatever has been produced has been stored in the granary. You can check the amount*'. If it was enough for the whole year then the harvest had been good. These days the Tharu have started to calculate their yield. But one piece of land is harvested in the traditional way: without measurements so as to please the family god.

Forests and water resources are declining in Dibya Nagar. There are no longer any community forests, although some 10 kms away there is a forest belonging to the Royal Chitwan National Park. It is a restricted area and no forest products can be collected there. Occasional conflicts have arisen between the Park Authority and the community most affected by these regulations. The Narayani is a major Nepalese river close to Dibya Nagar. Large industries have been established upstream and as a result aquatic life, drinking water and fishing has been affected. Fishing in Narayani River has been forbidden by law, the river has eroded cultivated land. The situation for the people in the area is miserable and it is very difficult for them to maintain their livelihood.

Farmers have started to grow some timber and fodder species for household use on their own land. The most important species are *Dalbergia sisso, Melia azedirach, Azedirachta indica, Bombax ceiba, Dendrocalamus spp., Terminalia spp., Syzgium spp., Ziziphus, Amala, Ficus religiosa, Ficus benghalensis, Ficus lacor, Artocarpus lakoocha, Ficus benjamina, Bauhinia spp.* Most of the land is now being cultivated and crops are being grown under seasonal irrigation on the lowlands and rainfed agriculture in the uplands. The most important crops grown in the area are paddy, wheat, maize, mustard, lentil, and seasonal vegetables. Local fruits include mangoes, litchi, papaya, pineapple, jackfruit and some citrus. The various ethnic groups have their own live-stock traditions. The most common livestock are buffaloes, cows, goats, chickens, pigs and sheep.

Building on indigenous knowledge

There is some awareness among the NGOs in Nepal that use can be made of farmers' indigenous knowledge for sustainable development. Over the centuries, farmers have developed their own, location-specific, holistic and harmonious knowledge and prac-tices in agriculture, health, social norms and natural resources management. This knowledge is based on spirituality, culture and traditional values. Due to processes of globalisation, liberalisation and the free market economy, Nepalese life has changed dramatically over the last decades. The government has invested considerable amounts of internal and external revenue in modernising agriculture and forestry. Since the 1960s, there has been a subsidised chemical approach to agriculture that has favoured educated and rich farmers. It has also lead to the degradation of the environment and to decreased productivity. Until 1988/89, Nepal exported food grain. Today the country imports it. In order to achieve sustainable development and solve the agri-cultural, environmental and social problems caused by modernisation, study and documentation, synthesis and dissemination of indigenous knowledge systems is a priority. Fortunately, there are still many opportunities for such studies.

Based in Chitwan, the Ecological Services Centre (ECOSCENTRE) is a small NGO which started implementing field programmes since 1995 in the Devghat region of the mid-hill region of Nepal. ECOSCENTRE is mainly active in natural resource management programmes which contain components of education, agri-culture, forest management and protection, rural infrastructure development and other community development programmes using participatory approaches. The major focus has been on sustainable agriculture and studying indigenous natural resource management practice amongst the people of Devghat Region.

Based on farmer workshops held in preparation for the programme, it would appear that farmers in Dibya Nagar have two expectations of the COMPAS programme. One is to create a level of awareness among the youth about their culture, the merits of traditional agriculture and to try to create an interface between traditional and modern agriculture. The last sentence might seem a little controversial because of the two polarities involved. However, we have tried to compromise and to begin building a strong network of people from both traditional and modern agriculture. Both farmers and ECOSCENTRE realise that there is an opportunity to integrate cosmovision into the experimentation of our action-oriented, sustainable agriculture programme. Secondly, farmers are interested in trying to find an effective alternative to chemical farming that will help to save the soil, the people and their identity. Given this background we decided with the farmers to work on the following six topics:

- Study and document farmers' indigenous knowledge and cosmovision.
- Develop a procedure for experimenting with crop cultivation according to the recommendations of the Panchangam, the traditional astrological calendar.
- Execute these experiments.
- Involve the youth using an exchange programme between farmers and school pupils.
- Write an article on the subject and publish regularly in the local newspaper. This will also help to build up local level networks.
- Organise lectures at the Central Agriculture and Animal Science College, which is located in Chitwan some 10 km from Dibya Nagar.

We would very much like to compare the cosmovision of the original Tharu population with that of migrants and to explore the interactions between the different ethnic groups. There is encouraging support and participation from farmers in Dibya Nagar. It is a challenging task for us, as Devghat and Dibya Nagar have different agro-ecological conditions, social structures and other phenomena. Although there are Gurung communities in both working areas, there are some differences in the festivals, rituals and other cultural ceremonies celebrated. However, the ultimate objectives of farmers are very similar: sustaining food security and cultural identity.

ACTIVATING ALL POWERS IN SRI LANKA AGRICULTURE

G.K. Upawansa and Rukman Wagachchi

The Buddhist priest was just about leaving the temple of Kataragama in the south of Sri Lanka. When he learned about the aim of our visit, he decided to stay and take time for a lengthy dialogue with us. As our aim is to assist farmers to revitalise and to field test ancient knowledge, including its spiritual techniques, we wanted to ask the spiritual leaders for support. Monks and priests possess invaluable knowledge about indigenous techniques such as charming water and sand. They can also possibly train shamans and village priests and develop methods for testing and valuing traditional practices. The priest Mabima Pangananda is knowledgeable about such agricultural rituals as seed selection, preparing land for sowing, and determining the right moments for sowing and harvesting. During our visit it became clear that he is very willing to train the village shamans. He was pleased with our interest: until recently, agriculturalists were not interested in spirituality.

In this article, we describe how agriculture in Sri Lanka was essentially an integrated system with crops, trees, livestock and fish. Animal and crop production has always been based on three aspects: the relationship with spirits and supernatural beings, astrology, and ecologically-sound practices. We will also indicate how we established a system of field experimentation to test and improve indigenous and effective traditional farming practices.

Sri Lanka is a small pear-shaped island to the south of the Indian sub-continent. Altitudes are as high as 3500 meter above sea level giving rise to a varied pattern of rainfall. The several different agro-ecological zones range from tropical forests, to highlands and semi-deserts. The south and southwest regions receive rainfall throughout the year and are referred to as the Wet Zone. The northwest province, the central province, the Uva and the north and eastern provinces make up the dry zone. The dry zone receives an average seasonal rainfall of 75 inches. The northeast monsoons which provide this rain lasts from October till January. The ancient people used the undulating topography to construct *wewa's* or pond-like tanks. In these cascading water reservoirs, water overflows from the top most tanks to those lower down and ultimately flows into rice fields below. In some cases the *chena*, an agro-forestry type of farm on the highlands, was located above the tanks. Cultivation usually began in the highland farms before the onset of the rains. The food security situation was such that in spite of the renovation of almost all ancient irrigation schemes and the construction of new schemes, food self-sufficiency remained a distant dream. Heavy imports were needed to meet grain requirements. This contrasts sharply with the past when the country produced all its food.

During the first phase of COMPAS, Upawansa of the NGO Ecological Conservation Organisation (ECO) and other members of the network for agricultural revival documented the importance of cosmovision for farmers in different areas of Sri Lanka. Workshops were organised in which farmers who apply traditional practices based on their cosmovision as well as other resource persons, priests and monks and NGO officials participated and shared their knowledge and experience. Written sources were also consulted. ECO's main objective is to offer Sri Lankan farmers alternatives to modern high-tech and chemical agriculture and protect them from exploitation. Training programmes in ecological farming have been conducted since 1992 for university lecturers, graduates, NGO officials, farmers and students interested in ecological agriculture. The programme deals with indigenous knowledge related to agriculture and includes astrology and the influence of supernatural beings. Most of the traditional practices are used extensively in the north central, northwestern, southern and Uva provinces. In the north and east they are used as well, but with some variations due to Tamil and Hindu influences. In the more developed provinces these practices have largely disappeared due to the extensive use of chemicals. Because of the reaction against the use of chemicals, some NGOs are trying to revive these traditional practices. In the training sessions on eco-friendly practices, farmers bring up the spiritual practices they find effective. The aim is to have farmers testing these indigenous practices so they can be adapted and re-introduced among other farmers. The topic of cosmovision was very well received throughout the country and at present there are farmers groups experimenting with spiritual techniques in five different district of Sri Lanka. Most of them are being helped by NGOs and staff from the Ministry of Agriculture.

Sri Lankan agricultural cosmovision

Spirits and supernatural beings. The majority of Sri Lankans are Buddhists (70%) and 10% are Hindus. People believe in gods and other deities and it is customary to invoke their blessings. The help and blessings of the gods will protect them from dangers, ill-health and hardship. Gods inhabit trees and especially the Bo tree (Ficus religiosa). Other ficus species are venerated. Both Buddhists and Hindus construct temples along side Bo trees and make offerings to these trees. It is also believed that there are gods or goddesses protecting rivers, forests and mountains. On the other hand, demons are believed to haunt cemeteries, funeral houses, empty buildings and unclean places. People also believe in a category of spirits that are neither gods nor demons: *bahirawas*, who are believed to live underground and within air space. *Bahirawas* are believed to look after the harvest. People believe that a *bahirawa* can sometimes appropriate part of the harvest, causing losses to the farmers. Therefore, special *poojas* (sacrifices or offerings) are made to these spirits in the field in order to protect against losses caused by such appropriation.

The different spirits are placed in a particular hierarchical order. When gods are angered or not treated properly, deaths, epidemics, quarrels, crop failures, animal losses, and many more disasters occur in society. Bad gods also contribute to such calamities. The hierarchy from the bottom upwards is: the mountains, rivers and trees, through sub-divisional gods (*gambara*), regional gods, national gods and then the four worldly gods: Viruda, Virupaksha, Drutaraksha and Wesamuni. All matter is believed to exist in three physical forms: solid (*apo*), liquid (*theyo*) or vapour (*vayo*). Heat (*patavi*) determines in which of these three forms any matter exists. The cosmos, which was called *akasha*, exerts influence on the earth. These five factors are collectively referred to as Pancha Maha Butha in ancient literature.

COSMOVISION OF AGRICULTURE IN SRI LANKA

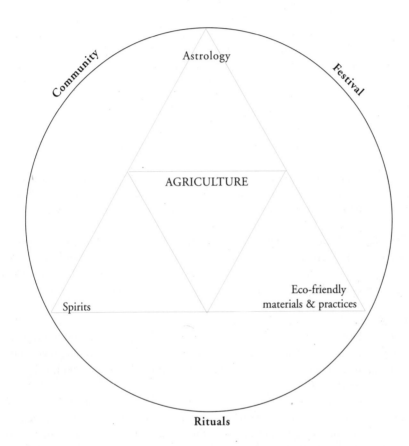

Mabima, the Buddhist priest from Kataragama explained his understanding of reality: '*In classical knowledge, upon which both Hinduism and Buddhism are based, reality is understood to function through a multitude of powers and forces. In western thinking, the most important powers are those of matter and energy. According to the theory of Einstein, matter and energy are just different expressions of the same phenomenon. In addition to these, Sri Lankan Buddhism recognises at least eight different forces and powers: the power of the moment (each moment has its special quality, hence the importance of astrology), the power of a certain location (sacred places, bad places), the power of sound (mantras), the power of symbols (yantras), the mental powers of certain persons (enhanced by training and pious lifestyle), the power of plants (i.e. the powers that go beyond the nutritional or pharmaceutical values), the power of place and space induced by certain events that have taken place there, and supernatural powers that have*

their origin in spirits or divine beings. It is important to understand all these different powers and know how to relate to them. But also the balance and synergy between these powers is important. This understanding cannot be achieved through mental efforts only. Also other levels of understanding are important: spiritual perception, feelings, intuition, using ordinary and extra-ordinary senses, dreams, visions. Words are too limited to explain the full richness and functioning of these powers and forces. Therefore, a prerequisite is personal spiritual development that helps overcome personal prejudices and biases. Spiritual development will enable people to be in full contact with all the powers and forces of life. A different language is necessary, of course: the language of metaphors, art and rituals. The traditional practices related to health, construction and agriculture are firmly based on the existence of these forces. Rural people have learned to handle this multitude of forces: local priests and shamans who live a pious life can perform rituals at auspicious times and at specific locations during which mantras *(sounds),* yantras *(symbols), and plants are used to create the good vibrations for plant and animal life and human health. These village priests or* shamans *acquire these capacities through training and initiation, during which they learn to develop their supernatural qualities, learn to overcome the prejudices and learn mantra's and how to perform rituals. The pious life style implies that they do not eat meat, do not consume alcohol, have no wrong sex, do not see dead bodies, do not lie and steal and are not attached to material goods.'*

Astrology. Astrology plays a significant role in the lives of Sri Lankan people. Rural people in particular have great faith in astrology and consult astrologers before embarking on any significant enterprise in their personal, educational or professional life. Astrology also plays a dominant role in agriculture, especially in the cultivation of rice. Farmers believe that certain days are good for beginning cultivation. They also avoid certain days which they consider inauspicious or unlucky. Usually a Sunday is chosen to initiate work relating to paddy cultivation. The work is begun on an auspicious day at an auspicious time. Most farmers follow the astrological calendar or *pancha suddiya* to ensure success and avoid bad luck. *Pancha suddiya* involves the following five aspects.

□ Adherence to 'good' and 'bad' days. For example, Thursdays and Fridays are considered auspicious or good days when important undertakings may be launched.

□ The position of the moon in relation to the earth. Twenty-seven such positions or *nekathas* are known out of which twelve are believed to be good. Also different *nekathas* are appropriate for different undertakings.

□ The auspicious *hora* or one-hour period. Seven *horas* are identified and each *hora* is divided into five *panchamakala hora* (12 minutes). Each of the latter is divided into three *shookshama horas* of 4 minutes and further sub-divided into periods of 36 seconds each.

□ Avoid facing certain directions on certain days. For example it is believed to be inauspicious to begin any important enterprise while facing the north on a Sunday. *Yogini* means facing auspicious directions.

□ The evil period. This period is called *rahukalaya* and one should not begin any important activities at this time. It lasts one and a half hour, and every day there are two such periods.

Eco-friendly practices. According to traditional practice, agricultural cultivation was a community activity. Individual decisions had to fall in line with communal decisions and the *gamarala* or village chief saw to it that all collective decisions were adhered to. Cultivation started with the making of a vow to the gods to ensure the success of cultivation. Then cultivation was initiated by the village leader in one area at an auspicious time. These activities were followed by several agricultural practices: minimal tillage of the land; mixed cropping and seeding wherever possible; fencing activities at auspicious moments; crop protection like the cultivation of a small portion of land to attract birds for pest management in paddy, performing *kems*, a ritual or a religious rite (see below), and if necessary supplement these actions with use of plants or plant extracts (biopesticides); Harvesting and heaping in the field for some weeks or months; threshing and separating a small portion for the Mangalya or other festival.

Spiritual practices

Since ancient times rituals have been used in Sri Lankan agriculture to support crop growth and animal husbandry and to chase away wild animals or pests that damage the crops. The combination of spiritual practices, astrology and eco-friendly technologies have become customs. Despite the impact of the green revolution, many of these spiritual practices still exist, but in some instances, their full meaning is not fully understood by the younger farmers. Frequently they are being practised away from the eyes and ears of outsiders. People have learned not to express their spiritual practices openly as they are often ridiculed or condemned by outsiders. Yet, our experience is that once we showed sincere interest in their spiritual practices, farmers were happy to share their experiences with us.

One of the most important rituals is the *pooja* or offering, carried out during the annual festival that is called Mangalya. In many villages this festival is held at the *devala*, a specific place, usually on the bund of the village water reservoir, the tank. On the day of the festival all items which are collected and purchased are taken in a procession to the devale premises. All men, women and children of the village are expected to participate. In the meantime some *poojas* are made to God Ganesh. These *poojas* consist of fruits, specially prepared oil cakes, and other items of food. Milk rice cooked at the place of God Ganesh is first offered to him. Then the milk rice cooked at another location is offered to five gods in a special stage decorated with betel leaves and sheltered with cloth. Offerings are made to two other gods, stages for which are made on either side of the main platform. It appears that one of these gods is responsible for the well-being of animals while the other is the guardian of crops. Finally, two more cups of food including fruits and milk rice are offered to Kadawara, the messenger of the god, who is also considered to be a powerful figure. A successful *pooja* is believed to usher in prosperity to the village farmers. If something goes wrong during the course of the *pooja*, the Kapurala (the caretaker or servant) will be punished. This festival is normally performed with a new harvest. There are certain rituals that have to be performed in order to remove curses, the ill effects of black magic, and to prevent crop losses caused by the Bairawas. Sometimes the participants wear masks and use fire torches.

There are three major sections to Buddha's teachings. One deals with the discipline of monks or priests; another section refers to the understanding of thoughts, mental activities and the process of thinking; and a third section is known as the Suthara Pitakaya which describes good ways of living. This section consists of many *suthras,* sermons preached by Lord Buddha. Reciting *suthras,* which is done to get rid of evil spirits and to invoke blessings, is called *pirith.* *Pirith* chanting is used to obtain protection for crops and cultivation. Farmers often chant *pirith* to prevent or obtain relief from crop diseases, animal epidemics and evil effects. There is nothing secret or confidential about these methods. But one important requirement is that the chanting has to be done by a devout person who leads a pious and righteous life. Fortunately, such people are available in our villages today. They are familiar with traditional religious practices such as charming sand and water for protection against pests. Many farmers in the villages obtain the services of these persons to protect their crops against pests and diseases. Many of them have reported that these traditional religions methods have proved to be more effective than chemical pesticides.

A *mantra* is a certain type of verse, a combination of carefully selected sounds that together create a nucleus of spiritual energy. It functions as a magnet or a lens to attract or create spiritual vibrations. According to the Upanishads, ancient writings from India, the *mantra* has its origin in the eternal and unchangeable substrate of the creation. *Mantras* existed in this substrate and caused the creation of the universe. Early seers and sages have made a study of the effects of sound or vibrations and in this way composed the specific combinations of sounds that are now established *mantras.*

In Sri Lankan Buddhism, it is considered evil to kill other forms of life. The use of chemical pesticides, therefore, is not consistent with the faith as it kills insects and other living organisms. In the tradition, several spiritual practices have been developed to relate to the spirits of the different living organisms. *Mantras* play an important role there. The spiritual leaders know what *mantras* to use to achieve specific effects. There are *mantras* to ask rats to leave the field, *mantras* to enhance a healthy crop and *mantras* to reduce the damage by paddy bugs. The *mantras* address some invisible spirits who is believed to grant redress. The words used, the sounds made and the rhythm of the reciting is important. Some *mantras* are very short and may consist of just a few words. *Mantras* are used in agriculture to obtain higher yields and also to protect crops from damage by pests and wild animals.

Yantras are symbols that have been given the powers by *mantra* or *pirith* chanting by a sacred person. It can have the form of a drawing, an idol or a structure. Some *yantras* are inscriptions on a thin strip of copper or palm leaves. These inscriptions can represent gods, spirits or be abstract geometrical figures or texts in Sanskrit or another language. *Yantras* are used to secure protection from ones enemies, the anger of the gods or evil spirits, ill effects of planets, forces of nature, envy and the evil eye. They can also help to ensure good crops or good health.

In agriculture, the use of *yantras* is widespread. Generally a *yantra* is placed in the centre of the rice threshing floor. An abstract geometrical drawing is used: three concentric circles and eight radial lines with different drawings on the outside: The *yantra* is placed or drawn on the threshing floor, certain items such as an oyster shell, a coconut, a piece of iron are placed on it, together with a few bundles of paddy.

During threshing operations no item is referred to by its real name. The idea is to mislead the spirits so they may not know that a threshing operation is going on. Other *yantras* are used for crop protection: against flies, rats, and for animal health.

During one of our field visits we discussed the use of *yantras* with the farmers. One of the farmers remembered that his father made use of these, and that he should have a booklet with the designs of the *yantras* in the attic of his house. He found the book. The pages had turned yellow and some pages were missing. It contained some 20 abstract geometric figures each referring to a specific plague or pest. We copied the booklet and have since shown it to several other farmers. In many instances they were recognised by traditional leaders as consistent with their own knowledge. Other farmers were eager to copy the drawings to test them in their fields.

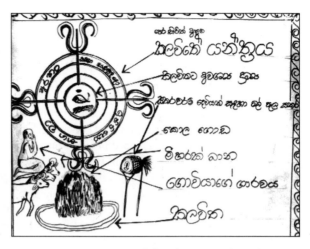

Drawing made by a farmer to indicate the yantra, mantra and rituals used when threshing rice.

The practice of *kems* is very widespread in rural Sri Lanka. A *kem* is a kind of practice, technique or custom that is followed in order to obtain some favourable effect such as relief from a specific illness. For example, washing in a pool of water immediately after a crow washes in that pool is believed to bring relief to people suffering from certain infirmities. A requirement in this *kem* is that the patient should wash without speaking or making much noise. The following *kem* is used for protection against the paddy fly. 'Go to the paddy field early in the morning, catch a fly at the entrance of the field, chant a specific *mantra* seven times and then release the fly'. Another one is: 'Charm some oil with a specific *mantra* and light an oil lamp at dusk at the farmers home and not in the field. To prevent crop damage by birds charm some sand and sprinkle it in the field'. Some *kems* combine the use of astrology with the use of certain plants or herbs. Other *kems* depend on the use of specific plants and *mantras*. These traditional practices have survived because they must be effective. If these had no real effect, they would have disappeared long ago.

There are also *kems* that do not involve any belief in spiritual beings or gods. These *kems* are based on a careful observation of nature and natural phenomena. The *kem* practised to destroy the paddy caterpillar belongs to this category. It works as follows: milk rice is prepared and put on circular slices of banana leaves, placed on tree stumps which are located in those parts of the field where caterpillars have infested the crop. This is done very early in the morning before the crows leave their nests. When the crows perch on the banana discs to eat the milk rice, the milk rice falls to the ground. When the crows pick up the fallen milk rice, they see the caterpillars and eat them instead of the milk rice. A variation of this practice is to keep roasted grains mixed with pieces of fruit in the evenings before sunset. This attracts carnivorous birds who destroy the caterpillars. Here, it is not the farmer who kills the caterpillars. So he does not commit any sin, which is an important consideration in Buddhism. This *kem* is an example of how traditional practices are based on knowledge of nature and religion.

Some *kems* are mechanical methods, like the lighting of fire torches. These torches are made using a piece of saffron robe for the wick and sticks of trees *wara* (Calatropis gigantea), *kadura* (Pagiantha dichotoma) or *gurula* (Leea indica) for the handle. The wick is dipped in butter oil or fat. A number of these torches are lighted and kept burning for about two hours at dusk. Most pests and insects are destroyed in this way. This is really a light trap. But the colouring used for the robe and the chemical properties of the selected sticks give extra effect. Today, some farmers may even use engine oil and cotton waste to make these torches. It is also believed that the torches will drive away evil spirits such as demons and *prethas*.

There are various conditions that have to be met to make the working of *kems* successful. For example, the farmer should not visit the field being treated for a specific period. This period of prohibition may be one, three or seven days. With some *kems*, women are prohibited from entering the field altogether, while other *kems* have to be performed by women only or even by pregnant women only. The effectiveness of a *kem* can be nullified if the person is exposed to a *killa* or impurity caused by eating certain food (especially meat). Attending a funeral also causes impurities. Another major impurity is associated with women's menstruation.

'Please accept this offering. Take care of my crops this season.
I'll promise that I'll do an offering at the end of the season.'

112

Cosmovisions of the Atoni, in Timor, Indonesia have shown a strong ability to survive and are translated in religion, economy and political structures or adat. ◆

5-1 A dukun *has spiritual powers and is consulted for crop diseases, human health and weather forecasts. On his advice the* pah tuaf, *or clan elder will perform rituals and sacrifices.*

5-2, 5-3 Lady harvesting sweet potatoes for own consumption. Soil erosion increases as traditional land use practices are abandoned and threatens food security.

One of the major aims of Timor Integrated Rural Development Programme (TIRD-P) is to realise a more just and democratic society where people can express their culture. In agriculture, learning and experimentation will be based on the Atoni cosmovisions. ◆

5-4 *Every clan builds an adat house, the meeting place of the elders of the clan. Here they decide about festivals, sacrifices and farming activities.*

5-5 *The adat houses have a location where animal sacrifices are being held. Especially pigs have great ceremonial value.*

5-6 *Traditional rulers (*rajas*) have great political influence and play important functions in rituals for crop production. Here the first harvested maize is kept and worshipped in the adat house.*

114

In Africa, ancestral ownership of land is widely accepted. The living are temporary possessors of a heritage to be passed on to yet unborn generations. Before adopting an innovation, spirits have to be consulted through ancestors. Soothsayers, traditional priests and spirit mediums can communicate with the ancestors and divine beings in the environment. ◆

5-7 In northern Ghana, sacrifices are made on the ancestral shrines in the courtyard of a farmers' house.

5-8 The chief fetish priest prepares to sacrifice a white chicken for reconciliation.

Chiefs are responsible for administrative and judicial functions. The spiritual world is the major driving force and regulates the performance of traditional institutions in Africa. ◆

5-9 *Young chief sitting in state with his sister after he has been initiated and installed.*

Antoni cosmovision and African ancestors

Indigenous institutions

Indigenous knowledge associated with the practice of agriculture and irrigation survived for over 2000 years due to the unique institutional system that supported it. This institutional system was made up of many components and organised as a hierarchy. At the base, there was the village – the smallest unit. Each village was under a *gamsabha* or village council. Each village also had a village chief. A number of villages formed a *korale* which was the next higher level. Next came *rataymahattayas* and even larger divisions were called *disawas*. At the apex of this pyramid was the king who possessed unlimited power. Any problem that could not be resolved at the local level was referred to the higher levels. Village temples and *devales* with their priests also enjoyed a certain degree of power. Then there were practitioners of Ayurvedic medicine.

The *pirivena* was the only formal education institute. This is a school attached to a Buddhist temple of worship. While religion was taught by Buddhist priests, the other three sections of the indigenous knowledge system, namely medicine, astrology and ritualism were taught by masters (*gurus*). In the passing down of this knowledge from master to pupil, some important sections were deliberately kept back without being passed down to the pupils. This practice of retaining some knowledge was referred to as *guru mushtiya*. The knowledge was hidden for the pupil and only given when the master died. In many instances, knowledge retained by the master in this way was lost forever.

This entire knowledge system is written in ola scripts. Young leaves of palmyrah trees are treated and seasoned in a particular way to produce a writing surface. The teachings of Lord Buddha are also written on these ola scripts. These writings can be categorised into four main fields: *dhamma*, medicine, astrology and the category dealing with spirits, *yantras* and *mantras*. The *dhamma* books also contain remedies for crop damage, pest attacks, damage from wild animals and also advice for improving yields. The medical book contained methods of treatment for crops. These remedies are described as Vrkshayurveda: Vrksha means trees and Ayurveda means treating sicknesses and physical disorders. A large number of remedies, rituals, and the use of spirits can be found in the section covering astrology and spirits. These prescriptions have been safeguarded as secrets and some have been passed down orally.

These indigenous systems began to disappear with the advent of westerners. The *gamsabha* was abolished in 1832. The gamarala was replaced by an officer called the *velvidane* in the 1860s. The *velvidane's* functions related only to the cultivation of paddy. Other components of the farming system such as highland and livestock farming were neglected. Agriculture in the villages came more and more under the influence of bureaucrats who were outsiders. Then modern technology entered village agriculture. The Waste Lands Ordinance was an enormous blow to indigenous agriculture. This law introduced by the British, enabled them to buy up land at very low prices. Coffee plantations were established and later tea and cocoa were planted. Natives lost access to the land and this destroyed village agriculture. Christian missionaries came from an entirely different socio-cultural and religious background and did not appreciate the value of indigenous practices or beliefs. Some of them deliberately suppressed and ridiculed them in order to introduce their own beliefs and practices.

The present institutional arrangements favour individual activity rather than communal or cooperative efforts. Paid labour was introduced into village agriculture that until then had depended on the mutual exchange of labour. Agriculture became an economic pursuit, and no longer a way of life. As a result, human values, respect for nature and cultural considerations all began to disappear.

The introduction of science-based education accelerated this process further. Modern science has not seriously studied indigenous knowledge. Instead of subjecting it to scientific study to test its validity, scientists tend to dismiss it as a myth. Agricultural scientists do not seem to have much faith in indigenous knowledge. Yet, the rejection of indigenous knowledge has led to the disturbance of the ecosystem. Crop failures are frequent due to non-adherence to cultivation time-schedules.

One can also observe a revival of the interest of agricultural scientists in traditional practices, including their spiritual aspects. One promising feature is that Integrated Pest Management methods in agriculture are likely to gain popularity over chemical methods in the next few years. Many traditional methods are now included in IPM of rice pests in Sri Lanka.

In the north, central and the northwest Province, although certain changes have occurred in the practices, methods and techniques related to agriculture, by and large the traditional way of farming has been preserved. Many farmers use both modern as well as traditional methods. Almost all farmers use fertilisers and agro-chemicals. At the same time they adhere to traditional practices such as making a vow to gods when cultivation begins. They fulfil this vow at the end of the season. This also takes place in the colonisation schemes established by the government. More farmers are now using modern pesticides rather than indigenous techniques. This is due to the propaganda carried out by agricultural officers and chemical companies. In some places, for example, conditions favour the adoption of traditional techniques. The availability of practitioners of ancient techniques helps to get them adopted in some areas. Many farmers have now realised the serious negative consequences of modern methods.

Our challenge within COMPAS

It has to be accepted that a large section of the farmer population has more or less abandoned most indigenous practices and techniques and adopted modern technologies that are often directly antagonistic to astrology, supernatural beings and the ecosystem. However, the number of individuals or formal institutions interested in indigenous knowledge is gradually on the increase. Ecological Conservation Organisation is experimenting with farmers on both eco-friendly practices, *kems*, rituals and *poojas* to the gods. We follow the technique of observation and experimentation by several farmers and then meetings are organised where farmers share their experiences. Almost every phenomenon that was subjected to testing has produced satisfactory results. The re-introduction of indigenous practices needs careful planning. Such a plan should have the following steps:

□ Identification of areas where aspects of indigenous and cosmovision-based knowledge is currently being practised.

□ Collection of available information on availability of competent persons that can apply these methods and techniques and comparing these practises with modern technology.

☐ Examination of constraints, if any, that may prevent the widespread application of cosmovision-based techniques.

☐ Verification of the effectiveness of cosmovision-based methods and techniques practised by farmers. These verifications can be carried out by volunteer farmers who carry out tests on their own fields.

☐ Techniques found to be effective are introduced to farmers by training resource persons and making the services of the latter available to them.

☐ Increasing awareness in the form of seminars and workshops for farmers, NGO officials and government officials, in which the experiences of farmers and researchers are discussed.

☐ Successful case studies to be given publicity through the mass media.

The above programme was implemented in Polonnaruwa District and generated a lot of interest among the farmers. Many more farmers will participate, as over 100 demonstrations are now being planned. These demonstrations will show the farmers how the application of cosmovision-based technologies can help them solve the problem of low yields, persistent losses and damage to the environment. Most of these techniques, practices and methods are environment friendly, do not involve high costs and are also culturally accepted. Fortunately many participants have offered to train selected youths from different parts of the country to use these techniques, practices and methods. There has also been a suggestion that a private library be organised that would be accessible to recognised practitioners.

The next step is testing on a small scale. Small plots are selected for this process. Observations are made and tests carried out in these plots. Since these tests are duplicated in a large number of plots, the results are acceptable. Successful techniques are immediately adopted by farmers in the neighbourhood. This ensures that successful techniques spread to other areas. Buddhist temples are important places with respect to indigenous knowledge, because priests in charge carry out indigenous practices such as charming water and sand. The close relationship that exist between the rural people and the Buddhist temples are a great help in popularising indigenous knowledge. Buddhist priests have close contact with farmers and moreover they command respect among the farming community.

When we organised workshops in the context of this study, the participants became so interested, that one of the NGOs - Janodaya - offered to organise a workshop in a temple so as to provide practitioners with the opportunity of contributing more towards popularising indigenous knowledge and cosmovision. The chief incumbent of this temple was himself a resource person. Another workshop was held in Kaudulla, in the Polonnaruwa district and was attended by resource persons, NGO officials and practitioners. This workshop too was very successful and many participants revealed the effective techniques they used. The meeting ended with a resolution to apply indigenous methods in agriculture together with certain modern ones. The success of this workshop led to the organisation of two more similar workshops that received assistance from the local agricultural society. Now the farmers themselves have organised another workshop and have even undertaken to provide its participants with lunch and refreshments. Since farmers have now realised that farming is not profitable with modern technology, they are looking for alternatives. There is clearly scope for the popularisation of indigenous knowledge and cosmovision.

The Ministry of Agriculture is also now involved in experiments with cosmovision - based practices. At the end of 1997, a series of farmers exchange meetings were organised for their staff. Kalyani Palangasinghe, one of the Sri Lankan COMPAS partners, describes how such a meeting was organised. *'With the help of farmer leaders, I identified key people: those who have a spiritual function, knowledgeable farmers, Ayurvedic doctors. Also people with an interest in the subject were invited. Farmer leaders are respected in the community and know their own culture well. The objectives of the meeting were discussed with the resource persons: to present to farmers the spiritual practices that are being used in the tradition and specifically how they should carry out their roles. In Sri Lanka, shamans carry out rituals to influence the good growth of the crops by enhancing the powers of sound (mantras) and symbols (yantras). These rituals have to be performed at auspicious times, to be determined by astrologers. The shamans undergo extensive apprenticeships, have to be inaugurated and should live a pious life. These shamans were asked to reveal the* mantras *they are using, show some of the* yantras *and make a demonstration of a certain ritual. Other shamans were asked to make a drawing of the ritual they generally perform on a piece of paper of a size large enough to be presented to the meeting. My role was to prepare and facilitate the meeting.*

According to the farmers, mantras and yantras create vibrations leading to a harmony in the plot.

We made use of traditional symbols and ceremonies to introduce the meeting. An oil lamp was lightened and mantras *were intoned. There was a demonstration of a ritual in the farmers' meeting. It is very important to search for the right resource persons. We also made a kind of healthy curative oil, and gave a small demonstration which immediately shows its applicability. The farmers were very enthusiastic. They sensed that in this way their knowledge, their culture and their spirituality was respected. The meeting lasted longer than usual. Even after the meeting farmers continued discussions. Most of the participants wrote down the mantras, and in some cases they recognised them from the time their parents had used them.*

During the meeting drawings of spiritual practices were shown. They provoked so much reactions that we only needed to ask: 'What do you see in this poster, and do you think it is useful?' to get a very lively discussion going. At the end of the meeting we asked which farmers were interested in

120

experimenting with some of the traditional practices that had been presented. We got more than twenty volunteers and I promised that I would help them in carrying out the experiments. I now need to define the methods for field experiments. My colleagues of the Ministry of Agriculture were surprised about the degree of participation and the self-respect shown by the leaders. Nobody said it was nonsense. Apparently the idea was well received and the idea to start testing them appealed to both the farmers and professional scientists.'

Recent activities

The results of the work by COMPAS further helped build the network and different organisations, farmer groups and individuals in different parts of the country are now working on cosmovision. The most important lesson was that during sharing workshops, farmers readily accepted the idea of testing, experimenting and further validating the methods. The involvement of officials of the Ministry of Agriculture, and various other government departments and research institutions, and district administrative officials in various capacities needs to be further strengthened so that use can be made of their capacities in order to further understand and develop cosmovision-based ecological agriculture.

In the coming years, we will engage in a number of activities. First of all, we will reinforce the interest among farmers in experimentation in order to test and improve indigenous and effective traditional farming techniques. Farmers will be the main actors, but we will also intensify the relations with support organisations. Possibly, collaborative experiments will be executed with other national and international research institutes. We also hope to contribute to building theory to explain the results.

We also intend to continue collecting and documenting information on indigenous knowledge and cosmovision, their concepts of life, and indigenous institutions. Key persons, both men and women, will be interviewed, life histories will be studied and village workshops will be organised to study and discuss the topic and share information with other traditional farming systems. Participation in village festivals, rituals and other important events will be central. The documentation will not only be in written form, but also in audio and video records, slides and photos, and also through indigenous expressions with local media, local symbols, music, songs and designs. It will be interesting and challenging to conduct exchange visits between villagers, village leaders and spiritual leaders. In order to present the information to a wider audience, we also intend to conduct national and international seminars and workshops.

Field staff will be further trained and supported in order to assist field staff implement these activities with farmers. We hope to establish clusters of traditional leaders and farmer groups, in which the methods used by the various farmer groups will be documented, discussed and their effectiveness assessed. In order to exchange and agree on the approaches to be used, national, regional and village level working groups will be established. We also intend to do intense networking with governmental and non-governmental institutions, but the farmer groups who intend to continue with indigenous practices will have most of our attention.

To meet the demand of partner organisations that are working with farmers and are interested in this approach, we offer support with documentation, testing and the improvement of traditional techniques themselves. We hope to establish a field laboratory where we can also do some of the testing ourselves and strengthen our cooperation with Buddhist priests and traditional shamans.

ATONI COSMOVISIONS IN AGRICULTURE IN TIMOR

Johan Kieft and Marthen Duan

The Atoni, or Dawan as they are called in the Belunese language, live in the western part of the island of Timor, Indonesia. They are still mainly subsistence farmers and have some livestock which are free ranged. They collect non-wood forest products such as candlenut and Tamarind and they also produce handicrafts. For centuries Timor was famous for its sandalwood. In an early Chinese report of 1225 by the Chinese inspector of overseas trade, Chau Ju-Kua, Timor was mentioned as being rich in sandalwood [Krom, 1931]. From 1511 onwards, the Portuguese became interested in the island's sandalwood trade. They needed sandalwood to trade with the Chinese because there were no European products that were of value to China. In Europe, there was hardly any demand for it. The Dutch became interested for the same reason, but they were unable to control the trade. The competition for sandalwood led to Timor being divided between the Dutch and the Portuguese. The east became Portuguese and the west Dutch. The western part became Indonesian in 1949 when the Dutch withdrew from Indonesia. In 1975 East Timor became a part of Indonesia.

Compared to the other Indonesian islands, Timor is dry. Average rainfall depends on topography and the mountains generally receive significantly more (over 2000 mm) than the surrounding flat lands (1000-1400 mm). The western part of the island is influenced by the north-west monsoon and receives rain in a relatively short three-month period from December to March. More to the east, the importance of the north-west monsoon becomes less significant and the chances of drought during the wet season increase significantly. In the east, the southern monsoon brings occasional rainfall, especially to the south of the island. Cassava can grow there all year round, and short season 90 days crops like mungbean can be produced during the dry season [Pingin, 1995]. According to Fox [1995] the effects of ENSO (El Niño Southern Oscillation) are marked and these limit the boundaries within which agriculture can be carried out. Farmers must contend with the certainty of uncertain rainfall and at least implicitly attune their activities at the beginning of each raining season to the worst case scenario. This, according to Fox, is the only reasonable perspective for agricultural development.

The island is not volcanic. The parent material of the soils consists of uplifted sea bottom, a process that is still going on. This geological background means that soils are not as fertile as on volcanic islands such as Flores and Java. There are five major agro-ecosystems in Timor [Alderick & Anda, 1987]. First, there are alluvial marine plains and basin agro-ecosystems: generally flat to sloping land where the soils close to the rivers are loamy. During the monsoon percolation is limited which means that these soils, especially the clayey ones are suited for rainfed *sawah* (rice) cultivation. Land is also used for *ladangs* (swidden cultivation) and grazing. There are also palm forests that provide materials that can be used for house building. Farmers have developed an indigenous system of fallow management [Kieft, 1997]. Secondly, there are the coral plateau agro-ecosystems These gently sloping reefal limestone soils with reddish clay have a low swelling and shrinking potential. The soils are often too shallow for crop production, but as groundwater is close by (4-5 m depth), there is good potential for small-scale irrigation with the help of windmills. Then there are limestone and marl upland agro-ecosystems. This moderately sloping land consists of limestones and marl. There used to be a lush, mixed tropical hardwood forest, but this has now been removed and the area is now covered with coconut palms, fruit trees and home gardens. These soils are favoured by the Timorese farmers. Fourthly, there are Bobonaro clay soils, which are basically uplifted marine clays with poor physical and chemical properties. They are extremely hard when dry and very sticky when wet. With a very low infiltration rate, these soils are also very sensitive to erosion. In Amarasi (Kab Kupang), farmers developed their system of fallow management based on the use of Leucaena on these soils. This system is seen as a successful example of indigenous fallow management and land rehabilitation [Field et. al., 1992]. Fifthly, there are old alluvial terrace deposits in which the soils are neutral and slightly acid red clayey. These lands are not used intensively, mainly because of dryness. Farmers themselves have developed their own land use characterisation system. For Unab, a hamlet 30 km east of Kefamenanu farmers mentioned 4 major soil types: black, red, stony and clayey. In other areas farmers use a comparable system [Kieft, 1997].

Cosmovisions

Cosmovisions, or how people understand relations between mankind, spirituality and nature, has a significant impact on the way people organise their lives on Timor. The recent problems between the local government and the indigenous people on land rights can clarify this. According to the law, land which is under forest is government land. The people living in these forests and living from it believe that it is theirs. They are convinced that the land has been given by the Almighty to their ancestors. If they loose it, because they are not able to defend it, their ancestors will be very angry [YTM, 1997]. The way cosmovisions are worked out in religious, economic and political structures is called *adat* in Indonesian.

TIRD-P or Timor Integrated Rural Development Programme is a network of four NGOs (Haumeni, Tafenpah, Tafentop and Timor Membangum). Alfa-Omega and Justisia are also partners in TIRD-P, the latter providing juridical support to farmers. The aims of TIRD-P is to realise a more just and democratic society, in which there is room for people to express their culture and cosmovision. The partners are currently working on integrated crop development and part of the programme is dealing with farmer experimentation, in which attempts are made to use indigenous forms and concepts of experimentation.

An important concept in the cosmovisions of the Atoni is the *le'u* concept. It means holy, sacred, something that provokes awe. It is a force that can be either dangerous or beneficial. Anything might become *le'u* as a results of a ceremonial act or a dream. The Atoni distinguish the following kind of *le'u*: *le'u nono* or fertility; *le'u musu* or hostility; *le'u fenu*, a medicine used during pregnancy and child birth; *le'u abanut,* another medicine used for taming buffaloes; and *le'u kinat* applied in conjunction with the manufacture of dyes for weaving (*kinat*).

In the literature there are no creation myths mentioned [Schulte-Nordholt, 1971; Asche, 1995]. However, every clan has its myth of origin. An example is the myth of origin of the Teakas village. *'Long ago, around the year 1400, Neno ani tei and Amaina were the first people originating from nature. They were originally a piece of wood and a stone. They saw the sun for the first time when they left the cave Popnam. They lived in a place where now there is* rumah adat *(temple). After a while they separated and one lived in the area close to the cave Oekanaf popnam and the other in Faotkanaf Naisolat'.* [YTM/Kehati, 1997].

Cosmovisions still play a very important role in economic life. Agriculture and handicraft production are closely related to cosmovisions. Still people perform the ceremonies. On every garden plot the farmers build a small temple of stones. It is there they offer to the spirits, their ancestors and Uis Neno and were farmers try to influence nature. However, the relationship between experimentation and their prayers has to be clarified.

During discussions held in the village of Panthea on technology development, farmers stated that if a technology is to be accepted they ask for signs from their ancestors. A typical example was the introduction of a hybrid maize variety in the mid-1980's. The variety Arjuna was introduced by the government under force. Initially it developed well but when the cob was ready to harvest, it was attacked by a weevil. The introduction failed completely and it meant a set back in agricultural development from the governments' point of view. The farmers experienced it as a sign from their ancestors that this variety was not good for them. The farmers have their own concept of experimenting which is called *cobal tit*. It means try out something first and when it is suited, use it. Still it is not clear what indicators they use in this adaptation process. Research on this issue is still on going.

The table shows the ceremonies performed in Kainbaun in 1996. When the calendar is compared with the one described by Schulte Nordholt [1971] which is based on data gathered in 1947, there were hardly any differences. The only difference is that the buffalo has been replaced by the cow.

How do cosmovision relate to costs? For both maize and rice crops, the major costs involved in terms of time and money are related to hedging to protect the crops from free ranging animals. Costs for *adat* and ceremonies are only a small part of the total cost, some 5%. It is not true, as is often assumed, that *adat* negatively influences income due to the expense involved in ceremonies. The major cause of low profits are low yields caused by low soil fertility [Piggin, 1995].

AGRICULTURAL EVENT	ADAT AND MEANING	CEREMONY
Land clearing	**Feknono Hauawa:** adat elders determine which fields are going be used, which wood will be cut and the ropes made of wood beans.	Enter maize into the adat house.
After burning the fields	**Si fon nopo:** to cool down the fields which are just burned.	Sprinkle the fields with bamboo sprouts.
Planting and sowing	**Simosuak:** to prepare for planting.	Every member of a clan gets a planting stick from the head of the clan and plants 3 to 4 holes of the head's field before starting on his own fields.
Land conservation	**Eka hoe:** to avoid the field from erosion.	At the lowest point of the field the head of the clan slaughters pig and chicken (to contact ancestors).
Pests, diseases and climatic problems	**Doa adat:** to ask for protection for the crops.	Pray to get in contact with the ancestors.
Harvesting	**Seka pena:** the young maize season.	People are not allowed to eat the maize just after harvest. The newly harvested maize has to be entered into church and the clans' house. After this every clan collects its cows and fries maize and prays under the ficus tree. Then the people dance around the cows and break a melon/cucumber on the back of a cow, so that the herd will not enter the gardens and eat the harvest.

To answer the problem of soil fertility, Sloping Agricultural Land Technology (SALT) has been introduced by NGOs and government projects. SALT aims at contour hedging, non-burning of fields and the recycling of organic matter. However, its adaptation has been low. In a discussion on soil fertility, farmers said that they believed strongly in the use of fire to increase fertility when they open land. They mentioned that yields of land burned earlier are higher that those not burned. Our research confirmed this statement. Also here cosmovisions play an important role and determine the choice of technology. Still many questions are unanswered. SALT clearly cannot compete with the traditional way of agriculture. Also there is a strong relation between burning and cosmovision-based concept of farming, as has been indicated in the table [Kieft, 1997].

Agriculture and handicraft are closely related. Cotton is only produced for making *ikats*. In more isolated villages in the Biboki kingdom most of the old women use home grown cotton to weave *ikats*. *Ikats* are one of the most specific expressions of the Timorese culture: each clan has its own design. *Ikats* symbolise feminity and have an important function in rituals and the exchange economy of the Atoni: it opposes the masculine gifts of money, weapons and animals [Asche, 1995]. Some clothes have magical powers. People believe that these clothes can have a protective function in times of individual weakness such as childbirth and sickness [Asche, 1995]. The relationship between clothes (*ikat*) and *adat* is the main reason why it is difficult to 'rationalise' its production. The major aim of weaving is not to increase income but to make sure that when *ikats* have to be exchanged (marriage, death etc.) there are

Timorese farmers use home-grown cotton to weave ikats.

127

clothes available. However, one of the NGOs in TIRD, Tafenpah, has proven that if the women receive a reasonable price for their work, they are willing to increase production. Asche proves that the poorest are the most active weavers.

In 1998, TIRD started with an integrated crop management approach in which experimentation is a major activity. TIRD is using the indigenous concept of *cobal tit* to stimulate farmers to look for opportunities to develop farming. It is in a sense a way of testing by transforming technology coming from outside the community and synthesising it with local culture. It is similar to what has been mentioned by Van Veldhuizen (1995) in his article on farmers' experimentation. In one village a farmer was farming on very steep slopes. He had experienced erosion and was wondering what to do. After an NGO had carried out training on how to plant hedgerows and how this could be used to prevent erosion, he decided he should also plant hedgerows. Instead of using legumes as proposed during the training, he used cassava. He planted the cassava close together: 5 cm within the row. He mentioned that one of the main advantages of his adjustment was that he had cassava leaves which he could use as vegetables.

The economic performance of agriculture is low and in the long term will lead to marginalisation. Labour and land are not paid and the availability of food is insecure. Farmers are not accumulating capital to develop agriculture but instead they are using capital (silver, gold, *ikats*) to purchase food. This is one of the biggest push factors in urbanisation. It means that young people are not attracted to work in agriculture any longer, although they have very few other alternatives. This is a big challenge for TIRD. TIRD wants to support these processes in the field. It wants to improve the performance of farmers through learning by doing and experimenting. TIRD had made a small start but still needs to do more. One of its major aims is to realise a more just and democratic society in which there is a place for people to express their culture. Cosmovisions in the area have proven to be resilient and have a strong ability to survive. Although the church and the Indonesian State have challenged their existence, they are still being practised by people in the area. TIRD needs to do more. It has to develop a framework for development that is based on the cosmovision of the people.

References

Alderick, J. M. and M. Anda, 1987.
   The land resources of Nusa Tenggara, Technical report 3 Nusa Tenggara Agricultural Project. Melbourne: ACIL, 96 p.
Asche, 1992.
   Dialogue in development, Unpublished Msc-thesis. Darwin: Northern Territory University, 230 p.
Carson, B., 1987.
   In: Alderick & Alda, 1987.
Fox, J., 1995.
   Social history and government policy of agricultural development in eastern Indonesia. Paper presented on the international conference on agricultural development in semi arid areas of East Nusa Tenggara, East Timor and South East Maluku. Kupang, Indonesia, 8 p.

Kieft, J. A. M., 1997.

The use of Sesbania grandiflora as a farmers' answer to declining soil fertility in North Central Timor. Paper presented at the regional workshop on Indigenous strategies for intensification of shifting cultivation in South East Asia. Bogor, June 22nd -June 27th., 24 p.

Krom, N. J. (1931)

Hindoe-Javaansche geschiedenis. In: J. Ormeling (1957: p.93), 's-Gravenhage.

Ormeling, F. J., 1957.

The Timor Problem, second impression. Groningen/Djakarta: J.B. Wolters / 's-Gravenhage: Martinus Nijhof, 285 p.

Piggin, C.M., 1995.

Agronomic aspects for agricultural development in semi-arid regions. Paper presented on the international conference on agricultural development in semi arid areas of East Nusa Tenggara and South East Malluku. Kupang, Indonesia, 24 p.

Schulte Nordholt, H. G., 1971.

The political system of the Antoni of Timor, Den Haag: Martinus Nijhof. 511 p.

YTM (Yayasan Timor Membangun), 1997

Pengelolaan Sumbur Daya Alam secara Berlanjut dan Lestari: Lokakarya Jaringan Masyarakat Adat Timor Tengah Utara. Kefamenanu: Unpublished, 42 p.

YTM / Yayasan Kehati.

Berpikir bersama, berbuat bersama. Kefamananu: Unpublished, 39 p.

Van Veldhuizen L., 1995.

Experimentation by farmers. In: COMPAS Newsletter (2), pp. 20-21.

Uis Neno

Uis Neno, crocodile: water of the moon, water of the sun.
He bestows righteous, gives coolness and coldness
A shinning body, a splendid body, as we say: Uis Neno of the water.
Uis Neno, the radiant one, the brilliant one, the sun
Neno who arts a vault, who dost give shelter, who dost give shade
He who brings about change, who alters, who provides and supports
Who burns and scorches
Who raises up and administers justice
Mayest Thou give coolness and cold
Star, morning star and full moon
are the younger brothers of Uis Neno.
The moon is the wife of Uis Neno.
His spouse is the moon
When Uis Neno sleeps we do not go forth
The divine man we call sun
The divine woman we call moon
Le'u moon, Le'u sun
Thou are both radiant,
Thou are both brilliant

In this Atoni prayer, Uis Neno means the Lord of heaven. In the first four lines he is compared with three other gods, Uis Pah, the Earthgod; Uis Oe; and the god of water, symbolised by a crocodile. Uis Neno is the one who makes the earth fertile. In these lines he is identical with Uis Pah, the Earthgod, who is his pendant and the deity that is complementary to him though its nature is entirely different.

Uis Pah also refers to 'the earth spirits'. In every garden the Atoni build a small temple of stones to honour him. Uis Neno is as the sun, radiant and fierce and makes the earth hot. He provides humans with rice and maize. He is also the *le'u* (awe springing) and a taboo (*nuni*) and stands above everything. Mankind is surrounded by a host of spirits and invisible forces. They stand between humans and Uis Neno. People believe that Uis Neno is responsible for all good things. If bad things happen, a mistake was made in the rituals or a taboo was broken.

TRADITIONAL AFRICAN WORLDVIEWS

FROM A COSMOVISION PERSPECTIVE

David Millar

'*The common awareness that the earth we are part of has been entrusted to us and can in no way be considered as property or commodity to dispose of as we please (like the Whiteman does), has always been deeply embedded in our traditional beliefs. Traditional philosophy ascribed a sacred significance to land. It was commonly believed that basic property, in particularly land, belongs to the ancestors. This principle of ancestral ownership made the living temporary possessors of a heritage which was destined to pass to generations yet unborn. Land was an ancestral trust, committed to the living for the benefit of the whole community, in particular the unborn generations. It is intended for the benefit of ourselves and the generations yet unborn. We, the living and in particular the Chief and the Tindambas, are the custodians of the land. Land, therefore, is the most valuable heritage of the whole community, and cannot be lightly parted with.*'

This philosophical pronouncement was brought very recently to my attention by a Konkonba Elder, Femme Biligon in northern Ghana. Although this encounter happened a short while ago, it translates back into several historical discourses I have had in various parts of Africa on the subject of cosmovision. It also finds expression in several writings of scholars interested in the sociology and anthropology of Africa. I take the position that in all these narratives, the common thread flowing through the African perspective is 'The Triad': the principle of ancestor (representing the dead), the living, and the generations yet unborn. It is similar to the three-persons-in-one-God concept of the Christian religion: Father, Son and Holy Spirit. F. W. Bartle alludes to a similar position in his article 'The universe has three souls' [Bartle, 1990].

Land is the most revered property of all African traditions. It is in the ownership, management, and use of this common property that African traditions best express their cosmovisions. Reverent Father Globus, in his paper presented to a national Eucharist Congress in Ghana on the Church and the Environment puts it like this: '*According to the northern ethnic groups, land was the property of the earth spirit who was the giver of the means to live. The Gas (living in the coastal area in southern Ghana) attributed ownership of land to sacred lagoons, while the Ashanties regarded land as a supernatural female force - the inexhaustible source of sustenance and the provider of the most basic needs. The earth was helpful if propitiated, and harmful if neglected. Land was the sanctuary for the souls of the departed ancestors.*' The late Nana Sir Ofori Atta I, an Ashanti chief, spoke the famous words: '*Land belongs to a vast family of whom many are dead, a few are living and a countless host are still unborn.*' A well-known Ashanti saying that sums it all up goes as follows: '*The farm is mine, but the soil belongs to the stool.*'

Land belongs to a vast family of whom many are dead, a few are living and countless hosts are still unborn.

It could be argued that it is very difficult, if not impossible, to take a common position for a continent so huge and diverse as Africa. This does not seem to be the case when it comes to the subject of cosmovision. When the focus is on 'The Triad', and the focus is on land as a common property, a common vocabulary and knowledge, and therefore a common culture, sweeps through Africa. In my own researches and field studies, I have constantly been reminded of the commonness and similarities in positions taken on 'ancestor-centrism' and land, as a medium expressing cosmovisions. I came across these reminders when I was in Casamance, Senegal, as part of a Farming Systems Research team in 1984 and in Zaria, Nigeria, as part of the Institute of Field Communication and Agricultural Training team. But also in Burkina Faso, where part of my own ancestral home lies. With Burkina, I have been able to gather more information from the work of R. A. Swanson on the Gourma and from Malidoma P. Somé's book 'Of water and spirits'. In 1992 in Zimbabwe, when I was member of an international workshop on research-extension linkages and also during my over twenty studies and researches in both northern and southern Ghana similar impressions have been confirmed. With these encounters as a spring-board, what are the details of the common characteristics of the African perspective of the cosmovision paradigm?

The African cosmovision concept

The cosmovision notion originates from a culture which has a holistic worldview, integrating the world with the cosmos. In this perspective, the whole of nature is conceived as a living being, like an animal, with all parts interrelated and needing to perform. Human society is part of nature and mankind works and communicates with nature. Nature does not belong to mankind, but mankind to nature. Thus, human society does not stand in opposition to nature, as in the western view where mankind is considered the conqueror of natural forces. This relationship is not static, but dynamic and involves continuous domestication and transformation of the environment which must not be abused or flouted.

Cosmovision is a social construct that includes the assumed interrelationships between spirituality, nature and mankind. It describes the role of supernatural powers, the natural processes that take place and the relationship between mankind and nature. It also makes explicit the philosophical and scientific basis on which interventions in nature take place. Being a social construction implies that it is not a uniform concept. However, cosmovisions often indicate a hierarchy in divine beings, spiritual beings (especially the ancestors), natural forces (such as climate, diseases,

COSMOVISION IN NORTHERN GHANA

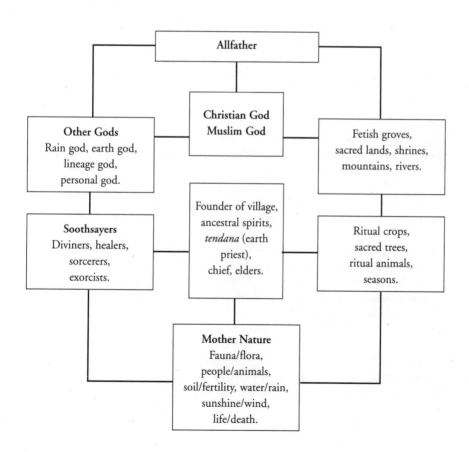

133

floods), soil, vegetation, animals, man and woman. These hierarchies, when they exist, give rise to several rituals in which the elders, priests and soothsayers play prominent roles and prescribe the way problem-solving and general experimentation can take place. This presupposes the way people go about knowledge and technology development. Because of the holistic nature of the worldview, the hierarchies are often difficult to discern. Below is a diagrammatic representation of the interrelationships mentioned above in the northern Ghanaian context.

Several studies have drawn attention to spirituality as an essential component of rural people's way of life. Though research in this field is by no means exhausted, the cosmovision paradigm provides an added framework for studying indigenous knowledge, with emphasis on wholeness. Earlier anthropologists have documented how spirituality is a vital component in the lives of the people of Africa. Fortes [1962], Goody [1972] and Brown [1975] do not refer to cosmovision and do not make the interrelations spelt out above. They have underscored the importance and the need to take the link between spirits of the dead, the yet unborn, and the living very seriously and shown how this link influences the use of resources in Africa. Kassogue et al. [1990] have thoroughly discussed the role of nature and mankind and their relationship with the spirits among the Dogon in Mali. A more advanced form of this discourse can be found in Firth [1967; 1970] in which he describes 'the freeing of the land' which takes place before the yam planting among the Tikopia. With a few differences, the Tikopia also make a clear link between spirituality, materiality (nature) and mankind. Recent attempts at drawing attention to African folk spirituality can be found in the studies of Huizer [1991; 1995]. His findings reflect the work of Zimbabwean organisations like ZIRRCON - the Zimbabwean Institute of Religious Research and Ecological Conservation. Also AZTREC - the Association of Zimbabwe Traditional Environmental Conservationists as presented by Cosmas Gonese in this publication, has a similar orientation. Gonese's description of the philosophy behind the management of natural resources reinforces the position of the Elder (as Femme Biligon, quoted in the beginning of this article) on the land and their images of the land. The work of Sibanda [1997] and Mahir and Millar [1994] focuses on the spirituality of trees in Zimbabwe and the Sudan. The livestock sector has received its fair share of spirituality. Toure [1990] elaborately described traditional livestock herding and spirituality in Senegal. B. J. Linquist and David Adolph described in Blunt and Warren [1996] the rituals and use of sacred proverbs as part of veterinary knowledge among the Gabra, camel pastoralists in Northern Kenya. Two of my recent studies (yet to be published) are on Fulani herdsmen in Ghana and on cattle track management and spirituality.

The role of different functionaries in perpetuating the worldviews of traditional African societies, as they influence of development interventions, is vividly elucidated by Professor Kofi Asare Opuku in two publications 'Traditional attitudes towards nature in Africa' [1993] and 'The traditional foundations of development' [1989]. He mentions the institution of chieftaincy and their prescribed functionaries, griots and town criers, the various leaderships and their structural arrangements, and describes their functions as traditionally supportive to the chiefs in rural development. He puts the chief at the centre. Beumers and Koloss [1992] take a similar position with their article 'Kings of Africa'. The chief or king is really central to rural development in cephalous societies (with chiefs), but for some acephalous societies (without chiefs) in Africa, the land priests or land owners may occupy centre stage. Swanson [1980] reveals to us development and spirituality in his article 'Development interventions and self-realisation among the Gourma': *'The Gourma of Upper Volta (now Burkina Faso) have a highly developed worldview that incorporates specific concepts and perceptions of human beings, souls, God and destiny. Individual actions that result in failure or success, are seen as a reflection of destiny.'* From his viewpoint, destiny becomes a factor in sustainable development. Hence, with destiny as a social construct, he argues for endogenous development among cultures with such strong ties. Kirby [1995] puts together a long list of cross-cultural differences between Europeans and Americans, and between Ghanaians and Africans. He draws a very clear parallel between the two spiritual realms and how they influence perceptions. He posits a perspective for endogenous development that is cosmovision-based, in order to go around cross-cultural biases or stereotyping.

A paradigm shift

Enriched by such knowledgeable reflections, how could a paradigm shift towards endogenous development be made that caters for the African worldviews? Endogenous development means working through indigenous structures and institutions. It is my experience that the spiritual world is the major driving force and implicitly regulates the performance of all other traditional institutions in Africa. Chieftaincy is responsible for administrative and judicial functions in traditional societies but the power position of the chief is mitigated by parallel institutions.

Installation of a chief in northern Ghana.

135

The revered spiritual world has a weak link with chieftaincy but a very strong link with the land owners or earth priests (Tindabas) and the institutions that have spiritual roles to perform. They regulate the powers of the chief, they prescribe punishments in the case of excessive abuse of power by the chief. This ensures morality, accountability and transparency in a chief's performance. The family heads are empowered by the support of their family members and some of them form the council of elders which advises the chief. This council is instrumental in influencing policy direction, formulation, execution, and sanctions. In addition to the fact that the people are represented by the council of elders, who themselves are members of families, it will be noticed that the people have an even stronger link with the Tindabas and the spiritual offices than with the chief. They have daily contact and access to these institutions.

There are multiple opportunities for influencing local policy and its implementation, and for redress and hearing. All of these functions are supposed to be life long positions, hence the elaborate regularity mechanisms and multiple communication channels established by rural communities. This structure is, almost invariably, politically stable with opportunities for the people to influence or contribute towards their future. These same structures are used for conflict prevention, resolution and management, be it wars or civil disagreement [see also Huizer, 1991]. They deal with issues of population, migration, and the environment, and all development that is community-based. The people are governed by unwritten laws and regulations that are guided by history, posterity, and their spirituality. These laws define and protect the rights of the people and regulate the community. They guarantee freedom within specific confines. Amongst other issues, the laws prescribe that access to production resources are negotiated and rarely traded-off for money. On the whole, the structures emphasise endogenous development and endogenous guarantees of food security.

The presentation above seems to have made a wholesale choice for traditional systems of endogenous development. This has deliberately been done in order to draw attention to a neglected area. By this line of action, I wish to drum up my proposed choice which is a blend of traditional system of governance with western democracies if food security is to be achieved. For these reasons, I advocate a blend of external and internal structures and action possibilities for sustainable endogenous development.

'Democratizing' development

My premise for evolving such a framework for endogenous development stems from my twenty years experience in development. When we intervene in rural communities to assist in improving their living conditions, we often think that the local communities are either so ignorant that they exacerbate their problems or that they are simply not doing enough to solve them. The reality is that often what we encounter is their 'best-option scenario', resulting from protracted efforts to resolve the problem - an endeavour they would continue with or without us. For them it is a question of survival and continuous existence within that environment. For us, it is one of plugging in and plugging out. So with their limited tools, techniques, information, know-how, and know-what, coupled with their spirituality and worldview, they keep at the problem, year after year, trying out a wide range of possible experiences, learning from them, and planning new action: learning from experience.

What this means is that while we are beginning to enter into their lives, they are engaged in trying to improve them. So, when we eventually get to acting, there are, in fact, two parallel action programmes on the same issue running concurrently: one (ours) with a temporary life span, and the other (theirs) perpetual. We often come in as intruders into their on-going world of discovery and re-discovery, then we enrol them in our activities, dictating the rules of participation, without allowing them to enrol us in their style of participation. The Empathetic Learning and Action (ELA) framework tries to come to grips with these parallel realities. Negotiation, consensus building, and establishing of dialogue are the objectives within the ELA framework. Most attention is focused on building communication bridges through what I call 'learning shades'. The details of ELA are available in Millar (1996) and also the article 'When the spirits speak' in this book takes this discussion further.

References

Bartle, P. F. W., 1992.
   The Universe has three souls. Notes on translating Akan culture. (Unpublished).
Beumers, E. and H. J. Koloss, 1992.
   Kings of Africa: art and authority in Africa. Foundation Kings of Africa, Utrecht, Netherlands.
Firth, R., 1967.
   The work of the gods in Tikopia. University of London, The Althone Press.
Firth, R., 1970.
   Rank and religion in Tikopia: a study in polynesian paganism and conversion to christianity. George Allen and Unwin Ltd. Ruskin House Museum street, London, England.
Fortes, M., 1969.
   The web of kingship among the Talensi. Antropological publications. Oxford University Press, London, England.
Gonese, C. 1998.
   Culture and Cosmovision of Traditional Institutions in Zimbabwe In: The Earth, Food and the Divine. COMPAS/Books for Change.
Goody, J., 1972.
   The myth of the bagre. Oxford University press, Ely House, London, England.
Goody, J., 1990.
   The political system of the Tallensi and their neighbours 1888-1915. Cambridge anthropology 14: 2.
Haverkort, B. and D. Millar, 1992.
   Farmers' experiments and cosmovision. ILEIA Newsletter 1/92.
Huizer, G., 1991.
   Indigenous knowledge and popular spirituality: a challenge to developmentalists. Unpublished paper for international workshop 'Agricultural knowledge systems and the role of extension'. Bad Boll University, Hohenheim, 21-24 May 1991.
Huizer, G., 1995.
   Agriculture and spirituality. Inter (agri)cultural dialogues. Essay from the crossroads conference at Wageningen Agricultural University.
Huizer, G., 1991.
   Folk spirituality and liberation in southern Africa. Traveaux et Documents. No. 29-30.
Huizer, G., 1994.

Indigenous Knowledge and Popular Spirituality: a challenge for developmentalists. In: Schuurmans, F. Current Issues in Development Studies, Verein für Entwicklungspolitik Breitenbach, Saarbrücken, Germany.

Kassaogue, A., J. Dolo and T. Ponsioen, 1990.
Traditional soil and water conservation on the Dagon plateau, Mali. Gatekeeper series, IIED paper 23.

Kirby, P. J., 1995.
Cross-cultural differences. (Unpublished).

Linquist, B. J. and D. Adolph, 1996.
The drums speak - are we listening? Experiences in development with a traditional Gabra institution - The Yaa Galbo. In: Indigenous organisations and development. P. Blunt and M. Warren, IT Publications, England.

Mahir, S. and D. Millar, 1992.
Disappearing trees: myths and realities. (Unpublished).

Millar, D., 1992.
Understanding rural people's knowledge and its implication for intervention: from the roots to the branches. Case studies from northern Ghana. Msc. thesis presented to Wageningen Agricultural University.

Millar, D., 1996.
Footprints in the mud: re-constructing the diversities in rural people's learning processes. PhD. Thesis Wageningen Agricultural University.

Opoku, K. A., 1989.
The traditional foundations of development. (Unpublished).

Opoku, K. A., 1990.
Development intervention and self-realisation among the Gourma. (Unpublished).

Sibanda, B., 1997.
Governance and the environment: The role of African religion in sustainable utilisation of natural resources in Zimbabwe. In: Forests, Trees and People Newsletter, September 1997.

Somé, P. M., 1995.
Of water and spirits. Ritual, magic, and initiation in the life of an African shaman. Penguin books ltd.

Toure, O., 1990.
Where herders do not herd anymore: Experience from the Ferlo, northern Senegal. Gatekeeper series, IIED paper 22.

WHEN THE SPIRITS SPEAK

David Millar

During one of my visits to the Frafra area near Bolgatanga, northern Ghana, I went to a village called Vea where there was a big government irrigation project. Besides the rice and vegetables that were growing on the fields, the land both on the farming side and on the opposite side of the dam was very bare. You see only a handful of trees. I knew that those on the farming side were cleared to enhance mechanised agriculture, but what about those on the opposite side? I asked the chief, who was about seventy years old then, what had happened to those trees. He told me that, '*Long ago my people and I showed our concern about 'the disappearing trees' since the dam was constructed by consulting our ancestors through the soothsayer. The ancestors told us that the gods were protecting those trees, because for them, the trees were living creatures just like humans, and so needed protection. When the irrigation project came along, it did not give us the opportunity to consult our gods, and went ahead and cleared the trees on the farming side. So all the trees got annoyed and walked away from the area; never to come back again*'. Although there was a government nursery nearby, there was very little planting going on in the area, because the people were not keen and the gods were still annoyed. So I asked what if they were given the opportunity to make sacrifices to pacify their gods, and then asked for their permission to plant trees in the area again, with the gods' consent. The chief said: '*That is the way to go about things. We would have protected some of the trees or would have planted some back. They will not be the same but we would have pleased our gods.*' For me, the response of the chief is a guarantee that they would do their best to fulfil the wishes of the gods, once the gods have agreed that trees should be planted.

This article highlights some encounters with cosmovisions in northern Ghana. Firstly, the cosmovision and agricultural experimentation among the Talensis is described, followed by an exploration of the importance of gender in cosmovision among the Boosi. As outside interventions are still male biased and also have paid too little attention to spirituality and indigenous learning, a new methodology which allows for a 'twin-track' is needed. I have labelled this methodology 'Empathic Learning and Action (ELA) [see details in Millar, 1996]. Within the context of COMPAS, this learning and action framework will be tested in Bongo. Its brief description will close this article.

Walking the development path

In the course of my field work as manager of a church-based agricultural development programme, I realised that the discourse referred to above about tree-planting in the Vea area was not just an incident. Looking back, my education in modern agriculture and extension methods prevented me from seeing the rural reality with the eyes of the rural population. In the 1970s and 1980s, the work of the agricultural extension programmes of the government and the NGOs in the area were based on the assumption that we, the outsiders, would have better agricultural technologies and ways to organise them, than those being used in the traditional farming system. In order to help the farmers to increase productivity and earn more profit, we demonstrated fertilisers, encouraged tractorisation and the use of agro-chemicals, distributed high-yielding varieties to replace traditional ones. We were part of the 'Green Revolution' [Benor and Harrison, 1977; Röling, 1988]. These activities were based on the assumption that the farmers' objectives were to increase yields and maximise their income, and that a demonstration with 'better' technologies would be sufficient to convince farmers of their usefulness. At the end of the 1980s, we gradually realised that small farmers have very limited control over the environment and face many risks and uncertainties due to drought, pests and diseases. Hence, they pay much attention to the environment, study it critically, and use it as a reference for choosing production methods. We concluded that their choice of varieties to grow, tools to use, what crop-crop or crop-livestock combinations to adopt, where to grow what, and the timing of farm operations have all been a response to existing ecological conditions. This also means that in the traditional form of production, primarily locally available inputs are used. This system has supported itself over generations. Technologies introduced from the West have disturbed it and have led to a degree of instability that would not have existed if they were not introduced.

Realising this, we emphasised technologies that were based on the local resources, natural as well as human, and through Low-External-Input and Sustainable Agriculture (LEISA) programmes we tried to address the location specific needs of the farmers. However, the traditional forms of farming in our country, as in most other developing countries, were not well documented in writing. The knowledge was maintained and developed through oral tradition. The origin of LEISA should be the knowledge-rich small farmers who may not always have received enough yield from their plots, but still survived. Early in 1990 we applied the methods of Participatory Technology Development (PTD), which implied the joint experimentation with farmers on topics that farmers themselves identified as useful [Jiggings et. al., 1989]. Finally, farmers' knowledge was taken serious, we thought.

In the course of these experiences we started to realise that farmers in Ghana have a worldview that is different from that promoted through the extension programmes of the government and the NGOs. This 'official' worldview was based on so-called modern agriculture, with its origin in Europe and embedded in the concepts of science and technology. However, we gradually realised again that it is not the maximum yield or commercial value of the crop that is necessarily the most important motivation for farmers. Nor are individual farmers taking their own decisions independently. For the majority of farmers in northern Ghana, farming is rather a result of the cosmovisions and social organisation in their communities [see Millar, 1990; 1992; 1994; 1996]. We gained more insight into the farmers' cosmovision from 1995 onwards by doing case studies in Tongo, Bongo and Vea and by looking deeper into the role of traditional leaders in the communities as well as of sacred lands such as shrines and groves.

In order to get a more complete picture of a cosmovision [PRATEC 1991], we went to the Tongo village in northern Ghana, where the people belong to the Talensi tribe. This village was chosen, as it became clear from other research in northern Ghana [Millar 1992] that religious practices play important roles in farmers' experiments. At crucial moments, farmers make sacrifices, read omen, consult soothsayers and traditional priests. Yet, the concrete mechanisms and the logic for these practices were not known. For a good understanding of existing farmers' practices, it was found necessary to make an in-depth analysis of the interaction between agriculture and indigenous institutions, which in northern Ghana have a distinct spiritual character.

On the basis of interviews with several traditional functionaries, the Talensi cosmovision could be reconstructed. The Universe has been created by the Almighty God or Allfather. God presents himself in other gods such as the rain god, the earth god, tree gods, house gods or personal gods. Certain people are endowed with special powers to call upon, for example, the earth and wind to cause certain things to happen. Also each individual or family has his or her personal god. Certain trees, groves and animals are sacred. Man has a soul which is of divine origin. Between the gods and the living humans are the ancestors. Ancestors can communicate directly with the gods, as well as with the living people. The spirits of the ancestors, especially the male and those who have had a long life and have exerted special spiritual power during their living time, are believed to be present in the community and the guide people's behaviour.

The tindana or earth priest seated on the grave of his ancestor.

Of the living people, the *tindana* or earth priest, has the power to communicate directly with the god of the earth. He exercises both spiritual power and especially power over the land. For our acephalous societies, the Chiefs are recognised for their political, administrative, and judiciary functions. Chiefs do not have spiritual powers or powers over land. They are seen as a choice of the ancestors to provide leadership functions, guided by the *tindana*, soothsayers, a council of elders, and various functionaries. The soothsayer has supernatural power in seeing the intentions and wishes of the gods, either directly or through the ancestors. They can act as medium, predict the future and they can advise on the type of sacrifice to be made. Their capacities are tested during the initiation ceremonies. Villagers are free to consult those soothsayers who have the best reputation. Soothsayers who are consistently proven wrong may be consulted very little or even abandoned.

Nature is sacred just as certain crops and animals. Gods can be pleased by sacrifices: offering drinks, food or the life of an animal. Sacrifices can also be made to encourage ancestors to plead to God on behalf of the living person. Sacrifices generally take place before the growing season and after the harvest. There is an intimate relationship between the traditional calendar of festivals and agricultural activities. No planting is allowed before certain festivals have taken place. Towards the end of the growing season, agricultural activities come to an end at a moment indicated by the Tindana and is associated with drumming, dancing and sacrifices [see also Fortes, 1969; Goody, 1972; Riehl, 1990].

Innovation and experimentation

In the Talensi worldview, there is no clear distinction between the past and the present. '*We live by the lessons accumulated by our ancestors and thus are guided by our ancestors.*' Change is a relative new phenomenon in the Talensi society. Till the beginning of the twentieth century exposure to outside systems and information had been limited: slave hunting and tribal wars made travelling even to nearby villages risky. Transport systems were very limited and education and alternative job opportunities were virtually absent. Since the 1940s outside contacts increased through mission, formal education, government agricultural and health programmes, road construction and transport systems.

These contacts have led to a number of structural changes. One generation ago people were generally very scantily dressed. Now, even the smaller children wear clothes. Food habits change as people have started to take breakfast and children are being fed externally manufactured foods, which was not the case in the past. New fields have been opened for farming and new crops and new varieties of traditional crops (such as sorghum) have been adopted. Animal traction and mechanisation has been introduced and at present certain crops are being grown for cash (cotton). Young men and, to a lesser extent, women receive formal training and acquire jobs outside the village and they transfer money and consumer goods to the village. This migration leads to a labour shortage in farming (especially weeding) and is seen as a fact adversely affecting agricultural production. One remarkable change in Bongo is that a Catholic church has been built in the village. The land was provided by the *tindana*, the earth priest, on a strategic location between two fetish bushes to allow the indigenous gods to keep an eye on the 'White-man's-god'.

These changes are substantial and in conflict with the belief held by some outsiders that the society is conservative and resists change. New ideas can come up and be implemented as long as the ancestors' consent and advice is sought. If a new idea does not deviate substantially from the existing practices and above all, is not seen to cause calamities to the individual or the community, people are free to experiment, adapt or adopt. If the innovation is considered a major change from traditional practice, the approval of the gods and the ancestors has to be sought.

The soothsayers play a role in these experiments by performing certain rites: He or she makes use of a 'reading stick' which is held in the hands above a number of items poured on a goat skin. Supernatural powers move the stick in a certain direction and the meaning of this direction can only be read by the soothsayer and his or her assistant. Then dice are used to confirm or reject the interpretation. The general requirements are that experiments with innovations are approved. Before the experiments are carried out, sacrifices are made and the traditional rituals are respected. The success or failure of an experiment is not only indicated by the relation between the physical or economic costs and the effects of the innovation, the total environmental (physical, economic, economic and spiritual) response to the innovation is assessed. Apart from yield responses, attention is given to the incidence of accidents, illnesses or diseases, snake bites, and so on. Non-material indicators supersede the material ones and this may lead to a rejection of an innovation if the farm family's welfare has decreased despite good performance. A snake bite or an accident or disease during production has a meaning which can be related to the experiment. In the interpretation of the results of the experiment, the soothsayer can play a decisive role.

Sacred groves and shrines

Comparatively recently, shrines and groves are beginning to attract the attention of development workers. They are found to be a library of vital information on ecological preservation and a response to environmental concerns [see Shrines and Groves in Dorm-Adzobu et.al., 1991]. According to the elders of Winkongo and Tongo, two villages in the Bolgatanga district, the gods demarcated these areas as their sanctuary and informed the fetish priest through a vision. Usually the chosen spot for shrines and groves stick out as closed canopies of baobab and ebony trees, perched on slightly raised pieces of land which are otherwise bare. The Tongo shrine stands close to the market square and adjacent to the Catholic Church.

These sacred groves were established when the first settlers came to that area. So far, these areas have been very significant in their socio-cultural and spiritual roles. They have served as grounds for festivals, sacrifices, spiritual worships and a place for humans to get closer association with the gods. The need to maintain this relationship with spirituality has contributed to their continued existence. Stories can still be heard about forest situations that existed in these parts 70 years ago. The joint actions of humans and nature have caused this to disappear. The droughts and bush fires of the early 1980s have left behind permanent scars. The groves have managed to persist, although their flora and fauna have been transformed to some extent.

At the end of each farming season, the groves are protected by sacrificing to the gods. Unwritten regulations permits grazing only at the fringes of the groves. Within the groves, hunting is restricted. Felling of trees and picking of firewood is controlled. The control and restriction measures include what species can be harvested, how often, at what time of the year and by whom: priests, men, women or children. It is true that groves have shrunk in size and been transformed with time. The increased human activities, population pressure on limited resources and an increase in hazards have contributed to these changes Even from the religious or spiritual perspective, the advent of Islam and Christianity has diluted the values of groves. However, the largest culprit in the destruction has been development or modernisation. The reductionistic position that development has assumed so far has limited the active role of groves in time and space. Centralised authority militated against the integration of traditional institutions into development. The cosmovision of these rural people is counter to reductionism. Nature, the visible form of the groves, is intertwined with people, spirituality, even Christian and Muslim gods, to the Allfather. There is a cause and effect relationship which is not necessarily linear. This inter-relationship has developed an awe within the rural people which influences the way resources are managed. The groves are the identity of the people.

The Boosi

Being aware of religious practices in farmers' experimentation and the cosmovision of the Talensis, we were interested to further explore the gender dimension in cosmovisions. The first phase of COMPAS (1995-1996) enabled us to study this aspect. The people living around Bongo are called 'Boosi'. There is clear evidence of pressure on land, with estimates of about 300 people per km^2 of land. The land is strewn with extensive rocky out-crops. Land holdings average around 3 acres, including the rocky out-crops and are continuously under cultivation. On average the yearly precipitation is 800 mm and average crop yields estimated at 300 kg per acre cereal. To supplement the little that comes from the harvest, crafts, cottage industries, and livestock rearing have found a special place in the lives of the Boosi. Like everywhere else in northern Ghana, the traditional form of worship is the cult of the ancestral spirit. The Boosi sacrifice to this ancestral spirit for various favours and the earth spirit is central amongst the spirits worshipped. While the ritual control of the land is vested in the land priest, legal control is vested in the chief.

Although women are not directly involved in sacrificing to the ancestral spirits, they play very important contributory roles in sacrifices as they fetch water for sacrifices and grind flour from early millet, sorghum, and late millet for the rituals. They brew the local drink (*pito*) for sacrifices and also do the cooking for them. The women also take care of the animals that are used for the sacrifices or sometimes provide animals for the sacrifices. They occasionally get the men to sacrifice for the women's personal interests, which may also be for the common good of the family. The women are the 'diaries' of the local home. They advice the men about the need to sacrifice or remind them of the time for sacrifices.

There are no written rules or organised bodies (social groups) to ensure the management of the land. The simple fact that land is a sanctuary for the gods seems to be the most active factor regulating its use. The sacrifices and festivals serve as a reminder and binding mechanism. The women welcome spiritual restrictions and see them more as social controls or regulatory mechanisms, than as oppressive systems. So, the gods forbid married women to go into the granary without their husband's permission. Women do not own land and so cannot perform sacrifices on their own, so the husbands do it on their behalf or for them. Women are not allowed to search for firewood in the fetish groves or around that area, outside the specified periods for entering the groves. Women are also not allowed to flirt, but if this happens, the gods require that they perform a ritual for purification before they are allowed into the farm. Those women who have their menstrual periods do not go into a farm.

In the field of agriculture, Boosi women have a wide range of activities. Groundnuts is a common crop produced by most women on their own plots. It is used both as food and as a cash crop. In the few instances that women cultivate cereals, their preferred choice is millet, which is the major staple in their diets. Women also grow vegetables by taking advantage of the borders or bare patches on their husband's plots. They collect millet and sorghum stalks to be stored as firewood throughout the year as a major source of fuelwood since there is very little vegetation left in the area. Women have small livestock, especially poultry and a few goats or pigs. Poultry is produced either for sale or for sacrifices, rarely for food.

Women farmers' innovation

The study focused on experimentation, spirituality and gender. As mentioned above, the man is supposed to sacrifice on behalf of the woman and so it was extremely difficult to find women interacting directly with soothsayers to resolve their concerns for experimentation. During this survey in Bongo, I encountered the evolution of a tool used for planting. Planting of seeds is principally a woman's job. Nearly all the cereals and legumes are planted by women and the few roots and tubers are planted by men. Since the principal crops are cereals, it was relevant to discuss planting with the women. The research captured an aspect of the system that has received very little attention in the literature on the area - this is 'mixed seeding'. A typical example of mixed seeding is the mixture of early or late millet, sorghum and *neri*, a vegetable - usually a legume. The mixture, in a calabash, is held in one hand; the second hand holds a simple hoe which is used to make the seed hole. Seeds are then dropped into the hole from the receptacle and with the hoe, earth is put over the seeds to cover them. Though the seeds are different, the seed sizes mixed are about the same. The seeds invariably have different maturity dates and are of the small grain seed types. A small calabash serves as the receptacle for the seeds and is held between four fingers of one hand. This is the 'planter'. An average of two of each

The mixed seeding technique was an innovation of the women and the spirits were taken into account.

of the three kinds should be placed in one hole at the same time.

The women told me that it was quite a tedious balancing-act to hold the calabash in one hand and between the four fingers. It was demonstrated to me and I tried it with very little success. Seeding this way needs a lot of mental effort and concentration to regulate the number of seeds that come out of the calabash into one hole and to ensure that there is a mixture. Beginners and children often find it very difficult to hold the calabash in one hand. For the experienced, it brings a lot of pain and strain on the back, the fingers, and on the hand that is holding the seed, especially at the beginning of the planting season. It takes a woman one day (10 hours) to plant 2 acres if she is planting large seeds like maize and legumes such as groundnuts and cowpea. It takes the same amount of time to plant 1 acre when planting the small seeds I mentioned earlier.

The use of the calabash for planting and for mixed seeding is said to be as old as the Boosi. The women are not prepared to abandon it or substitute it for something else for fear of punishment by their ancestors. However, two major modifications have been made to improve upon the technology over time. Firstly, a simple mechanical modification has been done to solve the problem associated with seed rates and to ensure balanced planting of seed. An equal quantity of pebbles of about the same size are added to the seeds in the calabash and mixed thoroughly. The women then plant the seeds plus the pebbles thus evening out the probabilities. One does not put pebbles gathered at random. They must have been collected from farms that have been spiritually processed for the current cropping season - cleansed of evil spirits. Those from uncleansed farms would introduce evil spirits into the farm and this would result in a poor harvest or some other calamity. The women told me this modification was done by their grandmothers and mothers, and has been passed on to them. They stated that it really reduces the strain on the mind and the eyes.

Another modification deals with the problem of handling and thus saves on labour time. Some of the women showed me a clever attachment of animal skin on the outside wall of the calabash stitched in the form of fingers. This leather glove-like attachment accommodates the two fingers next to the small finger on the outside; the small finger is placed in the inside of the calabash and the thumb and the index finger are then free to fetch the grain from the calabash and put it into the hole. By doing this, the women claim they have doubled their planting time for the small seeds (2 acres in 1 day) and it has considerably reduced the strain and pain in their backs, fingers, and arms. As for the type of skin used for the support, the women said it was often the skin from goats used during traditional sacrifices related to purifying the land for farming. Where the skin is purchased from outside or is from a non-sacrificed animal, the quality is guaranteed by first offering it to the ancestral spirits for cleansing before use. This modification is not very extensively used since it is relatively new and a few women are trying it out. The women 'innovators' however, admitted that they saw the technology in other villages. Their own adaptation to what they saw was to make provision for four different finger sizes when attaching the leather. This allows for multiple users of different finger sizes - you choose the two that best accommodate your fingers.

Development intervention strategies and population pressure on land have resulted in the flagrant violation of the traditional regulations on land. Now land is increasingly commoditized by land lords (sold for cash or for kind or both). A proliferation of agro-forestry programmes (Government and NGO) in the area show a concern from the 'outside'. However, these concerns first of all marginalize the women as is the case in most intervention programmes, and do not take into consideration the cosmovision of the people.

Men are open to more opportunities as far as production resources are concerned; the benefits of production are largely appropriated by the men which limits the woman's role in investment decisions to increase productivity. The indigenous technologies and production information, especially for women, is very limited. Outside intervention, in the form of extension services, is male-biased which make the predicament of women even worse. These intervention strategies do not know how to deal with the people's cosmovisions. The women have realised changes in their agriculture when they compare the past situations with the present situations. They list these changes as reduction in crop yields, land fertility degradation, drought (water bodies for drinking are drying up), and the loss of vegetation (their fuelwood is now far away). What are the response signals from development intervention?

Empathic Learning and Action (ELA)

After 20 years in development work, I have come to realise that the 'project approach to development' gives little room for exploring indigenous knowledge. Where there is an attempt to go a bit more deeply, urgency from project results rapidly causes a relapse into hasty generalisations based on very minimum exploration. CECIK, the Centre for Cosmovision and Indigenous Knowledge has emerged as a supporting institution to rural development, focusing on indigenous knowledge that is linked to people's spirituality. CECIK's vision is to see cosmovision-based development grow and become sustainable in northern Ghana. The type of development in which communities themselves become the experts, own and control the pace of development. Several activities will be undertaken like collecting already documented information, generation and dissemination of information, building strategic alliances and developing indigenous communication systems.

In order to evolve field-level extension strategies to legitimise and integrate cosmovision into development in a participatory and a sustainable way, the Empathic Learning Action (ELA) programme will be initiated. ELA will provide the main framework to come to grips with two realities [see details in Millar, 1996]. While we development interventionists are using our philosophy, methods, tools and resources to resolve issues in development, the so-called beneficiaries are doing the same in their own way. The rural people are processing their responses within their spiritual orientations and traditional institutions. Enrolment and being enrolled is an essential part of the process and trust, confidence-building, respect, and reciprocity are pre-requisites for ELA.

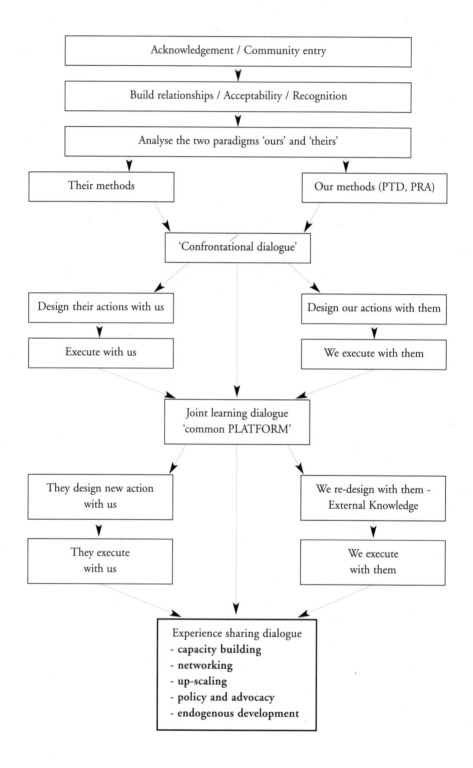

There are no written rules about the management of the land. The simple fact that land is a sanctuary for the gods seems to be the most active factor regulating its use. The sacrifices and festivals serve as a reminder and binding mechanism. ◆

6-1 Women are not directly involved in sacrificing to the ancestral spirits. They play an important role in preparing food and drinks to be offered.

6-2 Music and rhythm supports the rituals. Drumming and dancing enhances contact with the ancestors.

In countries like the Netherlands, traditional cosmovisions and spirituality have almost completely disappeared. There is widespread discontent about the materialism of modern farming. Currently an increasing interest in organic farming can be observed. ◆

8-3 *In organic farming, arable and animal production are integrated. Contrary to most conventional farmers, organic farmers keep cows on straw to produce good manure.*

8-4 *Organically grown products are being sold in farm shops (like shown here), in special shops and increasingly in supermarkets. Control and certification ensures that no chemicals are used.*

Organic farming and endogenous development

It is not wise to romanticise traditional knowledge, nor to reject everything that has been developed by Western science. It is a challenge to understand and appreciate traditional knowledge and look for possible combinations of this knowledge with outside knowledge. ◆

8-5 *Farmer workshops to discuss traditional practices. 'Seed Mela', supported by GREEN Foundation, provides a forum for exchange of indigenous seed varieties, knowledge and rituals.*

8-6 *Martin Duan of TIRD-P in Timor, Indonesia, with the clan elder or* pah tuaf *during a village meeting. More than 50 farmers have discussed crop and animal husbandry practices. The meeting is concluded with a ritual song, sacrificing a fowl and reading its signs.*

Organic farming and endogenous development

207

6-8 *The spirit mediums are the educators on how to live with nature. Nature as the habitat of both the spiritual world and the animal kingdom reaffirms the tripartite relationship between the people, ancestral spirits and the material world. After the war of liberation, spirit mediums, chiefs and war veterans came together to use their experiences in natural resource management and formed the Association of Zimbabwe Traditional Environmental Conservationists (AZTREC).*

Gender and spirit mediums

By this design there are a set of farmers (either as groups or as individuals, based on our design) that we would be working with, who are our collaborators. We would have enrolled these farmers in our participatory programme. Parallel to that would be some farmers, based within their own organisation, who would have us as their primary collaborator - they enrolling us in their participatory programmes. It is important to recognise and submit to this and not to try and usurp their power position. The ELA process means that we share our external resources with the farmers and they share their internal resources with us. This means that some of their own designed actions should receive financial support from our budget. That is, we fund their activities directly based on a 'dialogue of understanding'. The two action researches would, therefore, receive equal treatment. It would also eliminate some biases and most importantly, redistribute power. The right half of the twin-track is where project actions are located. This would also have aspects of spirituality related to project activities introduced, for example, a ritual before planting or harvesting new varieties or pest control measures. The farmers we have enrolled would be responsible for guiding and advising us on spiritual aspects and ensuring that they are fulfilled.

The starting point is a crucial departure from all conventional forms. We will visit the village (Bongo near Bolgatanga) and explain our interest and intentions, as clearly and in as much details as possible. We will then allow them to 'process us' within their cosmovisions to establish whether our presence there and our desire to work with them is 'acceptable' or not. If the response is negative, we will find another village. But if it is positive after consulting the gods, we will provide 'the necessary inputs' to enable the community to further consult their gods, make sacrifices, or prayers, so the powers that be show us what we should work on or guide us in choosing our areas of action. It is only after this is done that we will go into specific actions. During the course of actions, we will periodically review our action choices through the eyes of spirituality.

There are three main objectives in the CECIK-COMPAS programme in 1998-2000. Firstly, we want to research into and act upon secondary information on traditional practices, taboos, spirituality and astrology related to sustainable land use. Next, the aim is to understand the spiritual motivation and economic benefits for the involvement of rural people, especially the rural women, in sustainable practices. And finally, we will investigate indigenous management systems with respect to rural people's cosmovisions including shrines, sacred groves and water bodies. After exploratory surveys and in-depth surveys, actions within the ELA framework will start. Dialogue platforms are an essential component of the research as a forum for sharing the results and verifying the findings. Most often the discussions will be farmer-led and organised in the field. Next to professional analysis, we will periodically organise workshops with government bodies and NGOs working in the area and in other parts of Ghana to present findings. Another way of action-oriented analysis is to challenge the rural people to consult their gods or make sacrifices to find out why the results are as they are.

References

Benor, D. and Q. J. Harrison, 1977.
  The Training and Visit System.
Dorm-Adzobu, C., O. Ampadu-Agyei and P. G. Veit, 1991.
  Religious beliefs and environmental protection: The Malshegu sacred grove in Northern
  Ghana. By Centre for International Development and Environment. World Resources
  Institute, USA.
Fortes, M., 1969.
  The web of kingship among the Tallensi. Anthropological publication. Oxford University
  Press. London-England.
Goody, J., 1990.
  The political system of the Tallensi and their neighbours 1888-1915. Cambridge anthro-
  pology, 14:2, pp. 1-25.
Jiggings, J., B. Haverkort and P. Engel (1989, unpublished).
  Concepts and activities in Participatory Technology Development (PTD). Proceeding of
  the ILEIA workshop on operational approaches for participatory technology development
  in sustainable agriculture.
Millar, D. (1990).
  LEISA Where does this notion of farming originate? ILEIA newsletter 6 (1), p. 22.
Millar, D., 1992.
  Understanding rural people's knowledge and its implication for intervention: 'from the
  roots to the branches'. Case studies from northern Ghana. Msc. Thesis presented to
  Wageningen Agricultural University.
Millar, D., 1994.
  Experimenting farmers in northern Ghana. In: Beyond farmer first, edited by Scoones, I.
  and J. Thompson. Intermediate Technology Publications, pp. 44-50.
Millar, D., 1996.
  Footprints in the mud: reconstructing the diversities in rural people's learning processes.
  PhD Thesis. Wageningen Agricultural University.
PRATEC, 1991.
  Andean agriculture and peasant knowledge: revitalising Andean knowledge in Peru. In
  Haverkort B., J. van der Kamp and A. Waters-Bayer; Joining farmers' experiments: expe-
  riences in participatory technology development. pp. 93-112.
Riehl, V., 1990.
  The land is ours: Research on the land-use system among the Tallensi in Northern
  Ghana. Cambridge anthropology, 14:2, 1990, pp. 26-42.
Röling, N. G. (1988).
  Extension science. Information systems in agricultural development. Cambridge
  University Press.

CULTURE AND COSMOVISION

OF TRADITIONAL INSTITUTIONS IN ZIMBABWE

Cosmas Gonese

From time immemorial the tripartite relationship of the human, the natural and the spiritual world remained intact in Zimbabwe, and in fact all over Southern Africa. The existence of each world was dependent on the other. The respect and belief that mortal beings held towards the natural world as the habitat of the spiritual world and provider of foods, minerals and other resources, was in itself a manifestation of conservation consciousness. The spiritual world, as the supreme authority before God the creator, or *mwari* in the Shona language, would punish the entire society for transgressing certain taboos, rules and regulations that were meant to protect the environment. Large tracks of biodiversity and ecosystems were demarcated as sacred areas and no-one was allowed to tamper with them. Those sacred shrines, wetlands, woodlands were deemed spiritual habitat and the foundations of survival. Society, however, also depended heavily on the spiritual world for guidance. Communication with the spiritual world via the animal kingdom would not be possible if the environment was not conducive. Good and bad messages would be transmitted through various sacred species within the animal kingdom. Special ritual ceremonies were performed under specific sacred trees or shrines.

This scenario prevailed up until the period of European colonialism in the nineteenth century which introduced new philosophies on natural resource management. The indigenous spiritual world was deliberately substituted by Christianity which regards all sacred places and environments as the habitat of diabolical spirits. Some were turned into tourist centres, like Great Zimbabwe, Matopos, while at other sacred places mission schools were established. All this was done in the name of cleansing the society of satanic spirits. The destruction of the philosophical bases for the society's culture and cosmovision led to the desintegration of the interwoven relationship between the social, natural and spiritual worlds. The sacred animal species could not stand the invasion. The spiritual world was in disarray and this marked the beginning of a society without identity. This chaotic scenario washed away the values the environment used to have and conservation consciousness was eroded with it.

Spirit mediums were regarded as demons and all their functions were marginalised mainly because the colonial masters did not understand their role in society. New land tenure systems were introduced. These new land tenure systems resulted in the clear isolation of the three worlds and inter-connectedness vanished temporarily. The spiritual world could no longer educate the society via a mortal being - a spirit medium - as to which animal or tree species were sacred. The traditional and authentic administrators of the land, the chiefs or Mambos were forcibly replaced by district commissioners who viewed everything African as primitive, superstitious, unscientific and above all anti-God. New laws were enacted that sharply contradicted the African cosmo-vision and culture. District commissioners were armed with packages of land tenure systems which took little account of traditional land tenure systems. These conventional land tenure systems contributed enormously to the major environmental problems we are experiencing today, particularly in Mother Africa. Sacred woodlands were turned into Game Parks to promote tourism. No-one, not even the chiefs or spirit mediums, could access the sacred animal and bird species without paying the same entrance fees demanded from the tourist. In the agricultural sector external inputs, inorganic fertilisers and numerous chemicals were introduced and this resulted in sacred wet-lands running dry. Mermaids, fish-like spirit mediums that stay in water, and other mammals and reptiles which, according to African traditions, preserve the balance of an ecosystem could not stand the poisoned rainwater flowing into their habitat, springs, *vleis* (waterbodies) and other wetlands. This, coupled with monoculture, resulted in the depletion of the water table. Rules and codes of conduct which used to govern the maintenance of society's assets were abandoned in the name of progress and civilisation.

The traditional custodians of flora and fauna, the spirit mediums, were either exe-cuted [Mbuya Nehanda, Sekuru Kaguvi 1898] or silenced and replaced by priests. Laws were enacted to suppress any spirit revival. One such law was the Witchcraft Act. This law condemned the spiritual world of African belief. This further eroded the desire and interest in conserving the natural world. These scenarios provoked the anger of the spirit world and resulted in wars of liberation throughout Africa. In the case of Zimbabwe, the power of indigenous knowledge on war tactics reaffirmed the tripartite relationship between society, ancestral spirits and nature. Sacred wood-lands, wetlands and mountains were used as a refuge by both the combatants and masses during enemy attacks. In the war zones it was a taboo to be seen felling trees or causing *veld-fire* because everyone knew that without good vegetation they were like fish out of water. The spiritual world demonstrated its mighty powers during the trials of war by transmitting informative signals about the movements of the enemy. Various species in the animal kingdom such as baboons and snakes for example,

Chapungu (Barteleus Eagle) showing signs of an accepted ritual ceremony by the ancestors.

Chapungu (Barteleus Eagle) performing spiritual signs of a non accepted ritual ceremony by the ancestors.

were the most reliable spirit mediums. They could communicate with the spiritual world and transmit instructions that could guide the combatants. The enemy was left puzzled: how could they have been detected? All combatants underwent an orientation to enable them to interpret the messages passed on from the spiritual world via the animal kingdom. Biodiversity as the habitat of both the spiritual world and the animal kingdom became important hence reaffirming the tripartite relationship already referred to above.

In Zimbabwe, indigenous knowledge systems in natural resources management took root in the experiences of the liberation war. The traditional institutions, mainly the spirit mediums, were educators both for the masses and the combatants, and taught them how they should live with nature. Rules and regulations based on traditional beliefs protected the flora and fauna. The greatest 'drawback' of indigenous knowledge systems was that it had no written literature and this led the colonial masters to dismiss it as superstition and not scientific. Indigenous knowledge in natural resource management reminds us that knowledge and understanding is not only something that comes from scientists and textbooks. We need to be critical of all knowledge systems, scientific and indigenous and extract what is appropriate, combining the good from various sources to create a better and more sustainable environment.

The war of liberation was fought not only to gain independence but also to revive and resuscitate the tripartite relationship of the three worlds. After liberation, the chiefs, spirit mediums and war veterans came together to try and turn their war experiences to natural resource management. The development sector was most appropriate for the revival of African philosophy and identity and was the basis for the creation of the Association of Zimbabwe Traditional Environmental Conservationists (AZTREC). The three major objectives for forming AZTREC were to rehabilitate and/or conserve woody-biomass, to rehabilitate and/or conserve ecosystem blocks, and to establish a land-use management system that was based on indigenous knowledge and cosmovision. The basic goal was to draw to the full on indigenous knowledge systems in the process. Modern and scientific knowledge systems would be appreciated where they did not conflict with the status quo.

AZTREC's achievements

Zimbabwe has a population made up of many cultural and ethnic groups each with its own language, dialect, custom and belief. Part of the country is semi-arid whilst the central part is semi-humid and rains fall in the summer season. Annual rainfall is highly variable and there are often droughts, dry spells and crop failures especially in the semi arid regions. At the moment less than 10% of the country is covered by closed canopy forest, Fifty percent is savannah woodland and it is here where most of the grazingland is found. There is high pressure on existing vegetation because of increasing population especially in the communal areas where cultivation is being practised. General causes of environmental degradation are deforestation, uncontrolled grazing and inappropriate tillage systems. Serious soil erosion has occurred leading to siltation of rivers and dams, destruction of *vleis* and springs, and gully formation.

Biodiversity management. Since its inception in 1985, AZTREC has supported the establishment and management of a total of 10,000 ha of woodland in Masvingo and Mashonaland. The nature of the woodlands ranges from burial places of senior Chiefs (Mapa); sacred woodlands where important traditional rituals are performed (Marambatemwa); ordinary woodlands (Matondo) which are usually used for grazing and construction purposes; and shrines which are potential sites for eco-tourist development. These biodiversity management projects are directly under the control of the communities and traditional institutions; chiefs, spirit mediums, headmen and village heads give guidance.

Biodiversity management is considered the most crucial component of AZTREC's conservation endeavours for this is the habitat of the spiritual world. The traditional leaders that constitute the organisation's policy-making body have each re-identified the sacred woodlands in which their ancestors were buried. Rituals for the re-union of the three worlds have been performed throughout the country. Community-based local by-laws relating to the time for hunting, harvesting wild fruits, the authorisation of tree cutting for construction were spelled out by senior spirit mediums and enforced by chiefs, headmen and village heads with the full support of the population living near these sacred woodlands and shrines. The belief is that people must identify themselves with the socio-cultural values and myths embedded in biodiversity management before they take the preservation and rehabilitation of the denuded environment seriously. Once the communities and their cultural leaders agree on what needs to be done in order to preserve and promote their cultural identity, the project ceases to be seen as an outsider driven initiative and is perceived as a spiritually driven one.

The impact on the 10,000 ha of sacred woodland already under management has been very impressive. In some districts like Masvingo, Gutu and Bikita small game has been safely re-introduced. Sacred birds that had disappeared because of human interventions and vegetation loss are now nesting in their former habitats. The key message during the mobilisation and awareness campaigns is not simply that the environment has to be conserved but socio-spiritual values disappear when the natural habitat is not conducive to habitation. At the moment we are identifying other sacred woodlands and shrines in each and every chieftainship in the country and are using them as entry points in a massive conservation project. In Shona customs and belief, every chieftainship has such sacred places as Mapa and Marambatemwa. Some ordinary shrines of less cultural significance are being transformed into eco-cultural tourist centres. This is an initiative aimed at adding economic value to the conservation effort. Tourists from all over the world are received as guests of the local villagers and are served with traditional foods. This has proved very popular with both tourist and the communities themselves.

Ecosystem rehabilitation and conservation. Another dimension that aims at combating desertification using indigenous knowledge is the wetland conservation and rehabilitation programme. Wetlands, particularly *vleis* and springs, are considered to be the special habitat of water loving spirits namely the mermaid, or Njuzu. It is a proven belief that when this culturally important spirit is present water will not be a problem. The spiritual world, through a spirit medium, would communicate with the water-loving spirits about what needs to be done to recharge the ecosystems.

This communication process is carried out during a ritual ceremony specifically organised for that purpose. A special type of spirit medium, Nyusa facilitates the rehabilitation process. The Nyusa spirit medium is usually a man or a woman who is possessed by the spirit of the Njuzu. For this reason it would be very easy to determine the cultural procedures needed to revive or resuscitate the wetlands. These procedures would normally include the special rituals that need to be performed and identify who must perform them? Finding out where tree and grass species need to be planted and where? Discovering the rules and regulations that must be obeyed during and after the recharge? What type of utensils should be used to fetch water? What rodents, reptiles and mammals should not be killed and what herbs and other medicinal plants should be harvested and how? One very important message would be what crop production system needs to be applied in the wetland catchment in order to avoid water pollution. In the ten years that AZTREC's has been active, 11 *vleis* and springs that had completely dried up have been resuscitated. Thirty-nine five hectare wetlands (on average) are under management with the full support of traditional institutions. This has been achieved by showing what is lost when *vleis*, springs and mermaids are absent.

Land-use management. The other equally important programme aimed at combating desertification using indigenous knowledge is the crop production system. Since the introduction of mono-agriculture, pesticides and chemical fertilisers, life has proved very difficult for most rural people. The conventional agriculture system is heavily dependent on external inputs that are not only costly and therefore beyond the reach of many, but that are also very environmentally unfriendly. A piece of land treated by chemical fertilisers for last twenty years no longer produces any meaningful crop yields. Yet on the other hand the cost of these external inputs is increasing every season. The realisation of the negative effects of conventional agriculture is forcing our membership to shift to natural farming systems. In natural farming we are encouraging each other to utilise locally available organic soil and enrichment materials such as cattle, goat and sheep manure, ant-hill soil, crop residues, compost and humus from hill tops and under trees. Intercropping of various crops to combat the effects of drought has proved to be appropriate especially in ecological regions that have always receive an erratic rainfall. Other non-conventional crop production techniques which are integrated with organic farming systems are permaculture and holistic resource management. So far, all AZTREC staff have been trained in these land use management techniques. Twelve community demonstration centres have been established in Masvingo Province.

Framework for field-level implementation

Based on the COMPAS workshop in the Netherlands (February 1998), we present our framework for field-level implementation and testing with a cosmovision perspective of natural resource management.

How to get started. AZTREC's experience is such that development agencies must familiarise themselves with the cosmovision and the culture of the area by studying previous cosmovisions and anthropological and development studies. A non-bias relationship must be established with the traditional and spiritual leaders, since they are the authentic custodians of the indigenous knowledge. An interest has to be developed in how rural folk perceive their livelihood by attending traditional ceremonies and rituals in order to acquaint one-self with how indigenous knowledge and cosmovision are seriously discussed and strategies formulated.

How to develop a common agenda. One has to be culturally mature when introducing development topics to the rural population. This can only be achieved through a respectful and dignified approach to traditional institutions, which beyond doubt, still command a lot of influence. This will mean that unnecessary resistance can be avoided. A careful utilisation of modern participatory diagnostic tools such as PRAs for example, can be very effective. Sharing certain communication audio-visuals such as drumming, music, festivals, designs of structures, textiles and objects can be used to promote the way indigenous knowledge systems can be effectively employed to combat desertification. Extensive dialogue on the interconnectedness of these communication audio-visuals, the spiritual world, the natural world and social world constitute the backbone of African identity. A genuine respect for this identity would no doubt lead to a common agenda.

How to determine parameters. Obviously, as a technocrat and development practitioner you may have your own methodologies for determining parameters but it is always rewarding to evaluate these parameters against the indigenous cosmovision. Try as much as possible to incorporate spiritual elements as indicated by spiritual diviners, respect ritual calendars, astrological data, sacred places and other qualities of the project area as defined by the people's cosmovision, norms and values. Socio-cultural issues such as taboos, totems and the role of local authorities in decision making, project design, implementation, monitoring and evaluation are important in preserving the foundations of indigenous knowledge. Criteria for setting indicators and strategies should be in conformity with successful parameters in the communities' experiences. One has to be gender sensitive and make sex differentiation in setting parameters and indicators. It is always a fatal omission not to take into account a resource frame that responds to local perceptions and value systems.

How to design for action. The technocrats and development agencies should, at all costs, desist from designing a project using conventional methodologies and expecting the rural population to assimilate the process. The custodians of the traditional practices, the chiefs and spirit mediums must not only be consulted but fully involved if resistance is to be avoided. The design itself must be flexible enough to accommodate modifications during execution. One has to ensure that the traditional institutions give a full mandate and are accountable for the design to guarantee sustainability. We should find new ways for field experiments and trials. One can also carry out participatory case studies on experiments. Experiments should not simple be randomised square-block designs. Research of this type is based on the conventional western knowledge system. This does not mean that we should ignore everything conventional but we should select western techniques that are complementary to the beliefs, norms and values of the people's cosmovision.

How to monitor the process. The people who will be involved in implementation, whether farmers, chiefs, spirit mediums, women or young people, should always be at the centre of the process from the beginning. We should strive to cultivate some degree of confidence among the beneficiaries of our development efforts. The traditional institutions, once they develop a sense of ownership of the process would formulate and enforce community based by-laws. It is natural that no-one would want to be designated inferior in a development process which is claimed to benefit the same person in the end. Participatory dialogue during ritual ceremonies and festivals organised by the custodians of indigenous knowledge, at which interaction with the spiritual world takes place, would strengthen the entire monitoring process and instil conservation discipline.

How to judge the results. As mentioned earlier, the communities and the traditional institutions should be accountable for the project cycle. We should tactfully revisit the agreed parameters together with all stakeholders and authentic leaders with a view to undertaking an impact assessment. We should try to strike an equilibrium between their baselines and our baselines which must be established at the beginning. We have to be open for intended and unexpected results and modifications should be addressed in the process. If for some reason, the results are not satisfactory we should find a respectful way of ensuring success that does not demotivate the people's innovativeness. If the results are as expected then the traditional institutions should be requested to organise a ritual ceremony to appease the spiritual world.

How do we leave without creating a dependency syndrome. The whole project cycle from identification, project design, implementation, monitoring and evaluation should be strategically designed in a way that does not leace a vacuum when a development agent goes. One way of guaranteeing continuity is by ensuring that the entire process is embedded in the culture and cosmovision of the stakeholders. Traditional institutional networking and farmer-to-farmer reciprocal arrangements should be developed and adapted in order to internalise the process. The young generation, women and the aged usually integrated themselves into a process which fully respects socio-cultural practices. We have to cultivate some form of confidence in all segments of the population such that they identify themselves with the process.

Our link with COMPAS

We hope to support the COMPAS programme with the experience that AZTREC has developed over the years. Our participation in COMPAS will hopefully strengthen our own capacity to systematise our approaches in researching and building on indigenous knowledge and cosmovision which should result in community-based development, sustainable agriculture and natural resource management. One specific objective is to increase the capacity of the Charumbira community in Masvingo to autonomously revive and develop their indigenous knowledge, techniques and skills in order to meet the requirements of sustainable agriculture and natural resource management in a changing socio-economic and physical environment. Another objective is to develop methodologies that enable communities and organisations to start this process of endogenous development in other areas of Masvingo and Southern Africa.

By means of village-based workshops, observations during traditional ceremonies, participatory appraisal techniques like retrospective mapping and the study of existing literature, we want to further document the indigenous knowledge systems and strengthen the cultural identity of the Charumbira community. We will focus on topics like their concepts of life, regulation of community decision making and natural resource management by traditional institutions, the interaction of the traditional (local) with outside knowledge sources, the degree of influence of traditional worldviews in comparison to western worldviews, and options for endogenous development. We will also start up a process of indigenous experimentation using methods appropriate for sustainable farming and natural resource management. Farmer-innovators will be located, other indigenous knowledge in the Charumbira community that might be useful will be identified. In addition criteria and indicators (quantitative and qualitative) for success and failure will be defined. Once certain experiments are considered successful, we intend to facilitate a process of consolidation and dialogue between farmer-innovators. The experiments will also be documented and published in the local language.

We intend to network with local institutions to involve them in the dialogue on cultural identity and systematic approaches to attain endogenous development. We can share the results with others through workshops, field days, documents, training of field staff and policy makers of local development organisations. We are also thinking of developing a manual that can be used by networking organisations in Zimbabwe and the region. In order to publicise information on the cultural cosmovision of the indigenous peoples of Southern Africa, a magazine entitled 'The Three Worlds' will be circulated throughout Southern Africa.

We always knew
by **Backson M. C. Sibanda**

Lord as I cast my eyes
Across the African plains
I see the wild wonder
as the wildlife wander
and the elephants in their elegance
slowly blend into limitless biodiversity.
The lion wakes again
as the king of the jungle catches another prey.

I climb on high to the mountain top
as the early morning dew touches my skin
The smoke from the villages below
announce the start of another day
I listen to the early morning song
as the African wilds of the air
wake up and give praise to Thee.
I see the vulture sore on high to meet the air.
The Titihova still sings in abundant air.

I take in a fresh drink of air
In this serene solitude
as I look down the green beautiful valleys
of Mother Africa wake up from
a long slumber they call underdevelopment
Lord I thank you, for you delayed,
The coming of the motor car, and smoke puffing industrial complexes.
You delayed civilization and thy children starve.

There is still wilderness and the wilds here
The beauty of nature and diversity
Nearly frozen from creation to Eternity
Until they built that Safari treck
And then came the marrum road
They called it the dirt dust road
And finally came civilization with the motorway.
Solitude and serenity were broken forever.

Finally from the cities of the world
They came in hundreds, thousands
Oh Lord they came in their millions
From the bowels of the earth
They came to seek solitude here.
From concrete jungles they raced here.
To seek solitude and serenity
From this diversity-the hand of creation.

The endless plains of the Maasai and Serengeti
Those monotonous stretches of unbelievable distances
Land meets the sky in the horizon in a dusty day
Nothing vertical but the Maasai
man and beast are crushed into insignificance
by this landscape as the heavens kiss the earth.
Until the Safari treck and the jeep
shrink this vast landscape
and biological diversity into an envelop package.

Lord they will never understand
what this means to us, what they are doing to us
Our lives are interwoven into this metrix
of delicate landscape and biodiversity

Lord they called them National Parks
We call it home-mother Africa
They called it nature reserves, botanical gardens, finally biological diversity
For us this will always be life giving
Mother Africa, home and not jungle
For us this is neither garden or jungle
To us wildlife is part of us
Our names are elephant, lion, zebra, buffalo.
To us wildlife is life-our relatives
How can we kill wildlife-for that is life.
We conserve it for it is sacred
like milking a sacred cow
We sacrifice it to meet human needs.

It is life given in abundance
It is not a breath of fresh air
But a drink of life-life given in abundance
Now they call our worm fested water
Biological Diversity
For us this is just life and we have always known that.

The Wilderness is finally gone
The wilds and the forest have disappeared.
The wildlife no longer roams the African Plains
The Elegant Elephant is now trophy
The giraffe and the lion are now in the zoo
The Titihoya sings no more
The eagle flies high no more.
Only now do they understand
The hand of Creation.

We have always known that.

PEOPLE'S SPIRIT OF RESISTANCE IN LATIN AMERICA

Gerrit Huizer

In the process of the incorporation of traditional societies into the western capitalist system, people found in their cultural heritage the motivation for a spiritual persistence that at some stage turned into active resistance movements. In many parts of the world indigenous culture and knowledge had a special regard for psychic and spiritual forces which have been branded as superstitious, occult or even satanic by ruling ideologies both Christian and Capitalist. These forces have continued to appear and reappear as a 'counterpoint' in and a part of folk-culture and have had an impact into present times. They are apparently being re-discovered.

As a United Nations development worker, I have experienced the confrontation between our western worldview or knowledge system and that of the indigenous peoples in the Third World. I gradually discovered the limitations of my own western worldview and was helped to become acquainted with cultural and religious dimensions that I wish to refer to with the rather inadequate term spiritual. This spirituality is related to the 'resistance to change' that peasants, and particularly women, in non-western societies have shown towards the western economic and knowledge systems 'extended' to them by development agents. It became clear from various experiences that the 'indigenous knowledge' that formed the basis of their spirituality was different from, if not contrary to that of most western scholars. The psychologist Maslow [1966] has made a useful distinction between 'experiential knowledge' and 'spectator knowledge' and he stipulated that the former was a precondition for the latter. The latter is the kind of knowledge the orthodox scientist is generally looking for: neutral, quantifiable, objectified, detached and non-involved. Both kinds of knowledge complement each other, but, as also mentioned by Darshan Shankar in this volume, most of present-day science has neglected the experiential knowledge. For a real understanding, in addition to the objectivity of the spectator, a 'caring objectivity' is needed, which sees the object as much as possible 'in its own nature'. This approach is an essential part of what the social psychologist Kurt Lewin called 'action research'.

I have tried to come to grips with spirituality through active participation in the struggle for survival and justice of those with whom I have worked. This can be called 'research-through-action': there is careful reflection upon the experiential knowledge. In many cases the people I worked with shared this reflective process, making it 'participatory action research' in the perspective of a 'view from within and from below' [Huizer 1979].

Between 1954 and 1973, I lived in Third World countries. By trial and error I learned about, and particularly from, local people. During this learning process I gradually became acquainted with and began to some extent to share the worldview that enables men and women to survive and that inspires them at times to radical action. This worldview and inspiration is partly based on conscious and unconscious psychological defence mechanisms. There is often a dimension of spirituality in their approach to the natural environment, healing and witchcraft. It should be noted that these latter forces have not as yet been properly defined, categorised or understood by western scientists.

From the early days of my work amongst peasants, I experienced that seemingly distrustful and apathetic or fatalistic peasants were highly rational in their attitude when faced with 'modernising' agents or processes. My first real experience with the rationality of peasant distrust occurred in 1955 when I set out to live as a voluntary community development worker in a village in El Salvador. This was after a drinking water project which our agency tried to introduce had failed because of peasant non-participation. They did not come to work with us. I experienced the first crisis in my developmentalist ideology.

After deciding to go and live in that village, and to relax and 'wait and see', I soon learned that my neighbours - of whom hardly anyone had any formal schooling - were great and patient teachers. Not only in such relatively simple things as ploughing with unwilling oxen, tracing and hunting wild pigs or the use of herbs, but also their capacity to analyse the behaviour of outsiders particularly those 'from above'. Without ever using a term like 'class' they taught me, and made me feel, what 'class struggle' meant to them. This struggle was closely related to their deeply felt ties with the village land, Mother Earth as viewed in holistic pre-Christian indigenous cosmologies. They showed me how this land had belonged to their ancestors but was now gradually being 'washed away' by the erosion caused first by coffee cultivation and then by the extensive cattle-raising of the mostly absentee landlords who had appropriated these lands many decades ago. The peasants allowed and stimulated me to share all their traditional celebrations regarding life, survival, and death. These celebrations were frequently spiritual and appeared to be the source of their resistance to the desperate conditions of (mostly covert) struggle that characterised their existence.

Clear mind and spiritual awareness

Their patience and mild nature towards their oppressors gave me a feeling that in their material poverty lay the roots of an inner civilisation from which I could learn. Indirectly, they showed me the barbarity of the western 'civilisation' that had devastated theirs and had rather misused their Mother Earth to produce coffee and sugar on a large scale for the world market, while their children became increasingly undernourished. They were highly distrustful of any outside intervention. Peasants' non-participation, however, was a rationally and consciously adopted strategy of not letting themselves be further exploited. I also learned that under more encouraging conditions, their 'apathy' could easily be transformed into enthusiastic support and they were prepared to make considerable efforts when necessary even if their lives were at stake.

During such village-level work experiences over the years, I observed that there were certain people, men and women, with a special capacity to express clearly what their peers were feeling about certain crisis situations. I learned to recognise and collaborate with such people, men or women, as persons with charisma. These persons radiated a kind of spiritual force, knew how to inspire others, and were respected for this. Some of them took considerable risks in serving their community. Others used their charisma for their own benefit. Most had a deep knowledge of age-old cultural practices and survival strategies. When crisis situations became acute and confrontation with powerful elite could no longer be avoided, those with charisma were the ones who provided their peers with the crucial motivations to act against the physical and psychological power that landlords and rich farmers held over 'their' peasants.

In trying to answer the question of what kept peasants going under such oppressive circumstances I gradually came to the conclusion that two aspects of indigenous culture and spirituality were crucial:

□ A certain clearness in people's minds about those who are the main cause of their permanent crisis situation: a kind of 'common enemy'. This awareness was combined with a historical perspective, bridging generations, that gave them the (unspoken) conviction that, since their society had been more just and egalitarian in the past, it might or should be so in the future.

□ A permanent spiritual and holistic awareness which takes the continuity and the dialectical oneness of life and after-life, good and evil, natural and supernatural for granted. Something which is difficult for western, middle class, Christian-educated people, like myself, to understand.

These two aspects of the peasants' worldview often gave them the strength to endure what in western eyes were unbearable situations. It sometimes prompted them to resist or rebel as happened in some of the villages where I have worked in El Salvador, Mexico and northern Chile.

The spirit in which local people act is different from the system of knowledge or ideology of most westerners. It took some time before I was sufficiently familiar with indigenous wisdom and spirituality to be able to appreciate this. Non-western indigenous spirituality and knowledge systems are generally not purely traditional pre-western practices and beliefs. Rather they are part of survival and resistance strategies to cope with - often aggressively imposed - western ways. Knowledge systems cannot be seen outside the context of the mode of production (or exploitation) in which they function. Various studies show that the Maya knowledge system survived culturally thanks to a creative adaptation to colonial rule. It is probably not accidental that these areas in South and Central America have also been centres of endemic peasant rebellion until today's movement in Chiapas, southern Mexico.

The endurance with which the idea of a justified access to ancestral land was cherished is characteristic of peasant and indigenous societies all over the world. Such 'dreams' or 'counterpoints' can apparently be sustained for decades or even centuries and the movements that at times emerge from such counterpoints have been called utopian. But for those involved they have a permanent and strong topicality. Related religious views and cultural practices which for years, or even centuries, have appeared to foster passivity or withdrawal have also contained strong potential for sustained resistance and liberation struggle.

The survival of traditional indigenous cosmovisions was easier in those areas that Spanish colonialism considered less profitable. As Hans van den Berg [1989] shows, indigenous religion has survived most strongly in areas such as the high plateaux in

Bolivia with their poor soils that are inhabited mainly by Aymara subsistence peasant communities. The Aymara cosmovision with its supernatural beings, ancestral spirits, the earth, agricultural products and other forces that co-exist in an hierarchical equilibrium was such that Christian elements such as saints and angels could easily been incorporated. Van den Berg speaks of the Aymarisation of Christianity as a complement to the Christianisation of the Aymara. The Earth and the Earth Mother, Pachamama (identified also with the Virgin Mary), continued to play a crucial role in the Aymara religion as well as in agricultural rituals and practices. The Aymara tried to integrate the antagonism between good and bad, God and Satan, introduced by the Christians into their own views on harmony between opposites. Their cosmovision is still strongly alive.

That the observations made by the theologian Van den Berg, as well as those of PRATEC have considerable practical agricultural implications and usefulness has been demonstrated by AGRUCO, the Agro-ecology Programme of the University of Cochabamba in Bolivia. AGRUCO was designed to support Andean peasant communities through a transfer of ecologically sustainable technology such as those found in organic agriculture. There was a lack of enthusiasm among local peasants for these useful technologies. However, it gradually became clear that this 'resistance' was related to the fact that the community had its own locally tested, age-old knowledge about sustainable agriculture. University researchers and extensionists could learn from this. Andean civilisations have survived for over 3000 years by adapting them-selves to a great variety of climates and ecological situations in their mountainous homeland thanks to a holistic cosmology that combines respect for, and harmony between the natural environment, human communities and spiritual beings. Rituals, related to age-old knowledge concerning cyclical astrological influences (the moon, the seasons and supra-human influences behind those phenomena) have survived in Andean communities to the present day.

Traditional Andean footplough is still used today.

Similarly in the Huancayo region of Peru the TALPUY emphasises the importance of the Andean cosmology by inventarising traditional knowledge among peasants. The ritual relationships with the Pachamama,

The central notion in the native Quechua concept of life is Pacha, whose nearest equivalent in western terms would be 'the whole conformed by space and time'. Within Pacha there are three spheres: Pachakama: spiritual life; Pachamama: material life or Mother Earth and Pachankamachana: social life. From this confluence emanates a fourth sphere Pachankiri or daily life. ◆

7-1, 7-2 Rituals and music link people's microcosm with the macrocosm.

7-3 As part of its traditional organisation, the community has special people, jilakatas, *to protect the cultivated fields. They also have to protect the plots against negative influences which are perceived as the result of bad human behaviour.*

Reciprocity is an important principle. If people misbehave, nature will react with diseases or disasters. Through fasting, meditation, dancing and sacrifices people can redress the situation and create favourable conditions for crop growth, animal and human welfare. Rituals are performed in all important social and productive activities. The ritual calendar is in fact an agricultural calendar. ◆

7-4 For the Andean farmers, the landscape is alive in the sense that the spiritual world expresses itself in nature.

7-5 When negative influences prevail, the Jilakatas will order the community to pay tribute to Pachamama or to fast for a full day.

Pacha and potatoes

The Andean concept of life or cosmovision is pantheistic, which means that mountains, lakes, streams and trees are sacred. People observe signs in nature that indicate the balance between the lower world and the world of today. The area of Huancayo is known for its skilled artisans who carve their cosmovision on calabashes. ◆

7-6, 7-7 The calabash shows how the agricultural and ritual calendar coincide.

7-8 Celebrating 'Day of the Earth' during carnaval.

Pacha and potatoes

Farmers' knowledge has hardly been taken into account in agricultural policies. TALPUY is validating traditional knowledge with farmers and intends to make an in-depth study of the role of traditional institutions and rituals, particularly those related to agriculture. Field experiments involving traditional leaders are scheduled. ◆

7-9 When the potatoes are flowering and the new tubers appear, the 'Fiesta de la Candelaria', the day for the potato is celebrated in the highlands of Puno, southern Peru. Women collect potatoes from the plot, the mother potato is thanked and the new tubers are welcomed.

7-10 The elders sacrifice with coca leaves, alcohol and sweets.

7-11 The people pray and later dance through the fields.

172

Mother Earth, are still alive. For example, offerings are made when new roads are opened. Traditional values such as joint labour (*minka*) for community purposes are alive in spite of the migration of many people to the towns. TALPUY tries to conserve and enhance such community values by publishing a regular magazine 'MINKA' in a simple style and by helping to organise meetings.

That the Andean cosmovision and its related local agricultural knowledge has proved to be more appropriate for the cultivation of potatoes in the Andes than modern technical knowledge, has recently been highlighted by Salas [1996]. Salas' dissertation gives considerable attention to the work of PRATEC (Andean Project of Peasant Technology) an NGO in Peru, set up in 1988 with headquarters in Lima. Its purpose is to contribute to the quality of life of the Andean peoples and reaffirm their cultural identity, particularly in the field of agriculture. Age-old, sophisticated life-support strategies have been neglected by the colonial and post-colonial economy that one-sidedly concentrated on mining and production for the world market. PRATEC tries to recover and/or conserve the traditional knowledge that existed in the many mini-agricultures in the great variety of Andean ecosystems. In these knowledge systems, part of an age-old holistic cosmology, relationships with the world and cosmos continue to play a crucial role.

The experience of PRATEC in many ways coincides with some of my observations on the role of indigenous spirituality and knowledge. There is a dialectical, reactive or cyclical relationship with what could be considered to be a 'common enemy'. In PRATEC's case this is explicitly the influence of 500 years colonial heritage expressing itself in modernisation as promoted by multinational corporations through the inadequate technologies that have their source in the research stations. PRATEC itself observes and supports the revitalisation of a holistic approach which started thousands of years ago and made effective survival possible in a great variety of ecosystems. A main task of PRATEC is to co-author, together with local peasants, the inventarisation of the many age-old local technologies and to transmit this knowledge to agricultural extensionists. Farmer-to-farmer communication is particularly important. Participatory approaches are used in local meetings, bringing in those with most traditional knowledge, and high office holders. Further, information is gathered through transzonal exchanges between farmers; circulating pamphlets of technologies drawn up by the farmer themselves; and by cooperating with the network of existing farmers' unions.

Resistance based on local traditions

Recently the Mother Earth symbolism, including the Virgin of Guadalupe, has been used again in the indigenous peasant rebellion in Chiapas, Southern Mexico. The Zapatista Army of National Liberation (EZLN) came dramatically into the foreground on 1 January 1994. On that day the North American Free Trade Agreement (NAFTA) officially went into effect. A number of small towns in Chiapas were occupied by indigenous peasant rebel forces to demonstrate that they would no longer tolerate the brutalities and land usurpations of local landlords and politicians. These had been made possible by the changes in the agrarian legislation that had formerly protected

Small farmers' cooperatives in Chiapas, southern Mexico, grow coffee organically. Through direct marketing in Europe a premium is received which enables them to strengthen their cultural identity.

peasant land possession but which now - as part of the NAFTA agreement - favoured large-scale privatisation. Many cases of the violent displacement of peasants, and the assassinations of their leaders had been reported but the situation grew steadily worse. Armed resistance finally appeared the only way to get some kind of justice. The rebel action had been prepared carefully and was strongly rooted in the local indigenous context. One of the main leaders, sub-commander Marcos, allegedly a former communication scientist at one of Mexico's universities, had lived for many years among the indigenous peasants in the Lacandon frontier area. Marcos explained that he had been taught about local traditions by an old indigenous leader, Antonio, who helped him understand the local communities and their worldview.

During August 1996, in the Lacandon jungle area of Chiapas where the Zapatistas are dominant, a six-day 'Intercontinental Conference for Humanity and against Neo-liberalism' took place. It was attended by 3000 representatives of grassroots organisations from all over the world. Land reform, peasant organisation and sustainable development was high on the agenda. Scholars, knowledgeable in this field, made a considerable contribution. During the conference itself and in several of the preparatory meetings leading up to the conference I could observe that the ecological and earth conservationist component of the present Zapatista movement was highlighted in collaboration with environmental action groups. It was also closely interlinked with the cultural dimension. Of late, people's spirit of resistance under adverse conditions has attracted renewed attention thanks to the strength of its effects. Examples are the participation of people in the liberation struggles during the past decades through rural-based rebellions in countries like Zimbabwe, Nicaragua, Guatemala and El Salvador. It has been documented that in these cases spiritual and religious factors have played a crucial role [Huizer 1998].

The role of western science

Western development has been responsible for ecological disasters in many Third World countries through deforestation and the introduction of monocultures for the world market. Now, finally, increasing attention is being given to the ecological wisdom and traditional knowledge still available among indigenous peoples. This knowledge, often more holistic than the purely objective and mechanistic approaches that dominate western scientific endeavours, is now being seriously reconsidered by western scientists, though rarely in a participatory manner.

A question that should be raised is the extent to which western development agencies such as the World Bank will utilise these alternative approaches and knowledge systems to soften the worst effects of their structural adjustment policies rather than to modify the overall effect of these policies: the integration of every corner of the world into a global market. Can we expect a new openness? A western perestroika, towards an effective alternative to IMFundamentalist 'free' market economy?

The struggle of the Zapatistas and many other indigenous resistance movements have strong implications on the globalisation of the present world market. At present the western scientific knowledge system is not only challenged by Third World and feminist authors concerned with the deteriorating relation between man (male particularly) and the natural environment, but also by new discoveries in the (natural) sciences, particularly in the field of quantum-physics. Some physicists go so far as to show a certain convergence between the most sophisticated developments in that field and certain holistic indigenous knowledge systems and worldviews such as Buddhism and Taoism. This recognition is confirmed in research by LeShan [1982] into the activities and attitudes of physicists, mediums and mystics. However, the challenges of physicists like Capra, Bohm and Heisenberg to the current scientific paradigms and the mechanistic worldview have not yet had much influence on the social sciences. In biology, the work of Rupert Sheldrake [1991] gives considerable attention to crucial aspects of indigenous knowledge systems and could be useful as a frame of reference for the studies and experiments coordinated by COMPAS.

Western scientists should continue to search for knowledge from indigenous peoples and at the same time examine their own place in the overall context of dominant western developmental interests. This is needed in order to ensure that they really serve the sustainable development of mankind as a whole. Hopefully the late discovery of the disastrous ecological effects of the spread of western production technologies in the pursuit of thoughtless profiteering and capital accumulation will help western development scientists to moderate their too self-confident supposition that their way of life (and death) is fostering the 'best of all possible worlds', and open up the possibility for dialogue with other cosmovisions.

References

Berg, H. v.d., 1989.

La tierra no Da Así no Más: Los Ritos Agrícolas en la Religión de los Aymara Cristianos. CEDLA, Amsterdam. In: Latin American Studies, no 51.

Huizer, G., 1979.

Research-through-action; Experiences with peasant organizations. In: G. Huizer and B. Mannheim, eds. The politics of anthropology Mouton, The Hague/Paris.

Huizer, G., 1998.

Social mobilisation for land reform; Historical perspective and theoretical considerations. UNRISD, Geneva.

LeShan, L., 1982

The Medium, the Mystic and the Physicist. Towards a General Theory of the Paranormal. Ballantine Books, New York.

Maslow, A. H., 1966.

The Psychology of Science. Harper and Row, New York.

Sheldrake, R., 1991.

The rebirth of Nature. Bantam Books.

Salas, M., 1996.

Papas y cultura. Acerce de la interacción de sistemas de conocimiento en los Andes del Peru. University of Nijmegen, Netherlands.

ANDEAN COSMOVISION

AND SELF-SUSTAINED DEVELOPMENT

Stephan Rist, Juan San Martin and Nelson Tapia

Ten years of participatory research, education and support to Quechua and Aymará communities in the Bolivian Andes has enabled AGRUCO (Agro-ecology University Cochabamba) to learn from and with the farmers. In this article we will share our experiences at three levels. First we will describe the cosmovision of the Andean communities and their significance at a general level. Then we will give an example of the concrete way the cosmovision in a specific community shapes and organises daily life. And finally we will give an outline of how AGRUCO supports endogenous development through an intercultural dialogue of complementarity.

Ten years ago the programme AGRUCO started with the objective of promoting ecological agriculture based on the European concept of organic farming. In the course of the years it became clear that this approach did not work. In the first place it was realised that the traditional farmers in the Andes already apply most of the principles of ecological agriculture including crop rotation, mixed cropping, use of organic fertilisers, biological control of pests and diseases, soil conservation, conservation of genetic resources and the protection of wild plants and animals. Further, it was observed that the indigenous knowledge that forms the basis of these practices was eroding. On the basis of these experiences, it was concluded that rather than trying to teach farmers concepts, techniques and methods from another culture, the rural communities would be better served if outside agencies would help them to document, restore and strengthen traditional knowledge in order to reverse the process of erosion. For this role, AGRUCO implements a programme of participatory research in and with communities.

This research is not just a method of investigation; it is an approach that enhances development, considering the spiritual, ethical, social and technical aspects that are specific to the area. The starting point for this consideration is the perception and knowledge of the rural communities. Our main challenge is to understand and appreciate the indigenous reality, their concept of life and cosmovision and not to limit ourselves to conventional scientific and technological options. In order to really support the native communities, we have to evolve from the 'actor oriented' approach of research towards an approach of development that is 'actor involved'. The actor involved development approach is a cooperation between different actors in order to try to solve problems and learn how to live in the biophysical and to interact in the social and spiritual environment.

Rituals and music link people's microcosm with the macrocosm.

Pacha

A central notion in the native concept of life is *pacha*, whose nearest equivalent in occidental terms would be 'the whole conformed by space-time'. *Pacha* embraces the idea of 'totality' like the eternal and dynamic 'space-time' concept. The concept of cosmos is derived from *pacha* and is understood as the ensemble of all the elements the human beings are capable of attaining through their senses, thoughts, intuitions and inspirations. Within *pacha*, three spheres of life flow together and interact: *Pachakamak* - Spiritual Life; *Pachamama* - Material Life; *Pachankamachaña* - Social Life. *Pachakamak* refers to all the invisible forces, as a whole, proceeding from the outer cosmos. These forces eternally dynamise the total life and enfold or 'bathe' everyone and everything; it is what is related to the spiritual life. Mankind cannot take a direct influence in this sphere but it exists whether it is being ignored or not. *Pachamama* refers to all the forces, as a whole, that make life here on earth possible expressing themselves in all the aspects related to material life, in particular. These are the forces we can more easily perceive and with which living beings are in contact daily. *Pachankamachaña* refers to life within the society of the living beings that all share this space-time, in order to make life and reproduction possible.

From this confluence emanates a fourth sphere, *Pachankiri* - Daily Life. It is in this sphere where all the shared practices such as the necessary techniques and technologies for the continuity of life, and the social, material and spiritual reproduction take place, be it for agriculture, husbandry, forestry, art or other activities. In short, it includes everything that happens within the concept of the evolutive spiral of real life. The concept of *Pachankiri* refers to the sphere where human beings are in a state of 'consciousness': conscious of the own quality, independent of any natural, social or cultural determinism. This state thus creates a sphere of ample spiritual freedom. This spiritual freedom permits the Andean women and men to perceive themselves as a 'Microcosm' which is the reflection of the surrounding 'Macrocosm'. That is why their notion of society is not anthropocentric and why their highest aspiration is the continuous re-creation of a maximum harmony between Micro- and Macrocosmos (see the figure on next page).

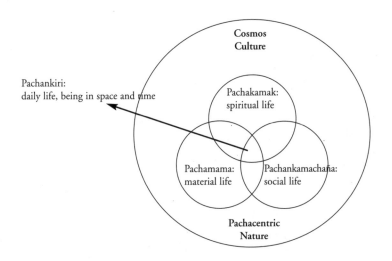

Pachankiri:
daily life, being in space and time

Cosmos
Culture

Pachakamak:
spiritual life

Pachamama:
material life

Pachankamachaña:
social life

Pachacentric
Nature

Pachankamachaña social life	Pachamama material life	Pachakamak spiritual life
Society - Nature Relationship Population - Demographics Organization - Hierarchies Population movements, migra- tions Housing sites Education - Formation - Positions Fair circuitry	Ecosymbiotic zones Agricultural - Ecological zones Territory - Community Soil - Water - Air Rainfed - Irrigation Forest - Orchard Flora - Fauna Rhythms - Cycles - Seasons Climatic astronomic cycles	Myths - Rites - Legends about nature 'Beliefs' - Festivities External return Art - Development within the habitat Music - Signs - Symbols Religious life - Behaviour Moral - Ethics

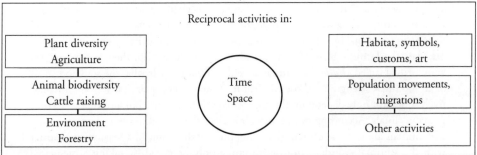

Reciprocal activities in:

Plant diversity Agriculture		Habitat, symbols, customs, art
Animal biodiversity Cattle raising	Time Space	Population movements, migrations
Environment Forestry		Other activities

Native concepts on evolution and 'development'

Up to the present day, the essential elements of the Andean cosmovision are widespread. In this vision evolution of life is seen as a spiral. This spiral notion of time leads to the understanding of life in terms of 'Jakakha' and 'Kutimithaya' corresponding to the concepts of karma and reincarnation respectively. 'Development' is perceived as the 'unrolling' and expansion of the past where only the context of every specific moment changes. Time is not a linear process from the beginning to the end, but a spiral process. This implies that the future is a repetition and expansion of cycles and rhythms. Development in this notion is the movement from the centre to the periphery. The moment obstacles arise, the movement will return to the origin, to the sources of knowledge and survival strategies that have been proven in the past. This is a phase of envelopment. Once the solutions for the obstacles are found and integrated, the development can continue but now with a renewed potential. Thus in the notion of the Andean people, the future is behind us and the past is in front of us. For example, in 1983/4 the people in the semi-desert area of Oruro experienced the period of drought as a punishment. People reacted by fasting and by searching and expanding their memory: they actively searched for former experiences and their solutions by different rituals and spiritual exercises. Older people remembered that some 50 years ago there was a similar drought, and they could recall a major remedy: the use of some 35 wild growing local herbs and vegetables for consumption. Once these vegetables were reintegrated into people's diet, development could continue again with a renewed potential.

The role of rituals

In the Andean worldview the human, natural and spiritual world are inseparable: they are in a constant dynamic interaction with each other. The notion that people have to relate both to the natural and to the spiritual world implies, therefore, that they not only develop knowledge and skills to survive materially, but that they also have to carry out their own spiritual activities in order to relate themselves to the spiritual world.

A ritual is understood as a spiritual activity carried out by humans in order to create the spiritual conditions for a certain material or social event that they wish to happen. In fact, through the spiritual activity a ritual should create room and a specific movement in the material world. Rituals are, therefore, performed in all important social and productive activities. The moment that farmers begin to create adequate physical conditions for plant growing (by ploughing), they ask *Pachamama* through a ritual to contribute to this by creating optimal spiritual conditions. Every year on Carnival Tuesday, the farmers go to their fields to celebrate their crop, then in full growth, with a ritual called *ch'alla*. This ritual is held in honour of Ispalla, the soul and spirit of all food that strengthens those who eat it. A good crop, quantitatively and qualitatively, does not only depend on the appropriate technologies, but also on the accompanying rituals. According to this view, it is clear that also illnesses in human beings and animals are not just caused by nature, but are the result of a negative encounter with the spiritual world. A disease cannot simply be cured by taking a medicinal plant. Along with the medical treatment, a ritual is needed to re-create adequate spiritual conditions for a healthy life.

For AGRUCO's work the most important thing to realise was that a new technology has a chance of being adopted only if a certain equilibrium exists between the three components of the cosmovision: nature, spirits and society. Rituals are the nucleus of both Andean religion and culture; especially those rituals related to agriculture. Because the inhabitants of the Andean communities have been and still are pre-dominantly farmers, their religion has evolved from agricultural experience. This emphasises the relationship of society and nature in a certain *Pacha* (space-time) and results in a ritual calendar that is in fact an agricultural calendar. This calendar permits them to synchronise the productive practices with the rhythms and cycles of the cosmos. The European and Christian colonisation could not change this: the communities chose to accept the Catholic feasts that coincided or were very close in time to their own most important festivals. Yet, below the cosmetics of Catholicism the fiestas still maintain their original meaning to a very large extent.

THE CONCEPT OF TIME IN THE WEST (ABOVE) AND IN THE ANDES (BELOW)

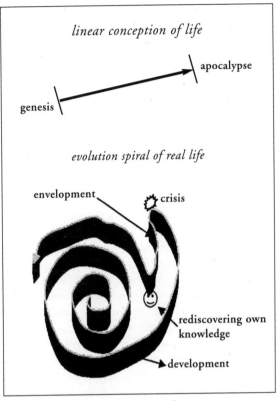

linear conception of life

genesis → apocalypse

evolution spiral of real life

envelopment — crisis

rediscovering own knowledge

development

Living astronomy and geography

Over 3500 years have passed since the Andean societies built observatories to register the passing of seasons, to measure eclipses, to observe planet rotations, moon and sun phases and the rising or setting of the stars. The careful and elaborate design of those structures show the importance attached to astrology and its relevance for the socio-territorial organisation of the agriculture cycle. Many of the most important spiritual moments, today marked by Christian feasts, are also important dates for astronomical observations. Many of these moments are used to predict the climatic characteristics of the coming raining season. Another important element in the organisation of social and productive activities are their interrelations with the moon-phases. Many activities such as sowing, the cutting of trees or animal castration, for example, are only done in certain moon phases. The interest of the Andean farmers goes beyond an abstract scientific interest in the movement of the stars and planets because they try to synchronise their social and productive life with the rhythms of the cosmos, and this leads to what could be called a 'living astronomy'.

When focusing on the interaction between spiritual and natural life, the configuration of a 'living geography' can be understood as that on which the entire social, economic, productive and technological organisation of the native communities is based. Understanding the living geography as the expression of spiritual life in nature is, therefore, important. One of the major challenges with which the native concept of life was faced, was their integration and harmonisation with multiple ecological and ethnic variabilities. The native cosmovision does not, therefore, lead to an 'overall socio-cultural system' but rather to a diversity of socio-cultural expressions that stands in direct relation to the ecological and cultural variabilities that characterise the Andes. The living geography does not only allow for the existence of spiritual life components, or simply permits the landscape to be structured by taking the ecological characteristics into account. It also constitutes the pillars of the social organisation.

San Antonio de Mujlli

We can draw here on a specific farming community to clarify the Andean concept of life further. The Ayllu of San Antonio de Mujlli is located in a mountainous area at an altitude ranging from 3,850 and 4,350 m.a.s.l. Its territory covers an area of about 18,400 hectares of which 92% is covered by native pastures used for grazing. Seven percent is used for crop cultivation and the remaining one percent is taken up by rivers, ravines and roads. The area is occupied by 769 families in 16 communities and has a total population of some 3000 - 3500 persons. The vegetation mainly consists of graminae and cactus varieties, characteristic for the *altiplano* (high plateau). In the raining season the annual plants develop a good vegetative cover, that serves as fodder, food, medicine, construction materials, and soil protection. The native fauna consists of cameloids (*llamas* and *alpacas*) and a large number of birds. The animals introduced have come to outnumber the cameloids and include cattle, goats, sheep and donkeys. The area, however, does not only provide a living for people, animals and plants. Through the concept of a living geography one is able to see and understand in a concrete way the interaction between the spiritual, social and natural worlds. Farmers in the area live together with the following important elements.

Spiritual beings. There are a great number of places that are feared, worshipped or respected, as a result of the presence of spiritual beings that influence the area in a positive or negative way.

Sacred places. The ceremonial centre of the community, also called 'head', is the village of Mujlli. Over 200 years ago, the ancestors of the present population chose this place as the centre of the Ayllu because, in the neighbourhood, there are two very powerful and sacred mountains: the female Mama T'alla and the male Achachila Mallku. Moreover, there is a sacred source of water that never dries out, something very important in the Andean Highlands. In the words of one of the members of the community: '*This water permits us year by year to call the rains when it is their time to come so that they can help the crops to grow that will feed us.*'

Feared places. There are places in the landscape where spiritual beings can cause severe diseases due to 'frights of the soul'.

Tower and square. Each ceremonial centre is represented by a tower, a male symbol and its female counterpart a square. During the festivals they are given ritual attention to ensure fertility and reproduction in the community.

Altars. Sacred places are also present in every home. On each patio there is a small altar of stone, which is used by the people to make their offerings to the sacred mountains, and to *Pachamama*, for the benefit of agricultural and social activities.

Corrals. Also the centre of the corrals where the animals pass their nights is a sacred place. Here people construct a tiny underground room where they keep their *illas*, miniature presentations of animals made of white stone. Every year or two these stones are taken out and are used in a ritual to ask for the further health and fertility of the animals.

In this way, the living geography constitutes a spiritual (or symbolic) landscape through which places and beings are related; from the most intimate place (the home) to the farthest place represented by the most powerful mountains some hundreds of kilometres away. Don Patricio explained the interrelationship of these different locations in the symbolic landscape by saying: '*When we express our thanks to the Virgin Pachamama, we call the mountains and powerful places, from the most remote places to the altars in the homes. This way every sacred place is invited to contribute to the welfare of the community.*'

AGRUCO staff noticed that the people often referred to certain locations as the 'head', the 'legs', the 'belly' or 'the tail' and held festivities for these body parts at these locations. A closer study of the map of the area revealed that the contours of the Major Ayllu, of which the Minor Ayllu of San Antonio de Mujlli is part, resembles the form of a *llama*.

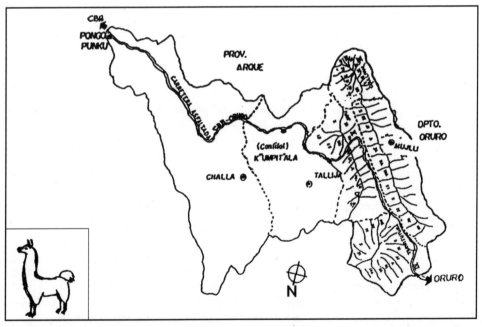

The socio-spiritual unit of the Mayor Ayllu of San Antonio de Mujlli is an example of living geography: it resembles a llama and the farmers celebrate the various body-parts with festivities.

The festivities and rituals continue to take place in the socio-spiritual unit of the whole Ayllu Mayor. There are 19 important festivals. These festivals mark religious activities, and at the same time are opportunities to express the reciprocity between people, plants, animals, nature and spiritual beings. At present the festivals are being threatened by religious sects, who discourage participation in cultural events and in the community activities.

The social relations at family, communal and inter-communal level, cannot be fully understood without mentioning the principles of reciprocity and redistribution, derived from the native cosmovision. According to the native cosmovision, opposites do not exclude each other but rather constitute the two poles between which the life generating forces are produced. Several forms of exchange of labour, land and of social relations and spiritual functions exist and optimise complementarity. This notion is not compatible with utilitarian and mercantile logic, but as the market economy penetrates the rural areas, the community members have to learn to combine mercantile economic relations with those based on reciprocity and complementarity.

The Aynoka land-use system

The Ayllu San Antonio de Mujlli has 4 different watersheds. The farmers of one watershed generally have access to the other three for crop cultivation and for grazing their animals. This is a mechanism of risk minimisation since the four watersheds have a great variety of soils and microclimates. Depending on the altitude, orientation to the sun and soil type there is a great variation in the vegetation, and sensitivity to drought, frost, hails, pests and diseases. Within this system the land is divided into 13 to 26 different sections of some 1000 hectares called *ayta*. This in turn is subdivided into three sections, the *aynokas*. The crop production of all the families of the community is concentrated in the *aynokas*. The crops are grown in a three year rotation starting with potatoes, followed by Andean grain crops (*quinua* or *cañahua*) and, in the third year fodder crops such as oats and barley are grown. The land is then left fallow for at least 10 years. During the fallow period it is used for free grazing and is available to all the animals in the community. All families follow this rotation which is decided by the community. The decisions on where to farm are influenced by the weather expected: if a year with drought or frost is expected, a place which is sensitive to this will be passed over for a year, and locations will be chosen which offer better protection. The access to land in the *aynokas* is not based on private property rights but is regulated by the community through family usufruct norms which also permit a redistribution of plots from smaller to larger families according to their basic requirements.

Indigenous Institutions

Two distinct historical systems underlie the communities organisation. The ancestral, pre-colonial organisation and a syndical organisation that was introduced as a result of the Land Reform in 1952. At present the incompatibility of the two organisation systems, based on two very different cosmovisions, is becoming increasingly clear. This incompatibility has led to a series of conflicts and raise question about the future of the social system.

The ancestral organisation. The ancestral organisation is a social replica of what has been described above in relation to the interaction between spiritual and material life. It allows the organisation of the productive system, and regulates the rotation and the complementarity of crop and animal production. Three *alcaldes*, the highest authorities, are elected every year. They divide the tasks of coordinating decision making about land rotation, the allocation of land rights and the performance of functions during festivals and are considered the 'fathers' of all the families of the Ayllu. Other important authorities are the *jilakatas*, persons who protect the cultivated *aynokas*, keep the animals out of these areas and sanction the owners of animals they catch grazing there. Because climatic problems are not perceived as arbitrary phenomena, but rather as the result of bad human behaviour, the *jilakatas* also have to protect the plots against those negative influences. If there is hail, frost or drought, the *jilakata* must order the community to pay tribute to *Pachamama* or to fast for a full day. This is followed by a ritual during which the people promise to live correctly. In this way they restore the balance between the two domains and thus remove the reason for the spiritual beings to punish the people.

The syndical organisation. As a result of the Land Reform of 1952, the agricultural production of the haciendas was supposed to be organised through cooperatives. As the Andean rationality and cooperativism was not compatible with

Three jilakatas (on the left) and three corregidores ensure protection of the plots and community against negative influences.

185

this, the syndicates suffered severe problems and were subsequently given other functions. In practice, the syndicates should regulate social and economic relationships, have political functions, solve conflicts and organise communal works for the construction of community buildings such as schools and health posts. They also have the function of establishing contacts outside the community: they represent the community on NGOs and GOs and explore markets opportunities for example. The way the syndicates function at present is problematic. With their focus on economic and material activities, they cannot respond effectively to the needs of community organisation based on reciprocity and complementarity between the spiritual, natural and social world.

Methodological instruments

In view of the existing difference between the conventional rationalism and the native concept of life, what are the options for the Andean population to develop and yet maintain their identity? One of the ways to express identity is through the native language. From an outside perspective, we should be very careful with the interpretations of local concepts. We are not only referring to the literal but also to the conceptual and the symbolic or figurative dimension of these languages. There is an urgent need for a new relation between the scientific knowledge system and the hundreds of native knowledge systems all over the world and to recognise that, after all, we are all immersed in the same adventure·or as the native people would say 'we are all fish in the same sea, we are all birds of the same sky'.

Some fundamental conditions and actions enabled AGRUCO to evolve from a conventional development programme into a position where it was able to try and initiate and practice an intercultural dialogue. Three questions are important here. Firstly, how can we establish an institutional framework that permits a harmonious and permanent interaction with native communities? Second, what are the main attitudes necessary to enhance social evolution both at community and university level? And finally, how can we encourage technical staff to overcome the limitations of a conventional and specialised education?

In order to establish an institutional basis for the intercultural dialogue we had to take two basic realities into account. On the one hand, the university of which we are part and its academic programme representing a system of scientific knowledge which has a different culture to that of native communities. And on the other hand, the native communities themselves presenting us an entirely different system of knowledge, objectives and concepts of life. For AGRUCO this meant that we had to find an institutional configuration that allows for a horizontal and reciprocal interaction at each stage of the communal management of knowledge. In order to achieve this, as a first step we systematised the main stages of the communal management of knowledge as shown in the figures.

The peasant families continuously generate, revaluate, validate and test existing and new knowledge and practices and communicate about them within and outside the family and community. Through this cyclical process they adapt their knowledge to new ecological and socio-economic conditions. Once we had been able see how the communities manage knowledge we could determine our institutional configuration. Since we wanted to ensure the interaction of our work with all parts of the communal process of learning and action, we could not organise ourselves as would be normal in conventional universities: into different departments for education, investigation and extension.

We have chosen to structure of AGRUCO into three units. In order to contribute to the educational process at universities, based on agro-ecology and the revaluation of native knowledge, it was decided to create a first unit called 'support of communities'. Based on this domain we could then establish the basis for realising the activities of the other two domains, 'participatory research' and 'education', both at communal and university level. Participatory research activities have particular characteristics. Because the investigation emerges from the support of communities it has to be in line with the necessities of the peasant families. On the other hand, since the domain of research constitutes the basis for the contents of the educational process, the education of the future professionals also answers to a higher degree the requirements of

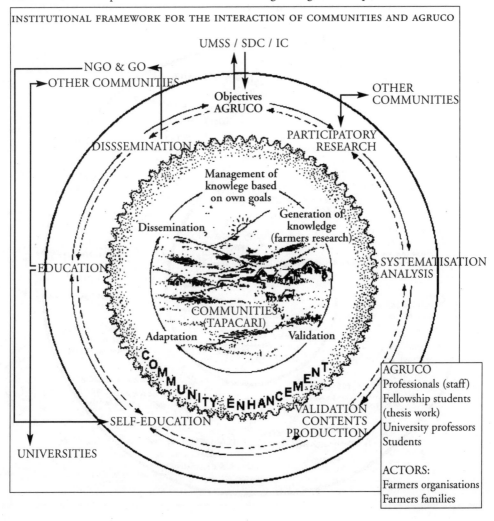

INSTITUTIONAL FRAMEWORK FOR THE INTERACTION OF COMMUNITIES AND AGRUCO

the communities.

The combination of education, research and support to the communities permits the integration of people from these communities into the educational process at the university. During theoretical and practical courses for students, university teachers and professionals in and with the communities, they will be able to transmit their knowledge and capabilities, their needs, preoccupations and aspirations to the external agents of development.

After we had overcome the artificial separation of research, extension and education we realised that the methodological instruments for conventional research, education and extension were not appropriate. In our case, when we make a description of a peasant technology or when a student produces a thesis in and with the community, we are simultaneously contributing to participatory research, support of the communities and reciprocal education. The figure summarises some of the main instruments or techniques used by AGRUCO for the intercultural dialogue.

THE STAGES OF PROCESS OF COMMUNITY DYNAMISATION AGRUCO-BOLIVIA

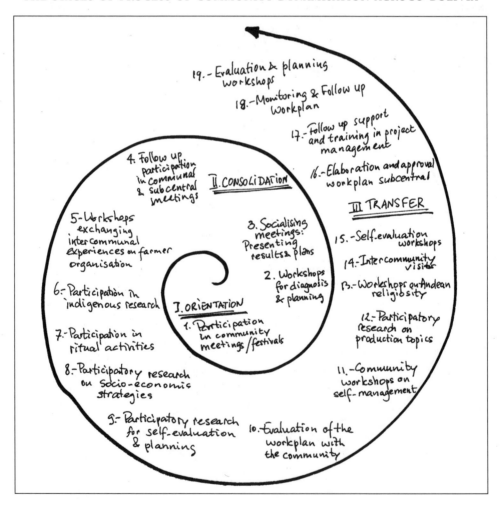

From extension to guidance

One aspect of utmost importance for the programme and the community is the appropriate education of the professionals involved. To integrate the work of the three units represents a challenge for individual professionals. In order for them not to limit their attention to a specific specialisation, it is important to involve each one in the three domains. We consider this necessary because their own learning experience is essential for the education of professionals who are supposed to conduct an intercultural dialogue. The limitation for this new challenge lies in the conventional education of professionals and, therefore, in AGRUCO we maintain a permanent and obligatory process of self-education for the whole staff.

The process of self-education started with a phase of de-schooling and an analysis of the experiences of conventional agricultural extension. The intentions of extension were to change traditional ways of production since they were considered old fashioned and obsolete. The experience of AGRUCO and other institutions has shown that it is possible to overcome the problems of extension by openly analysing the contradictions and the failures and by making serious efforts to achieve dialogue on an equal basis. There were many questions posed by professionals such as: How can we understand the reactions and decisions of the community? How can we learn with them about their reality and their strategies? What can we contribute considering the globalisation of the market distorts the way we should relate ourselves to nature? What is extension? Who decides what? What is it we all want and what can we offer? We came to the conclusion that we should move from extension to guiding the dynamics of community knowledge. But to really be able to give guidance, we need a self-education that will help us to see the community as it really is and not only to look at the community with a focus on the innovations they adapt. It means that we have to get to know and to understand the reality through an interpersonal dialogue in which we have to listen first and then support. It also means that first we have to learn to guide ourselves amongst professionals. We have to learn to behave as an interdisciplinary team rather than as a multidisciplinary one.

When looking into how we should go about guiding the community, we felt that we had reached a new approach to extension. An approach where we have to get involved in the total process of what the community learns, experiments and communicates. We should learn not to push anything that goes beyond the necessities of the community itself. We also have to be aware that the community is offering us the opportunity to learn about the potentials and the dangers of this kind of guidance. Factors that obstruct a diversified and productive interdisciplinary dialogue are, for example, the varying degrees of importance ascribed to different professions. This includes such aspects for example as difference in prestige and in remuneration. This is not surprising since professions are based on academic education where the professionals are constantly led to believe that their profession is the most important one and, therefore, they acquire the wrong attitude towards interdisciplinary work in support of rural communities. As we can see, the step of interdisciplinary learning is not a mere accumulation of new knowledge but implies a change of attitude amongst professionals. They have to integrate the same ethical criteria into their individual life as the ones that are guiding the behaviour of the community members. This is why we consider the self-education of the field worker to be the connecting link between the community's cosmovision and external knowledge and that is why we are giving so much importance to overcoming our orthodox scientific education. Once we have achieved this, we can continue with the following steps, where the present contributions of science such as philosophy, ethnology and new tendencies in physics or biology can help us understand more profoundly the support we should offer the rural communities.

SHARING THE FRUITS OF PACHAMAMA

Gloria Miranda Zambrano, Jesus Lindo Revilla and Raúl Santana Paucar

To understand the cosmovision of the people of the Peruvian Andes one has to realise that rural life is related to different ecological zones that go with different altitudes. Their culture and customs express the relationship with nature, gods, ancestors and family groups. In the higher areas (*sierra*), between 3500 and 4500 meters above sea level, plant, animal and human life originates. The people are the sons and daughters of the mountains and the brothers and sisters of animals such as the condor and llama. In the intermediary zone, of 3200 to 3500 meters above sea level people grow potatoes and other Andean tuber and grain crops. Farmers use ancestral knowledge about the phases of the moon and other natural phenomena in the planning of agricultural activities. They grow a variety of crops but still conserve the major quantities of indigenous seeds. Family activities are not only agricultural, but are artisanal and commercial as well. The lower zones, between 2800 and 3200 meters above sea level are the most privileged: irrigation water and milder climates allow for two harvests each year. Here farmers keep animals such as cattle, chicken, rabbits and even fish.

Cosmovision

The Andean pantheism is camouflaged by the impact of the inquisition. Ancient beliefs, practices and rituals for the traditional gods were continued behind the adoption of Christian saints. Grandparents tell their grandchildren legends, stories and riddles that refer to the happenings of the past. The cosmovision assumes the existence of three worlds: *Kay pacha*, the world of today; *Hanan pacha*, the upper world of the gods, the saints, sun and moon; and *Uku pacha* or *Lulin pacha*, the lower world of the ancestors. *Kay pacha*, the world of today, does not function well if one does not pay tribute to God and to the saints who are the intermediaries between humans and God. That is the value of the fiestas, festivities and folkloric dances: to please the gods and ask their blessings. That is also the reason why agricultural activities are programmed with a calendar of festivals.

The concept is pantheistic, which means that the mountains, lakes, streams and trees are considered sacred. People observe signs in nature that indicate the balance between the lower world and the world of today. Dust storms in the form of a snake are seen as an indication of imbalance. When the sons of the gods behave well in their families and in their relationship with nature, the gods will protect them. If not, they will be punished. Respect for nature is expressed in the rituals of 'paying the elements of nature' (earth, animals). The festivals also help to improve the relationships between members of the family, the community and between labourers and pastoralists. Divine beings are either male or female and things like food or places are either cold or warm. Both polarities bring about a balance in nature. Therefore, the activities of men and women are different. In general the men carry out the heavy labour in the field, whereas women take care of the household and the animals. Men teach the boys and women the girls. Women are more receptive to the cultural values and they practice them better then men. They tend to communicate better than men and if a decision has to be made they usually say: '*I have to consult my husband.*' In general they have better arguments and a better memory then men.

Since the time of the ancestors, farmers have attached importance to the existence and survival of all plants. They know that without them, animals and people cannot survive. From the simplest mosses up to trees, people depend on them for everything: medicine, fodder, fruits, food, firewood, timber, materials for housing and handicrafts. In nature, the most important element is water, but Mother Earth (*Pachamama*) supports everything created. Animals and people can be affected by the warm and cold qualities of the food they take. Therefore it is important to have a diet which is balanced with cold and warm food.

People deserve the blessing of the gods when they live without egoism, when they dance with enthusiasm. The cost of the festivities and ceremonial acts are paid for by the individual, the family or the community. Anybody who has contributed to the work will benefit from it. Jealousy, lack of respect and hate result in bad luck, provoked by the witches. The healers and soothsayers can help to correct these things with the help of gods. People explain the cause of welfare in society by the behaviour of people. They can cause confusion in the relationship with nature, the ancestors and the living people. The effect is damage, disease, abandonment and misery. If things are managed in a balanced way, the result is peace, mutual help and other benefits.

Paying tribute to nature and ancestors

Without the social values of reciprocity, survival in the Andean communities and in the families would not be possible. Reciprocity takes many forms such as the *minka*: joint work force; *uyay*: labour exchange based on the principle 'today for me, tomorrow for you'; *el shunay*: providing some new seeds of maize or potatoes or breeding stock; *el mallichi*: a meal for inhabitants of a section of the village organised on a rotational basis at certain occasions like during a harvest; *el kuyay*: a meal or drinks offered to the community at the occasion of family festivals such as marriage, baptism, anniversaries, or funerals; *el kutichi*: returning a favour to somebody; and *el pinachikuy*: asking somebody a favour when there is an emergency.

Despite 500 years of European domination and the effects of the Spanish Inquisition socalled pagan practices are still being held: ritual and pantheistic worships for nature. In some Andean villages there are *layas*, persons who know and act as intermediaries between nature and men, who read the signs of the mountains, lakes and springs and help in the planning of agricultural activities. They can perform the following rites:

□ Paying to the earth.

When opening a new road, building a house or ploughing a field before sowing, the soil will be disturbed. The people perform a ritual to pay the earth: chewing leaves of coca, making offerings of flowers, or of seed, coca leaves, cigars, liquor or juice (*chicha*) so that Mother Earth (*Pachamama*) can eat, drink, smoke and booze.

'We, the children of the earth give things back to her as she has given us our life.'

☐ Paying to the mountains.

People pay tribute to the mountains by building small pyramids of stones. Mountains can be divided in male mountains and female mountains. If not treated with respect, the mountains can cause damage, accidents or headaches. Today the sites of churches, crosses, or chapels are located in places where in prechristian times their gods and spirits were worshipped.

☐ Paying to the waters.

Lakes, springs, rivers and other waters are considered sacred, not only because they are the blood of the mountains, but because water means life for all living beings. No-one can refuse to give water to any being. Pacarina is the god of water and people make offerings for the benefits received from him. An unforgivable sin is to exhaust a water source.

☐ Paying the ancestral graves.

If a grave has been damaged or robbed, the place has to be treated with an animal body or grains.

Traditional institutions and customs

The *layas* can read the signs of nature including the stars and act accordingly. Yet this profession is scarcely found nowadays. There are several other traditional institutions. The *curandero* or local healer is somebody who understands diseases in terms of energy from nature or energy from persons who recently died. Elements that absorb energy of human beings are *chachu*. This is the case when the roots of a tree cause unhappiness, when a rock causes bad effects or when the land is wild. The healers can detect these energies and cure them. They make a diagnosis by looking at the face, eyes, hand palm and pulse. They are aware of their own powers and limitations. If they cannot treat somebody with the knowledge they have, they advice the patient to go to a doctor or hospital. Soothsayers and diviners can read the signs of coca leaves or grains of maize. These can indicate the fate of persons.

There is a clear symbiosis between indigenous gods and Christian gods in the agricultural calendar. There are special dates to celebrate festivals for planting, for the animals, the production, the harvest, the dead and the living. These festivals are frequent, spread over the year and are mixtures of pantheism and Christianity. The three different ecozones exchange their agricultural products during the festivals of the patrons but also during regular or weekly market days. *Parentesco* refers to ancestral customs that aim to establish family relationships. People seek to establish these family relationships with communities from other ecozones in order to look for material and spiritual support, security, better social status, cultural exchange and to reach equity in terms of dignity and labour. Marriage is of course the most clear case. Before marriage, there is a period of probation. The newly married couple help in their new relatives' farm and, as compensation, receive food. Baptism includes the choice of *compadres* and involves the exchange of a chicken, pig or other valuables. Friendship can be formalised in the form of oath brothers, *padrinos*.

Major decisions are taken by the community. The head of the community organises meetings, communicates the plans and has them discussed by community members. The tradition of oral communication plays a very important role in the communities and families, and has survived the influence of the political education of the state and the influence of the mass media. The elders teach the young people. It includes rules for good behaviour, justness, responsibility, equality and care. Words are important but examples are more important. Therefore, agriculture is taught in the field with the tools in hand. There are several codes for teaching: youth may be reproached in front of the community, or even physically punished when serious mistakes are made. But good behaviour is publicly recognised and awarded too. Satire is used indirectly, in addressing a person by pretending to joke to animals, tease them or reproach them. Because of migration to towns and terrorism, many people have left and those remain are wrestling with the issue of how to create autonomous development based on strong rural institutions.

Fiesta de la Candelaria

To give an example of how agriculture and cosmovision is interrelated, we share an experience how Greta Jiménez Sardón, a field worker from an NGO in Southern Peru benefited from participating in the fiesta de la Candelaria. In the time of carnaval, the town of Puno was vibrating with the fiesta. For a number of days in a row, from early morning to late in the evening, the streets were full of groups of musicians: rustic bands with pan flutes, drums and string instruments, and more urban-oriented groups with trumpets, clarinets and drums. Each group of musicians was

La Fajina is the festival for opening new fields with footploughs.

194

accompanied by dancers who performed the traditional dances of their regions.

One day a field trip had been scheduled to a farmers' meeting in a village in the province of Chucuito. The staff of the NGO, however, said that the field trip had to be cancelled because the fiesta would prevent people from joining the meeting. They said that on that particular day a tribute would be paid to the potato. It would draw all villagers to the potato fields and there a ritual was to be held. Yet Greta intended to go, she particularly wanted to be present at the ritual. Early that morning, the 'day of the potato' started with a ritual to honour Mother Earth, Pachamama. Every family made an offering of sweets on a small altar made of stone, dedicated to the virgin located in the house. This offering is done while praying to Pachamama and pouring a libation with alcohol. Usually the farmers have buried an *illa* in their *patio*, an amulette made of albast that represents a small farm unit: animals, stables, garden, house. The function of this *illa* is to ensure good luck in farm work, good yields, good reproduction for the animals and health for their owners. For the occasion of this ritual, the *illa* is dug out, subject to praying and libations in order to increase its beneficial properties and is then buried again. The farmers decorate the houses and patios with flowers and serpentines saying: '*Spirit of the potato, this is your day, take care of the food, accept the alcohol and coca leaves*'. Firecrackers are also used.

Then the families join the community and visit the potato fields. The older men, who have the role of spiritual leader in the community build an altar of stones while the women go to the potato fields. This is the time of the year when the potatoes are flowering and are setting new tubers. The women visit every plot separately, greet the potatoes and ask permission to take a few of the tubers for the ritual. They take the mother potato from one or two plants and 2 to 3 new potato seeds that are now the size of a dove's egg. The potato fields are then decorated with serpentines and flowers. A group of musicians goes through the fields, followed by the women dancing. The mother potato and the seedlings are then brought to the elder men. During a ceremony, the community offers coca leaves and alcohol. Everybody is silent for some ten minutes, during which he or she thanks the mother potato for its contribution and welcomes the young potatoes. Finally, the coca leaves and potatoes are burned on the altar. The direction of the smoke is important as it gives an indication of the spirits for future crops. The day is then concluded by visiting the house of every member of the community. Music, coca leaves and alcohol is abundantly available.

The presence of Greta during this festival was greatly appreciated by the community. It was considered a sign of respect for the communities' beliefs and strengthened their relationship. The community was proud to share their intimate knowledge. On this basis Greta was able to learn from the community and to make plans for cooperation that took indigenous concepts and spiritual leaders as the starting point.

TALPUY's activities

Farmers' knowledge has not been taken into account in the agricultural policies or development models. TALPUY is promoting ecological agriculture and autonomous agricultural development. Traditional technologies are being validated and promoted in order to reduce the costs of production. These technologies include organic fertilisers, integrated pest management, enhancing biodiversity through multiple cropping and in-situ conservation of genetic resources and ethnoveterinary practices. TALPUY supports the development of farmers' knowledge as well as adapted modern technologies when they are useful and feasible for the small farmer. TALPUY is making an elaborate inventory of essential knowledge for each of the three ecological zones. This knowledge is discussed and assessed in farmers' meetings, where technicians provide complementary information. It produces a regular magazine

'MINKA' with experiences of farmers, written in a simple style both in Spanish and in Quechua. Before intervening in any community TALPUY always makes a diagnosis of the specific situation: ecological, economic, social and cultural. It observes the family networks, the exchange of goods and labour, participation in the different local institutions and land use.

The aim of the staff is to become part of the community, to be able to give an opinion, or suggestion: to discuss, educate, and participate in an equal manner in decision making in the community. A curriculum based on indigenous and adapted practices has been formed. Farmers discuss and validate them and these sessions form a forum to express farmers' wisdom and knowledge.

In the context of COMPAS, TALPUY makes an in depth study of the role of traditional institutions and rituals in agriculture, particularly those related to potatoes. On that basis field experiments are scheduled and will be carried out together with the traditional leaders.

The Egg of Fire

In the time of silence that existed before the Creation: Purun Pacha,
in the Water of Time, Kon Akiri, the Eternal Supreme,
the Lord of Time, dreamt of the Egg of Fire.
And the Egg of Fire was born in the Night of Emptiness:
in the dream of the Eternal Lord.

And in the emptiness he moved blind and mute
in its flames it twirled and listened
to the recently created music of the abysm.

The fire, in its dance, twirled and in anguish cried
and called and did not receive an answer.
He asked and was not heard,
He dared to throw his anguish like a spark in the road of the lonely one,
of the indifferent, the Supreme Lord.

And Kon Akiri played in the obscure water and blew in the silence.
And from his blow, his play and the water his beloved son was born;
and he told him:
'Huaracocha, you will be the maker, the person with the ardent life,
and with the Fire and the First Light you will break the Egg.
And from this egg you will take the Shining Light.
And from the water and the Egg in the great Abysm,
you will create the sky and the stars.'

And Huarakhocha, with the Lightning, broke the Egg.
and he spoke The Word and created the sky and the world.
And in the sky he created the river of the night and the sun,
the circular fires and the road that they continuously take in the Great
Shadow.

And the Lord of the Time, knowing that he was lonely gave him
Khuno, the First Lady;
and he gave him Auki, the Lord of Darkness.
The three of them, embracing each other, created the earth.
Thus Tailka Pachamama was created:
..The one that is kind and the one that destroys;
..the one that fertile and that fertilises;
..the one that unites Life and Death;
..the one that receives, gives and takes;
Because it is the Light and the Shadow

And she went up to the mountains and snowpeaks
and gave birth from within herself:
from the fire in her womb,
... the forests, the mountains and the jungles
... and the seas, the rivers;
... the animals, the birds and the fishes ...

For the better understanding of this marvellous poem, Ing. Enrique Rocha gives some additional information. Tunapa was the 'Cosmic Christ' who appeared in the Altiplano of Bolivia in the region of Paria and who travelled in the area till the coast of Pachakamaj in Peru, more than 8000 years before Christ. Around 1550, this codice was given by an Aymara leader to the first Franciscan priest who arrived at Tiawanaku, as a token of appreciation that he has saved his live. The priest was punished by the Holy Inquisition for being too intimate with the indigenous people and transferred to Arequipa in Peru. The document remained unknown till 1950, when the relatives of the priest found the document in the crypt of the first chapel of the priest in the Bolivian Chaco. The person who published this document, Mr Avilla Echazu, presently claims the authorship of the document.

BIODYNAMIC AGRICULTURE AND SPIRITUALITY

Willem Beekman and Joke de Jonge

Europe is the homeland of western science and technology. The comparisons being made within COMPAS could be enriched if the experiences of those European farmers who are developing their farms on ecological principles and holistic paradigms are also included. Biodynamic agriculture is being practised today by a small group of Dutch farmers and is embedded in a biodynamic and anthroposophic movement of farmers, consumers and traders. These farmers regard the earth as a living organism and in their work they take full account of cosmic forces and spiritual beings. This article will begin by describing the historical roots of the biodynamic cosmovision and how Dutch farmers relate to it. Some comparisons with other cultures within COMPAS are discussed and plans for the future are outlined. COMPAS partners were able to visit biodynamic farmers during their stay in the Netherlands in February 1998 and this article provides some insights into this intercultural dialogue.

Roots of European agriculture

Although European culture, including the sources of (agro) science, is rooted in several worldviews and cosmovisions such as the Scandinavian and Celtic, its main roots are in ancient Greece. At that time, roughly between 2000 to 200 BC, 'new' concepts of thinking and acting in science and agriculture emerged. In the Greek myths, much cosmovision is expressed in poetic language and a deep understanding of the cosmic organism and human nature is revealed. Biodynamic farmers have a particular love for the myth of Demeter and Persephone.

Persephone is the young Goddess of the flowers and beauty in nature. She is the daughter of Demeter, the Goddess of the earth, mother of fertility and plant growth. One day, Persephone is kidnapped by Hades, the God of Death and the Underworld, to become his wife. Demeter desperately seeks her daughter and eventually comes in the courtyard of a royal family where the King has died. Demeter gives all her attention to a young prince, Triptolemos, who takes care of the land with his horses. He is a clever and hardworking man, the prototype of a dedicated farmer. Demeter has chosen him to be the mediator of earthly and heavenly forces in agriculture. Demeter initiates Triptolemos through fire but the queen intervenes and demands that Demeter stops. The queen does not understand what Demeter is doing and believes her son will be killed in the flames. Demeter is filled with sadness and hides herself in the mountains, angry and stubborn. From that moment onwards, she neglects the soil, plant growth and fertility of the seed. The land disintegrates. Zeus, brother of Demeter, tries to find her. He knows that only when Persephone is brought back to her mother, Demeter will start to take care of the earth again. Hades agrees to allow Persephone to stay with her mother for two-thirds of the year. The rest she must spend as his wife in the kingdom of death. Demeter agrees and life on Earth continues.

This myth contains the main elements of biodynamic cosmovision. First of all the existence of Demeter, Mother Earth. Demeter is the soul of the earth, the living principle in all soil organisms. A modern version of this idea is described in the Gaia concept of the British geologist James Lovelock. In biodynamic agriculture, the concept of a living earth is central: all farming efforts should be directed to improving soil fertility and enhancing soil life. This is the modern form of worshipping Demeter. Secondly, the existence of Persephone, the Goddess of beauty in nature, is the symbol of all spiritual beings that help plants to grow, seeds to germinate and fragrance to spread across the land. When Persephone is captured by Hades, the God of Death, nature loses its power and disintegration follows. Further, there is the notion of seasons: from early Spring to late Autumn, Persephone is in partnership with nature and with her mother Demeter. In Europe, this is the growing season. In the short winter season, nature hides in the earth (kingdom of death). Finally, there is also the notion of a 'real' human being (not a God or Goddess), the real caretaker of the soil. The young farmer can only do his job in the light of the spiritual world. This is symbolised by the initiation of Triptolemos in which Demeter gives her divine inspiration by means of fire.

Europeans have lived with such spiritual aspects for many centuries, but they have vanished in recent times because of the way European culture has dealt with knowledge processes. Natural science now plays a dominant role. Spiritual life has almost gone or is at least diminished and institutionalised in church religions. Yet, there has always been a minority who held a more holistic and spiritual worldview. These include the various gnostic movements such as the Cathars in France, who were forcefully suppressed by the church, as well as eco-spiritual movements such as the Franciscans who were accepted by it.

Goethe, the German scientist and poet, developed a more holistic and organic approach to research in the late eighteenth and early nineteenth century. Skills such as observation, lively imagination and intuition are meant to revive the cognitive powers of scientists and farmers in this phenomenological natural science. At the end of the 19th century Rudolf Steiner further developed the theory of cognition in Goethe's investigations in nature. Steiner's spiritual science inspired the anthroposophic movement and its biodynamic farming. Steiner often proclaimed that his worldview was a spiritual science for western people, and not a mixture of western and eastern esoteric wisdom.

Biodynamic agriculture was 'born' in 1924 with a series of eight lectures given by Steiner. This 'agricultural course' was an answer to farmers' looking for new insights into a biological safe and sound agriculture at the beginning of the era of chemical and pesticide agriculture. The dramatic decrease in seed quality was a particular reason for farmer concern. Steiner intended to connect his spiritual science, firmly based on his clairvoyance, with the modern western and scientific worldview. In the agricultural course more emphasis was put on the spiritual aspects of agriculture such as the quality of food, the role of the cosmos (moon, planets and stars), the use of hitherto unknown 'preparations', the revival of the Greek elements (earth, water, air, fire) and the inner quality of the protein elements as forces in nature rather than on material constituents such as composting and mixed farming. Steiner also introduced his ideas on the two main spiritual forces in nature, etheric and astral forces. He created a new language for understanding the forces of nature, which was not always clear to those farmers and researchers who took over the task of developing biodynamic agriculture. In the last 70 years, a lot of practical experience and scientific research has been obtained. Not every biodynamic principle and cosmovision could be developed in day-to-day farming practices.

Biodynamic cosmovision

Dutch biodynamic farmers have adopted varied positions and individual relations to the biodynamic cosmovision and to anthroposophy. They all share a basic attitude in which respect for nature and caring for the land is essential. Agriculture is not only an economic activity, it is also a cultural activity. There are various aspects within the biodynamic cosmovision.

Farm organism and farm individuality.
In Steiner's Agricultural Course some attention is paid to the organisation of the farm as a whole. 'Farm organism' refers to the interconnection of all partners in nature with the farmer(s) and other people involved. This term is not only meant as a metaphor, but expresses the existence of a real organism, whose constituents are all the living and non-living elements of the farm. The coherence of life-cycles is the core of this 'organism' and all processes are cyclically interwoven with each other. Related to the farm organism is 'farm individuality'. As the farm develops into a more ecologically, economically and spiritually balanced enterprise, it reflects the skills and aims of the farmer and the farm-organism and the farm individuality which can be seen as a higher order. The organism becomes an identity. Most biodynamic farmers stress the importance of this farm individuality and it is treated with respect and care. That 'the whole is more than the sum of its parts' is true of farm individuality and efforts are made to broaden farm (bio)diversity by means of shrubs and hedges, ponds, weed parcels, birds nests, mushroom corners and bee-keeping. The co-development of farmer(s) with their farm(s) is an essential element in biodynamic agriculture. The inner and spiritual development of the people are in a way reflected in the outer biodiversity of plants and animals on the farm.

Preparations.
The most intriguing part of biodynamic agriculture, at least for the layman, is the use of specific preparations. These are compositions of specific minerals (like silica), cow manure, weeds and weed parts, in combination with animal organs like intestine, bladder, skull and horns. The clue to preparing these compounds is given by Steiner in the Agricultural Course. Much effort was and still is being made in biodynamic agriculture to conceptually grasp the meaning and composition of the preparations, which obviously cannot be understood completely in conventional scientific terms. There is also cosmic energy, as planetary forces work

in the chosen weeds and animal organs. These preparations are not seen as material additives, but as forces in the realm of nature, coming from nature, embedded in nature and put back to nature, after very careful handling. Scientifically, much research has been done in proving the effects of preparation use with varying success. Here, as in the so-called sowing calendar (see below), the conventional way of thinking in science is inadequate for a full understanding and appreciation of these aspects. Farmers also have different experiences with these preparations. Some are committed users and have a good feeling about using them; others doubt about their effect.

Cosmic influences.

A sowing calendar based on the lifetime work of the German horticulturist Maria Thun is used in biodynamic agriculture. This calendar uses the position of the moon in the Zodiac as a guideline for practical handling. Thun made this her life-task and she paid special attention to the influence of the position (not the phases) of the moon in relation to four different qualities. Taurus, Virgo, Capricorn (earth): roots; Cancer, Scorpio, Pisces (water): stem and leaves; Gemini, Libra, Aquarius (air): flowers; Aries, Leo, Sagittarius (warmth): fruits. It must be said that in spite of the popularity of the Thun calendar its results are debatable. There is a clear distinction between those who use the calendar in their own (mostly amateur) garden, and the scientists who are looking for proof. Scientific research did not confirm the strong results that Thun obtained in her own garden. Therefore, the sowing calendar is not used as a law. One can also be a good biodynamic practitioner without it. On the other hand, it can be said that in biodynamic agriculture, there is deep interest in these cosmic aspects and a strong belief that the cosmic environment of the earth plays an important role in the ecosystem of the earth. In several places in the world research is taking place to ascertain this cosmic relationship, sometimes with positive results. As there are also relations between certain tree species and planets some people plant these trees in specific arrangements to symbolise the connection between nature and cosmos.

Spiritual beings.

In the anthroposophical work of Steiner one can find a tremendous effort to re-introduce spiritual beings into the western mind. Bio-dynamic farmers as anthroposophers are fully aware of the so-called 'elemental beings' and are working with them. The elemental beings are related to the well-known Greek elements: earth, water, air and fire. Via these elements the spiritual beings are thought to be connected with the corresponding parts of the higher plants: roots, stem and leaves, flowers and finally fruits. Only for the clairvoyant are these beings (also called gnomes, leprechauns, nymphs, sylphs, fairies and others) visible to the inner eyes. Some farmers are aware of the presence of these beings as a kind of feeling or mood in different parts of the farm and at specific times of the day. Also other spiritual beings like angels and archangels up to the Holy Trinity (Father, Son and Holy Ghost as aspects of God) live in the thoughts and feelings of many biodynamic farmers. Many spiritual beings are presented in this worldview, in a very complex but strictly hierarchical order, from the lowest (gnomes) to the highest (spirits of the heavens). Farmers have different experiences with these beings. These experiences are not limited to biodynamic farmers, though they may be more conscious in their observations.

Rituals and festivals. Biodynamic agriculture has a strong link with seasonal activities which are often embedded in festivals related to the rhythm of the year. Mostly these festivals are related to traditional Christian ones, which in turn were often proceeded by ancient cults. All farmers have a special day for making preparations. Each farmer has to create the traditions he or she considers important for the well-being of the farm, its plants, animals and people. Very often, the festivals take place in the larger social setting of the farm, consumers, volunteers, trainees and - if the farm is connected to such institutions - mentally handicapped people, prisoners and drugs-addicts.

Mixed farming system. According to Steiner's Agricultural Course, and in line with agricultural traditions in the nineteenth century and the beginnings of this century, the ideal farm is a mixed one. Farmers who have cattle next to arable crops see this as being very satisfactory, as animals and crops use each others' products so that external inputs can be minimal.

A fertile soil. The stability of a fertile soil, capable of producing healthy food for decades, is the ultimate goal in biodynamic agriculture. It is a prerequisite for healthy plants and healthy food. This refers to Steiner's Agricultural Course in which the soil is elaborated as a highly sophisticated living system composed of minerals, plants and animals. The soil is an interplay of cosmic and environmental forces: all regulatory principles and life-forces are directed towards fertility and the vitality of plants. Composting plays a major role. The soil is seen by the farmers as the skin of the earth and as a living being. Many farmers feel a great love for the soil and for what grows in it. They pay a lot of attention to her. '*The soil is almost like a second wife*', said one farmer.

Gender aspects. Gender plays the same role in biodynamic agriculture as it does in other parts of Dutch society. It could be, however, that on biodynamic farms female qualities are more desirable than on conventional farms and that there is a larger possibility to explore these qualities.

Social aspects. As mentioned before, Steiner provided new insights into the social construction of institutions and provided a wider perspective on society. Biodynamic farmers, trading firms and biodynamic related institutions often try to realise his vision.

Piet van Yzendoorn established with his family a new farm on the former seabottom according to biodynamic principles.

203

It is difficult for farmers to explain in words the biodynamic cosmovision, which is mainly a matter of feeling and intuition. Whereas there are some farmers who doubt the effect of preparations, others are becoming increasingly sensitive to the spiritual aspects of their farm and to nature. This is based on their knowledge and experiential learning. However, these seem to be strictly individual experiences which are difficult to put into words and thus even more difficult to communicate. One might ask if this is essentially different from organic farmers and if so, in what way. The failure of exchanging cosmovision with conventional farmers is partly due to the exclusive character and specific jargon of this vision. Many farmers experience this situation as conflicting.

Plans for the coming years

With the help of Coen ter Berg, a former farmer and currently an extension worker, the plans of the Biodynamic Association for the coming years as these relate to COMPAS have been defined. The aim is to stimulate farmer experimentation (amongst others on the preparations) and farmer-to-farmer approaches. There will be more interaction with other groups and approaches, but it will be emphasised that bio-dynamic agriculture is a way of searching and learning, a way of conscious dynamic development, both practically on the farm and personally. Some new courses for farmers to develop their personal spiritual skills will support this learning process. Conferences will also be organised and biodynamic seed breeding and improvement will receive more attention.

Various new extension approaches are emerging within the biodynamic movement. Firstly, there is the 'Coachings project' which started in 1997. Selected farmers are individually coaching fellow farmers during farm visits. Each of the ten 'farmer-coaches' work with some five to ten farmers each, colleagues who requested support in the development of their farm. The coaches are expected to be able to listen and stimulate the potential of the farm and the farm family. In doing so, they are a human sounding-board for the farmer and help improve his or her personal skills in order to develop more feeling and understanding of the cosmovision (the dynamic aspects) of biodynamic agriculture. The coach is expected to withhold his or her own knowledge and judgements, and stimulate the farmers' creativity. In the end, the assessments of the coached farmer and of the coaches themselves come together.

Another new project is 'Made to Measure'. This project has been started by the Louis Bolk anthroposophic research centre in order to find new ways in extension and alternatives to the negative effects latent in top-down relationships between extension-workers and farmers. The project will be finished by the end of 1998 and one of the outputs will be a handbook for extension workers. The typical attitude of conventional extensionists and researchers is still to 'solve' farmers' problems. This is done in a hierarchical relationship. In 'Made to Measure', a new method is tried out, which takes its inspiration from antroposophic cosmovision. The farmer and extension worker are seen as 'partners'. The approach demands from the extension worker or researcher that he or she is open to the whole: the totality of the farm as well as the farm family. But he or she should also be open for 'the unexpected' and

Organic farming and endogenous development

Europe is the homeland of Western science and technology but there have always been minorities who have held a more holistic and spiritual worldview. COMPAS is a platform for intercultural dialogue between knowledge systems in the South and the North. ◆

8-1 Biodynamic agriculture is based on the spiritual science of Steiner. To harmonise relations in the farm, certain preparations or 'medicines for the earth' are used.

8-2 In spring, the preparations are sprayed on the land.

In countries like the Netherlands, traditional cosmovisions and spirituality have almost completely disappeared. There is widespread discontent about the materialism of modern farming. Currently an increasing interest in organic farming can be observed. ◆

8-3 In organic farming, arable and animal production are integrated. Contrary to most conventional farmers, organic farmers keep cows on straw to produce good manure.

8-4 Organically grown products are being sold in farm shops (like shown here), in special shops and increasingly in supermarkets. Control and certification ensures that no chemicals are used.

206

It is not wise to romanticise traditional knowledge, nor to reject everything that has been developed by Western science. It is a challenge to understand and appreciate traditional knowledge and look for possible combinations of this knowledge with outside knowledge. ◆

8-5 Farmer workshops to discuss traditional practices. 'Seed Mela', supported by GREEN Foundation, provides a forum for exchange of indigenous seed varieties, knowledge and rituals.

8-6 Martin Duan of TIRD-P in Timor, Indonesia, with the clan elder or pah tuaf *during a village meeting. More than 50 farmers have discussed crop and animal husbandry practices. The meeting is concluded with a ritual song, sacrificing a fowl and reading its signs.*

Organic farming and endogenous development

207

In the design of the framework for their activities, COMPAS partners build on experiences with participatory farmer experimentation. The cultural and spiritual dimension will be part and parcel of the experimental design. ◆

8-7 *NGO staff and farmers during a lively discussion on traditional farming.*

8-8 *During a farmers' meeting, mr. Wijenayaka, the shaman or* kapu mahattaya *who performed the* kem *explains traditional rituals to other farmers.*

Organic farming and endogenous development

sensitive and curious. For the extension worker the emphasis is on the farm or farm management. Very subtle personal communicative (psycho-social) skills are needed in order to encourage the farmer to come forward with his or her experiences in dealing with the real agricultural situation. The extension worker withholds his own opinions and judgements for a long time. Of course, at a certain moment in the process he or she will also bring in other knowledge. For the researcher, the emphasis is more on a specific theme such as weed problems. The researcher will have to do outer and inner research on the 'character' of a problem. Questions are posed such as: What does it mean that there is a weed problem here? What quality is lacking on a farm that is taken over by this weed? In the end he will share his findings with the farmer in order to find out whether the farmer recognises the found ideas and concepts which visualise the problems in words and images. Both the researcher and the extension worker have to make a 'translation' by finding words that stress the positive potential of the farmer and his farm. They will put that potential into the actual process and development of the farm and the people who work and live there. Experience shows that, in doing so, creative possibilities for further developing the farm arise. We have noticed that when we presented this new approach to other COMPAS partners, they recognised certain aspects of their own work and were interested in this new approach to extension work.

A meditation course has started for farmers who want to improve their personal spiritual skills, in order to help them pay more concentrated attention to their farming activities whether these involve animals, plants or soil. After this course, they were able to feel the energy of living beings and improved their intuition. They had more awareness of the needs of their cows, crops or soil. Such a course enables some farmers to go beyond the strict rules of biodynamic agriculture as explained in the Agricultural Course. It widens the farmers' perceptions as to the possibilities inherent in themselves and nature.

An external study of the image of the biodynamic movement in 1996 revealed that many outsiders regard it as 'a closed society of farmers, who always know better'. This critique has been taken seriously and one way 'to open up' will be to organise conferences for broader audiences. The first one is planned to be on the theme 'agriculture and spirituality'. It will involve all those in the Dutch society who take this subject seriously, whether Catholic, Protestant or inspired by other forms of spirituality. The aim here is to remain open to other perceptions and be enriched in this way. A further conference may deal with the question of seed quality. Experiences with intercultural dialogue in the COMPAS workshops can be of inspiring value.

In recent years farmers have been searching for new ways of cooperating with consumers. Several farmers are experimenting with and developing the model of 'Consumer Supported Agriculture'. For them it is a way of freeing their farms from the hopeless spiral of economic pressure by sharing financial risks with consumers. Consumers get full insight into their book-keeping and they decide together which crops and what quantity will be grown. These consumers also help the farmer with weeding, packing and selling. Sometimes a group of consumers will even buy a tiny piece of land, to offer the farmer the possibility of growing a particular crop. Other farmers have chosen for a 'subscription-system': consumers subscribe for a certain amount of vegetables (and potatoes, eggs and fruit if available) at a fixed price for every week of the year, so the farmer is sure of a certain income. Within the context of COMPAS we will follow the development of this new strategy closely and can, for example, be inspired by the Andean cosmovision on reciprocity.

As genetic engineering and other technical ways of seed improvement have been introduced on a large scale into European farming, organic and biodynamic farmers have problems in obtaining the right seeds. The European Community has set guidelines for organic agriculture such that it should remain free of genetically modified organisms. Organic and biodynamic farmers strive to obtain regionally-adapted crops, which means that those crops are flexible in their interaction with different environmental circumstances. In conventional farming, the environmental circumstances are standardised as much as possible, while the environmental factors of each organic and biodynamic farm is different and unique. Together organic and biodynamic farmers have formulated their ideas on organic and biodynamic seed improvement. Firstly, the plant should be seen within the wholeness of it's natural surroundings. Secondly, the plant should have the possibility of being able to maintain itself. And finally, the plant should be able to multiply itself.

Biodynamic farmers do not agree with methods and techniques that destroy this wholeness, such as DNA techniques. This also means that they do not agree with growing methods that are not bound to the soil, such as growing on or in nutrient mediums. Not waiting for the governments judgements of their claims, a foundation called 'Seed-goods' started, which will stimulate the breeding of biodynamically grown seed. We hope that other COMPAS partners can help us with their knowledge on natural seed improvement and seed conservation.

Our role within COMPAS

We are surprised to note that in Bolivia, as well as in Sri Lanka, people are aware of biodynamic preparations and the sowing calendar. The Bolivian farmers' concept of living geography seems quite similar to the biodynamic concept of farm individuality. Interestingly, the Sri Lankan partner had compared the biodynamic sowing calendar with Asian almanacs. He had better results with the Asian almanac as not only the position, but also the phases of the moon are taken into account. Some Sri Lankans have a more elaborated personal sowing calendar to combine with calendars for farming activities. In India, some farmers working with Krishi Prayoga Pariwara are using horn preparations.

We are still in the process of digestion and of finding out <u>what</u> in COMPAS can be useful for Dutch farmers. Biodynamic farmers do have a basic, anthroposophic cosmovision from which they get their inspiration. The cosmovision from Steiner's Agricultural Course is young and has to be developed further through practical experiences. This often means a personal, and sometimes even painful, struggle. All the personal learning points can be fruitful for the well-being of the whole biodynamic movement. But it will only bring development if farmers openly and respectfully communicate about their experiences and conscious choices and if this is done in freedom. COMPAS enriches. It helps to reflect on our own position and cosmovision. Knowing how certain things are seen for example in India or in Peru is a starting point for our own reflections: how do we see it ourselves, is it different, is it similar, what are our own choices and what can we learn from others? We know how rich and wise other cosmovisions are. We have a great respect for all the COMPAS friends. Therefore, it is our wish to stay modest, but also to have self-respect and value our own search and our own rich initiatives.

A fantastic possibility of exchange with other COMPAS partners was given to a group of Dutch biodynamic farmers in February 1998. Nine farms invited two COMPAS partners to their farms in order to experience Dutch biodynamic farm life and to dialogue on agriculture and cosmovision. COMPAS partners felt at home because there were universal ideas even though the culture was very different. It was an exiting experience for both the Dutch farmers and the visitors. Though the COMPAS partners may have a longer cultural tradition as a basis for their search for holistic development, the commonalities were recognised in the same struggle against the materialistic mainstream. Asse Aukes, one of the farmers who received the partners from TALPUY and AGRUCO (Jaime Delgadillo and Gloria Miranda Zambrano) wrote a short report in the biodynamic movement's magazine.

Jaime Delgadillo, Asse Aukes, Gloria Miranda Zambrano and Willemijn Cuypers at Gerbranda State, a biodynamic farm in Fryslân, the Netherlands.

'It had been late the night before, due to the long discussions we had, but I get up early, before sunrise. Carefully, I gather some of the products our farm has produced: vegetables, some potatoes from the different varieties we grow, some hay and grass, goat milk and even goat droppings. I arrange them on a beautiful plate. When I woke our guests Jaime and Gloria, I saw that they were still wearing their coats and hats in bed. Despite the heating system, they felt the Dutch cold of minus eight degrees.

At dawn we will bring a sacrifice to Pachamama, Mother Earth, just like the farmers do in the Andes. Couldn't we find some flowers? No, unfortunately at this time in winter there are no flowers on the farm. A bit later, I make a hole in the frozen soil. While we see the sun rising, Jaime is praying, thanking Mother Earth. Willemijn, our translator, is explaining in Dutch the meaning of the prayers. We put the plate with the produce of our farm in the soil as a sacrifice and libate some home-made maizebeer. We all poured some beer on the sacrifice and closed the earth again. Then we were silent for meditation for a half hour.

It was curious to feel the mysterious power of the mountains of the Andes, which seemed to move our deeply religious Latin American guests in the freezing cold of the Frisian winter. It reminded me of a saying in the Bible: 'Where there are two or more gathered in My name, I am among them.' It was wonderful to host some people from a different culture, who so naturally experience God in nature. The respect they show to even the smallest detail of daily life was very heartening.'

Dream of the circular swings
by **Bertus Haverkort**

During the first COMPAS workshop in Capellani, Bolivia
I had a dream, the dream of the circular swings.

I saw a long cable hanging between two poles.
From both ends and towards the middle,
a swing was rolling over the cable.
In each swing there was a small girl,
both with enthusiasm and good intentions to enjoy life.
Coming from different directions and with increasing speed,
they were approaching each other and I was afraid that they would
crash.
Yet at the moment of contact,
both made a slight movement to the left and the right,
by which, instead of a deadly crash,
they started to make circular movements,
each in a different direction,
and with each circle coming closer to each other.
Finally they touched each other.
Then the movements started in the opposite direction and repeated
endlessly.

This dream represents what I hope COMPAS will be: confrontation of differences in opinions, avoiding a crash and the transformation of linear
and opposite opinions into circular movements leading to contact. The
most important experience of the two workshops was the enthusiasm of
the participants, their recognition and commonness. The time is ripe for
an approach in which both western and non-western sources of knowledge
and wisdom make contacts, are brought into an intercultural dialogue
and are being used to find solutions for future and present problems of
food production and health.

TOWARDS A METHODOLOGY FOR SUPPORTING

ENDOGENOUS DEVELOPMENT

The previous chapters show a great diversity of cultural expressions. A wealth of visions, concepts, techniques, institutions, customs, rituals and other cultural practices have been presented. Cultural diversity is linked with biological diversity and with diversity in epistemologies and systems of knowing. The case studies of the COMPAS partners show the way in which indigenous organisations support farmers and rural people in the processes of learning, teaching and experimenting within their own worldview.

The experiences and plans of the various COMPAS partners were discussed during a workshop in February 1998. This was a process of sharing between some thirty persons of fifteen organisations from ten different countries. The goal of the workshop was to lay the basis for future cooperation between partners and to formulate an approach for field-based activities. There was room for dialogues on concepts and approaches, but also for meditations, rituals and symbolic expression in the form of poems, sculptures, dreams and music. The partners worked on methods, activities and approaches for fieldwork with the aim of making the first steps towards a methodology and framework for action. In the mix of methodologies being used by COMPAS, each of the partners has its own comparative strengths and makes its own specific contributions.

This final chapter describes the beginning of a methodology and framework as defined by the partners. The ideas presented are the best approximations the partners could formulate. In the immediate future, an approach for joining endogenous development will be developed further on the basis of the experiences built up by the partners in field situations. The COMPAS programme implies four broad types of activities for organisations that support rural communities in endogenous development. First, the efforts to strengthen the cultural identity of local populations by learning together about cosmovision and indigenous institutions. Second, conducting local experiments in the context of the farmers' cosmovision. Third, self-development and the training of field staff. And, finally, sharing the experiences through networking and advocacy.

Learning from and with the rural population

Building a relationship. Partners have realised that one of the first requirements for any rural development agency to cooperate successful with the rural population is that it understands and respects the rural situation. Therefore, a relationship has to be established that makes it possible to learn about people's cosmovisions or concepts of life, with its three dimensions - the natural, social and spiritual world. It is also necessary to get a feeling about the way rural people learn, teach and experiment. An attempt must be made to learn about the roles of indigenous institutions such as elders, the political and spiritual leaders, the spirit mediums, local healers, the different classes and castes and the changes taking place within them. It is important to realise that this learning process can only take place if confidence, based on mutual respect, exists between the people and the outsider. Having respect for local concepts, values and institutions is very important.

Experience during the first phase of COMPAS teaches us that, in many cases, indigenous concepts of life are still very much part of a community's knowledge system and indigenous institutions are frequently very influential. Yet outsiders often fail to notice this, partly because villagers have learned not to express these matters openly. Out-siders often show a lack of appreciation for traditional knowledge and values. In many cases it is ridiculed as primitive, old-fashioned and full of irrational superstition. Modernisation is often considered to be a process of substituting traditional knowledge and indigenous institutions for more modern forms rather than trying to improve indigenous concepts by using local experiences or by searching for complementarity between indigenous and outside knowledge. Indigenous institutions are frequently neglected by development organisations or seen as obstacles to change. In many cases modern concepts have a higher status, and the confrontation between the tradition and modern may lead to conflicts between generations and socio-economic groups.

Often, in the communication with outsiders, villagers pretend to think and act according to the concepts of the outside world, whereas in reality, under the surface, they follow their own internal logic, maintain their own cosmovision and have their own values. In most cases there will be a mix of indigenous and outside knowledge and values. Scientists use terms such as acculturation or syncretism for this. For some communities, the elements introduced from outside can have considerable impact. Communities then receive the label modernised. Other communities may still be mainly governed by their traditions. Farmers in these communities are sometimes labelled conservative, risk avoiding and resistant to change. Traditions are hardly ever considered on their own merit. Age, gender, profession, traditional status, migratory experience and education may influence the orientation to tradition and to the modern world. There may also be conflicts or tensions between subgroups in this respect.

The relationship between outside organisations and rural communities needs to be established with care. When an agency has been working in a community for some time and wants to address the issue of cosmovision, a new definition of its role has to be made. It should be made very clear to the community that the agency has a sincere interest in learning about its cosmovision, traditions and spirituality. It may take a while, however, before the community feels confident enough to express itself in this way. In each situation, therefore, every agency has to address the question of how confidence can be built up. In the communication with rural people, the attitude of field workers is important. People's expression and values should be respected, even if it is hard to understand their reasoning. It is important to have patience, and not to disagree too quickly. Respectful disagreement can do no harm, if expressed at the right time.

There is frequently a limitation in the skills of outsiders, including COMPAS partners in establishing good relationships with local communities. Certain facilitation and participatory skills may exist including the capacity to speak and/or understand the local dialect. To a greater or lesser extent skills to act according to indigenous forms of communication and documentation may also exist. Listening is an important skill: one should be able to keep one's ears open to the ideas of another and recognise their ideas. But frequently one crucial skill is missing: the ability to act with empathy. Empathy means putting oneself in the position of the other and attempting to understand and appreciate how they think and feel.

Possible methods for building relationship

- Identify the population concerned: what is the boundary of the target population, their tribal name, socio-economic description and location?
- Compile existing anthropological, agricultural and other relevant literature and summarise existing information on the above. For this, the libraries in the area have to be consulted. Possibly libraries in other countries must also be used. In many cases, for example, anthropological data are more easily retrieved in the west than in the country they refer to.
- Also classical texts such as the Vedas and other scripts can be consulted. Cultural expressions in houses, painting, sculpturing, religion can give important information.
- When entering into a new community make sure to show respect and interest in their values. When already working in a community consider efforts to redefine the existing relationships.
- Agree with the population on the activities related to COMPAS. Agree on the goals and activities to be carried out as well as on the roles of the different leaders. As much as possible make a covenant on the process and ownership of the results. Use the principle of prior informed consent and joint planning.
- Agree about the methods to be used for learning about Indigenous Knowledge and Indigenous Institutions. Consider (a mix of) the following methods: Asking key persons about the traditional social structure and leadership; interview traditional leaders (men and women), be keen to learn about their worldview and about their role in teaching and experimentation; take note of oral life histories; use village workshops, village theatre, visual presentations, and linguistic analysis; understand folk stories, creation myths, songs, customs, rituals, visual expressions in painting, architecture and sculpturing; participate in festivals, rituals and other important events. Accept that you are a learner.
- Persons to be interviewed can be traditional leaders, spiritual leaders, healers, old farmers, young farmers or key persons with specific information.
- In all cases make sure that gender differentiation is being made.
- Make sure that the results of this process will be discussed and assessed

with members of the community and that conclusions will be drawn together, taking into account gender, age and power differences in the community.

☐ Ensure, as much as possible, that documentation is in a form that is in line with rural traditions and can be retrieved and used by the population.

Documentation and joint assessment. The aim of learning about cosmovision is to find the point of articulation for cooperation: the joint path for learning, experimentation and action. A cosmovision can be documented if this is useful for the cooperation process; it can help to make indigenous knowledge explicit and hence help in strengthening the cultural identity of the people.

Village documentation, assessment and a dialogue on these issues can play an important role in revaluing, reviving and improving traditional values. Cooperation of development organisations with indigenous institutions and traditional leaders may help the community to strengthen its own cultural identity and to integrate outside influences with traditions in a balanced way. These activities can lead to community testing, adapting local practices or experimenting with external innovations. Documentation and assessment of local tradition may strengthen the community. But how should this be done? Making a description of the situation as it is at the moment can be made in several ways. The most conventional way is to produce a paper that can be published in the local newspaper or that can be presented to donors and the international or academic public. COMPAS does not exclude this type of documentation, as long as it has been carried out in a participatory way, and its results can be used by the local population. Carrying out documentation in this way serves as a step in the process by which the local population makes an own assessment of the present situation. What are its strong and weak points, what are the opportunities and what are the threats. On the basis of this assessment, the population can (be supported to) experiment with different options to improve their situation.

It may be that documentation is good for the external relations of a development agency. But is it good for people? What are indigenous forms of communication? How do we use documented knowledge within the community? Documenting and assessing indigenous knowledge and practices should not be an extractive exercise. It should rather be seen as support towards the community. Participatory methods can be chosen that help self-assessment based on the values, indicators and experiences of the community themselves.

Ancient materials and literature can be looked for and folklore traditions, festivals and rituals can be included. These practices and community knowledge are an important and relevant aspect of living knowledge. Sometimes, groups practise these traditions, sometimes they are practised by individuals. It is also important to find out whether a certain practice is relatively new or has been tested and experimented with over a longer period of time. Its usefulness to certain groups of people can be described, as well as whether its use is limited to certain persons or it is widespread.

Support organisations should be sensitive and try to understand the cosmovision and look deeper into the background and effects of rituals, taboos and totemic relationships. In Zimbabwe there is a taboo that forbids farmers for going into the fields on certain days. In India and Sri Lanka, women who are menstruating are often not allowed to carry out certain farming activities. As an outsider, one should try to understand these taboos. They might have a very practical origin, but they can also have a deeper spiritual meaning. To give an example: in Sri Lanka, beef should not be eaten in front of a *yantra*. What will happen if someone does this? What is the taboo really about? Is it about the cow? Is it about eating of beef? Can this be an entry point for experimentation? In some cultures it is easy to find the logic behind certain rituals or taboos. But in other cultures it will be difficult to find the reasons. Sometimes one can and in other cases one cannot experiment with these puzzles. The community can guide the field staff on whether an experiment and the questions it involves is appropriate or not.

Another piece of the cosmovision puzzle is how secret knowledge can be dealt with. Often secret knowledge is only passed on to particular people so as to avoid misuse. This person may have undergone some specific training and initiation or may be part of a distinct family. There may be good reasons for not allowing the information to pass outside the initiated. Field staff should try to understand and respect these processes.

There will be many situations in which certain knowledge has disappeared or is disappearing. There may be certain things that grandparents still know. A contest or an exposition can be organised, and this knowledge might be revived. Rituals that have disappeared and certain traditional skills may also be restored. Registration can help to bring this type of information into the open, can help identify sources and lead to testing. A list can be made of the spiritual leaders in an area and the way they relate to other spiritual leaders can be described.

Another method of assessment might be comparison. What experiences do other knowledge systems or communities have and how do they value and think about these practices? In the field of health care FRLHT encourages local healers, Ayurvedic doctors and western bio-medical practitioners to exchange experiences about the use and effects of herbs. Such comparisons can also take place between cultures. A certain plant is used to cure hepatitis in Sri Lanka. This also appears to be the case in South America. When people see that the same plant is used for the same purpose in another culture, or has a slightly different use, it might encourage them to experiment with new options.

The theme of folklore, traditions and rituals should not only be restricted to two or three festivities in the year, it should be considered throughout the year given the differences during the seasons. Frequently the ritual calendars coincide with the agricultural calendars. Planting, weeding, harvesting and other activities may go together with or be conditioned by certain rituals or festivals. Folklore and spirituality is often integral in agriculture and feasts. A calendar could be made in which all the aspects of the lives of these communities are included. IDEA, TALPUY and AGRUCO have already made such a calendar.

Farmers could be encouraged to express their experiences. Farmers will not express their skills so long as they feel their ideas are not being respected. There may be traditional practices that have ceased to have any active role. People talk about them but they do not practise them anymore. School children can help with collecting information. Such a procedure can have several implications: one is raising awareness, another is motivation. If children are asked to bring seeds to school, they have to ask their parents. It makes the parents and the children aware of their own knowledge and culture.

It is important to work in local languages and put the 'documentation' in forms that harmonise with local tradition. The creation of a song, visual expressions in ceramics, textiles or paintings on walls may also serve the purpose, as it can continue to be part of community expressions. Information can be fed back to the community and conclusions can be drawn using a wide range of different methods: village workshops; village drama or puppet shows; visual aids such as slides, videos or more traditional media; publications in the local language or discussions in the local media. This feedback can be planned together with and implemented as much as possible by traditional and indigenous institutions. During these sessions the population is stimulated to value their own knowledge and culture, to assess its potentials and strengths, and identify ways and means to enhance endogenous development. The possible complementarity and conflicts between traditional knowledge and indigenous institutions and ways of handling them can also be discussed.

To present the conclusions to the outside world, an exchange of results and plans can be organised with adjacent communities, NGOs, government agencies, organisations concerned with research and development as well as donor agencies. Also the COMPAS partners are an obvious forum for presenting findings: both the results and the experiences with the methods used can be exchanged through the COMPAS newsletter, through workshops and through exchange visits. Care will be taken to give the rural people an active role in this.

Topics for joint documentation and assessment

The following items have been found useful and provide a checklist for documentation and assessment of rural knowledge.

- Cosmovision and concepts of life: creation myths; divine beings that play a role in the society; the role of ancestors, sacred persons, animals, places and objects; the concept of nature, the role of energy, rituals and spiritual technologies; the time concept, relationships of cause and effect; the relationship of mankind to nature and the spiritual world.
- Indigenous institutions: institutions that regulate community decision making, the management of resources and experimentation with new farming practices; persons who have special knowledge and power and who play a particular role in the community. Their roles, responsibilities and attitudes in agricultural experimentation and innovations.
- Indigenous practices and use of knowledge: What are the important practices relating to the management of natural resources, agriculture and health? What are concepts and explanations for the practices used by the local population? And how do they relate to western explanations and concepts? How do people learn, teach and experiment? What agricultural experiments have taken place and how have they

been carried out: subjects, methods, parameters, criteria, indicators? What changes take place with respect to the way indigenous knowledge is being used in learning, teaching and experimenting?

☐ Interaction: How do the indigenous knowledge systems interact with outside sources of knowledge? What is the focus of general and agricultural education, agricultural research and extension, religion and health?

☐ Changes in the traditional cosmovision of the local communities: Those that are the result of external influences and those that are a result of adjusting to ecological, technological commercial, political or demographic change? To what extent is experimentation and learning influenced by, or mixed with the western worldview? What are the contradictions or tensions: erosion of indigenous knowledge and indigenous institutions, creative adaptation, conflicts or parallel systems, underground knowledge, syncretism?

☐ Options that exist for endogenous development amongst the local populations: How can the local community develop in such a way that cultural identity is maintained and enhanced, local resources are used properly and opportunities for the use of external knowledge are carefully considered?

This list of issues for documentation is quite elaborate. It is important that the choice of the method fits local conditions. If required, possibilities for training of field staff in appropriate methods for documentation could be included. Therefore, the possible training needs of field staff could be considered in this stage and plans could be made accordingly.

Property rights. Within the COMPAS programme, care should be taken with publication of documented local knowledge. Sometimes local communities do not want their information to be published other than in their own language. It is always the community or its members that has the property rights over their own knowledge (see also the first chapter). Publishing should only be done when there is really something to share within the community or with other communities. The timing, the method and the medium need to be considered very carefully. As documentation and publication is a sensitive issue in view of property rights, COMPAS partners should be very careful in publishing local information. A code of conduct with various rules is therefore appropriate. The following points have been mentioned in this respect.

Elements of a code of conduct for publishing
☐ A risk assessment of documentation: the possibility of publication can be discussed, and risks be assessed together with the local population and possibly with national or international lobby organisations, that favour the protection local knowledge.

☐ Publication should only take place if it serves the purpose of the rural communities or other communities and should not be (mis-) used to further the (academic) careers of outsiders.

- Publication should be in a medium and language that serves the communities.
- Publication does not only mean an article in a news medium or scientific journal; it can also be a presentation in the community in the local language, using local symbols.
- The authors of publications should, as far as possible, be the original owners of the knowledge concerned. Publications by NGOs or universities should be co-authored by representatives of the community as much as possible.
- In publications it is important to state that the ownership of the knowledge is a particular community, ethnicity or population.
- When avoidable do not provide technical details.
- Anticipate the possibilities of monopolisation by private enterprises and enhance ownership in the public domain.
- Descriptions should not only be in terms of biology, chemistry and physics but should also be described in the terminology of the cosmovision and the worldview of the people which includes spiritual and cultural aspects. Limiting the description to the active ingredients of plants or to biological or physical aspects is an unjustified reduction of the richness of local knowledge.
- Where possible the COMPAS partners should endeavour to enhance the claim-making capacity of the rural population to help them negotiate fair exchange of their knowledge.
- Make sure that the data collected and publications made remain in the community. Do everything to ensure a sense of ownership by the rural community.

Exchange meetings. Farmer-to-farmer meetings are known to be very important ways of allowing farmers to exchange experiences and learn from each other. Such meetings may be important for persons with a comparable responsibility within the indigenous institutions such as spirit mediums, spiritual leaders, healers, village leaders and midwives. In some cases the role of the NGO can be supportive of the process of organising exchange.

. It is important to realise that the participation of spiritual leaders and/or spirit mediums implies a very special approach. Contacting these persons requires respect for or belief in the spiritual world they represent and a sensitivity to spiritual realities. General guidelines cannot be given, as the approach depends very much on the local situation.

Possible methods for exchange meetings
- Identification of the need and possibilities for exchange meetings within the project area by consulting the traditional institutions, including the spiritual leaders and spirit mediums. There may be political differences between different spiritual leaders. Given this situation, a meeting between spiritual leaders may be difficult and it may be better to look for a good combination of a particular

spiritual leader with a number of people who accept the authority of that leader.

- Building the responsibility for the meeting in the traditional institutions. An example is the case of AZTREC, where there is a coalition between traditional leaders and spirit mediums.
- Identification of the people who practise certain traditional roles in the community. The traditional leaders and spirit mediums or spiritual leaders should decide who are the right people to participate in the exchange meeting.
- Also the right time to meet should be determined by the village leaders. In some cases astrology, certain moon phases or religious dates are important.
- The location of the meeting should be left to the leaders. In cases where sacred places will be used such as temples or sacred trees, the necessary rituals should be observed and possibly be encouraged.
- If appropriate and acceptable, the government and staff of NGOs may also be invited to join to provide legitimacy and to help lobby.
- As a facilitating organisation, provide maximum opportunity for rural leaders to exchange their own views. Place yourself in the position of a learner.
- Ask the traditional leaders to prepare their presentation to the meeting by making a diagram or visual presentation of their knowledge and practices, by giving a demonstration, or by performing a ritual. Ensure that the contribution of each person is clearly defined and well prepared.

Conducting local experiments

Local or indigenous knowledge has been developed in the local ecological and cultural context. This suggests that it will be appropriate knowledge for that particular circumstance and location. Indigenous knowledge is often found to be holistic, to be related to community-based activities, to enhance the optimal use of local resources, to use genetic and physical diversity, to minimise risks, and to allow for site specific solutions. However, it is important to realise that indigenous knowledge can also have its limitations. It is not always uniformly spread throughout the community and individual talents for using and improving indigenous knowledge differ. Specialised knowledge, for example treasured insights into medicinal qualities of plants, are often kept secret or known only to a select few such as elders, midwives or healers. Certain knowledge may be tied to economic or cultural roles in the community and may not be known or not even be accessible to other members of the community, for which there may be legitimate reasons. Other knowledge may be related to magic or spiritual practices that are difficult to understand. Farmers' knowledge is frequently limited to what they can sense directly, usually through observation, and what they can comprehend with their own intuition or concepts. Even though these concepts grow out of their past experiences, it may be difficult for them to relate them to processes that are new to them like population growth, deteriorating natural resources and external markets. Yet it is also possible that their own concepts, rituals and insights, once taken seriously, may bring about important contributions to problem solving. Indigenous experimentation is also an important aspect of indigenous knowledge systems. Even in the most traditional societies farmers are found to experiment in order to improve their farming practices and to adjust to changing circumstances. In these experiments, farmers have their own experimental design, use their own criteria and their own indicators. In many cases these are appropriate, but in other cases there may be room for improvement.

Only through a good dialogue about these criteria and indicators will farmers be prepared to reconsider or to improve upon experimental design, analytical approach and measurement methods. Where indigenous knowledge and practices have gone underground, the traditional mechanisms for improving farmers knowledge through indigenous experimentation may have lost their significance and, as a consequence, the quality of indigenous knowledge may have been reduced. This gives extra importance to reviving and improving the experimental practices of the farming communities. Taking indigenous knowledge seriously means that romanticism should be avoided. There should be a preparedness to understand, respect and challenge it and look for ways to test and improve it. The way to do this is to cooperate with indigenous institutions, look for ways to test and improve local concepts, as well as to explore the applicability of certain external innovations.

Farm-level experiments can contribute to three goals. Firstly, the effectiveness and relevance of local practices can be tested. Secondly, the local experimental practices and skills of farmers can be improved. And finally, the experiments may help to build a theory to explain the effectiveness of indigenous technologies.

Testing effectiveness and relevance.
Farm-level experimenting may involve several aspects. When testing the effectiveness of local practices, a distinction can be made between effective practices on the one hand, and practices that are or remain doubtful, or appear to be based on superstition or the abuse of power. Subsequently, on the basis of the outcome, the farmers or support organisation can decide to further promote the development of effective practices or test or discourage the further application of doubtful ones. Testing may also give more insights into the full costs and benefits of traditional practices in ecological, economic and cultural dimensions. Further, the possibilities for upscaling certain local practices in the same cultural or ecological zone or for transcultural translation of the practices into other ecological, spiritual and social systems can be determined. An important aspect of testing is to find possibilities for combining local practices with science-based technologies and for developing synergetic combinations of traditional practices and western-based technologies. Also the potential of indigenous knowledge and institutions for improving the management of natural resources can be clarified through experiments. Some partners of COMPAS like IDEA and AZTREC build on indigenous knowledge and practices in their programmes for erosion control, reforestation and nature protection.

Carrying out farm-level experiments based on cosmovision is a considerable challenge. The design should be made together with spiritual leaders and rural people. The local concepts should be included in the design. This implies local criteria, local parameters and local record keeping. However, there are also practices which go beyond the scope of testing in the conventional way. A practice might be emotional or spiritual and thus rather difficult to explain and to test. Therefore, establishing the parameters is important. Such a parameter could be that the ancestors are satisfied, or that the vibration sensed by the spirit mediums are good. A parameter also might be social, as is often heard in Latin America. One can establish parameters from the perspective of the people.

Before embarking on experiments, access to information from literature or other people is important. In this way an awareness of external ideas and technologies can be built up. In order to find out if a technology from outside is complementary with the values and concepts of an area, the three dimensions of the cosmovision - the spiritual world, the material world and the social world should be taken into account. Complementarity might be possible in one of these three aspects. But, being accepted by the community is important. We should not always be looking for higher production, things can also be measured in the spiritual or social domain. Endogenous development is a permanent process in the community, that takes place with or with-out support institutions.

Framework for experimenting within a cosmovision perspective

To develop a framework for experimentation and testing, the following questions for field staff of outside agencies are suggested.
1. How to (re)enter the self-development process of the community and build up a good working relationship?
2. How to develop a working agenda together with the community?
3. How to determine the parameters for testing and experimenting together?
4. What common strategy to use to realise the common objective? And how to design the experiments?
5. How to keep track together of the process (monitoring, assessing, assisting, supporting, sharing and developing)?
6. How to judge or determine the results or products of the process, considering the three aspects of spiritual, material and social growth?
7. How to leave their process such that the community can continue the growth and self-development process (how to continue, how to up-scale, considering the spiritual, material and social equilibrium of the community)?

By elaborating the methods for each of these questions, the COMPAS partners have formulated the following framework for the activities of development agencies.

1. How to (re)enter the process of self development of the community and build up a good working relationship?
- If a field worker is approached by somebody from the community with the request to offer some help, it is important to find out what is

it that the community wants and what can be considered good experiences so far. An appointment can be made during which all senses should be open to existing knowledge and the institutional context. Also openness and transparency about the interest in cosmovision including its spiritual aspects is needed.

- In case the process is renewing older contacts, make sure to follow-up on a previous dialogue. In is important to make clear to the community how cooperation is foreseen, also indicating the interest in cosmovision and its three dimension (natural world, social world and spiritual world).
- When possible and relevant, participation in ceremonies and festivals is desirable, thus learning about the cosmovision, indigenous institutions and cultural identity.
- Familiarisation with the cosmovision and the culture of the area by studying previous cosmovision studies, anthropological and development studies can provide important background information.
- It is important to establish contacts with and have discussion with traditional and spiritual leaders, spirit mediums, healers and elders.
- When meetings are organised, reflect on including traditional ceremonies and rituals as performed by traditional and spiritual leaders.
- Develop intuition and spirituality. Listen to dreams and other signals from the unconsciousness.

2. How to develop a common agenda?
- Starting with positive experiences on the issues brought forward (yours and theirs).
- Consulting spiritual institutions.
- Meditation and reflection.
- Using participatory diagnostic tools.
- Carrying out visits and cross-visits.
- Having extensive dialogue with villagers.
- Using local means of communication audio-visuals such as drumming, music, drama, ceramics, designs on houses, textiles, and art objects.
- Participating in ceremonies.
- Participatory involvement of interest groups / stake holders.
- Being aware of possible resistance and confrontation and respect limits set by the community.

3. How to jointly determine parameters?
- Asking the spirit mediums about their parameters and to what extent is it possible for them to carry out and be involved in experiments.
- Identifying the successful parameters in the farmers' experiences.
- Evaluating project parameters against those of the indigenous cosmovision.
- Using a time frame that respects ritual calendars and astrological data.
- Taking into account the location; respecting sacred places and other

qualities of the location indicated by the cosmovision.
- Taking into account a resource frame that responds to local perceptions and value system.
- Incorporating socio-cultural issues such as taboos, totems, class and caste, and involve local authorities in decision making and the management of natural resources.
- Being gender sensitive and make sex differentiation in parameters and indicators.
- Incorporating spiritual elements as indicated by the spiritual leaders: respecting signs of the ancestors, indications by dreams and visions.
- Dealing more with qualitative than with quantitative data.
- Developing criteria, indicators and strategies gradually.

4. How to design actions?
- Using traditional institutions in the design process and if suggested include indications given by dreams, visions and intuition.
- Being open for modifications of the design during execution.
- Letting the local institutions be accountable for the design (for the whole action).

For example, the traditional astrologist in Sri Lanka sets the time for the meetings and experiments; the spirit mediums in Zimbabwe design rituals during tree planting activities. New ways have to be found for field experiments and trials. Case studies on single experiments can be carried out and not just randomised square-block design experiments. Research of this type is based on the conventional western knowledge system. This does not mean these certain methods should be excluded, but the idea of not randomising can also be accepted.

5. How to monitor?
- Building the strength into the communities and traditional institutions.
- Using relevant monitoring components from tools of participatory approaches.
- Letting the spirit mediums monitor.
- Setting up community code-of-conducts and by-laws.
- Making observations and reflections by meditation.
- Conducting participatory dialogue, ceremonies, festivals, parties.
- Emphasising participation in special ceremonies, festivals and consultations.
- Using field notebooks and diaries, community registers, indigenous recording forms, village albums, reports and audio-visuals.
- Giving attention to school children, women, and the elders.

The people involved with the action, whether farmers or spiritual leaders, should be right in the centre. Spirit mediums do not have to do the experimenting, but at certain critical moments their advice should be asked.

6. How to judge the results of the experiments?
- Going back to or revisiting the parameters with all stakeholders.
- Making a comparison with project baselines and the community's baselines established at the beginning.
- Doing impact assessment.
- Being open for intended and unexpected results and modifications of the experiments.
- Have open discussions on the results: Is everybody satisfied, can results be felt, tasted, parameters measured? Can symbols or signs indicate the results?
- Spiritual results can also express themselves in the physical world.

7. How to leave the community?
- A periodical follow-up, a social conversation, a call.
- Consulting spirit mediums.
- Being sure that the 'process' is embedded in the culture, especially when you duplicate or scale-up.
- Still being part of the community, especially for festivals and ceremonies.
- Ensuring networking with traditional institutional networking throughout.
- Developing farmer-to-farmer reciprocal arrangements.
- Involving women and the youth early, looking for signals from them and asking for their commitment.
- Having various forms of documentation available locally. Leaving a summary as a point of discussion.

Improving experimental practices and skills. The mere fact that an outsider takes indigenous knowledge seriously and wants to cooperate with indigenous institutions in testing and experimenting, may give a boost to the self-respect of the traditional system. Likewise, a joint reflection about the way experiments take place traditionally and a systematic community activity to decide about the experimental agenda may in itself have a positive effect on the communities' capacity to experiment. This also accounts for the parameters for the work, the design of the experiments, community involvement in monitoring, and judging the outcome on the basis of concepts that have their origin in the community itself. They are stimulated to make their own process and the concepts they use explicit and transparent. In the course of the joint exercise they can adjust and modify their process, and thus the local experimental activity can be seen as a learning process for all actors involved.

Various skills are to be developed: skills for improved sensibility; experimental skills; quantitative skills; monitoring skills; training skills; social skills; communication skills; analytical skills; skills for support and encouragement. Gender and age-specific training needs of each of these skills for the different actors (farmers, political leaders, spiritual leaders) could be assessed and the necessary action be taken.

Theory building. A third goal for experimentation may be to validate traditional and classical knowledge and contribute to theory building. Positivistic scientific development in the west has followed the guidelines of Descartes. These guidelines imply that those aspects of the reality that cannot be measured quantitatively are neglected in research and development. Therefore, there is a lack of recognition of the relevance of spiritual practices and a lack of theory about spiritual phenomena. Many of the practices that are encountered in non-western traditions cannot be explained by conventional western science.

In the history of mankind other sources of knowledge have existed besides the Cartesian one. These persist today. This is relatively well known in a number of medical traditions. Chinese, Ayurvedic, Andean and Mayan health systems have been documented and are recognised as valuable and effective or complementary to western bio-medicine under particular circumstances. Local health treatment is common and widespread in Africa, Asia and South America, not only amongst illiterate rural populations, but also amongst intellectuals. They often give considerable attention to the spiritual and psychological aspects of health. Herbs are used for treating different types of disease. The Chinese and Ayurvedic medical sciences are based on a systematic theory, documented in scripts in languages that are difficult for westerners to access (such as Chinese, Sanskrit and local Indian languages). In India and Sri Lanka a very large number of hospitals follow the classical approach and there are universities that teach and do research in the Ayurvedic tradition. Ayurvedic hospitals have incorporated certain products of western development such as X-rays. Where they are unable to cure a disease, they may refer the patient to a western bio-medical hospital.

Contrary to medical science, in agricultural science hardly any attention has been given to classical science, notwithstanding the fact that in India classical texts and scripts exist about animal health, crop production and crop protection. It looks as if there is an under-utilised stock of knowledge available for testing and development. FRLHT works this way in the domain of health, whereas CIKS, GREEN Foundation and KPP work in the domain of agriculture.

In Sri Lanka, traditional spiritual practices are influenced by Buddhist philosophy. The use of *mantras* and *yantras* are based on a notion that sounds and symbols have a power that can be influenced by certain tones and words (*mantras*) and symbols (*yantras*). Also the influence of cosmic forces are acknowledged in biodynamic agriculture and by leaders in Sri Lanka, Nepal and the Andes.

Several methods may be applied to contribute to theory building: studying classical texts; identifying the experiences of practitioners (spiritual leaders, healers and/or villagers); trying to link new insights in science to provide explanations, as in the case of astrology; revitalisation of the (ecological and social) meanings of certain festivals; including classical knowledge in the experimental designing.

It is important to include local practice and wisdom in university curricula. One could try to see how to develop and include other cosmovisions and knowledge systems into university teachings. One could study the concepts used in local languages to get deeper access to indigenous concepts within cosmovision. An example can be found in the book on the indigenous people of Tojolobales in Mexico where Carlos Lenkesdorf analysed the language and cosmovision in detail. Much can also be learned from the work of AGRUCO which operates in a university context.

Certain skills are needed in order to understand the broader perspectives behind a practice. More use can be made of indigenous ways of communication and expression like music, art and dance to give new insights into classical texts. And also modern information system as well as computer and laboratory equipment can be helpful. There should be an ability to appreciate alternative experimental explanations or designs. It might not be possible to repeat some experiments or practices but it may well be possible to challenge them. A proper investigation should be made of rituals, symbols and festivals. But care should be taken not to fall into the trap of stereotyping, romanticising or trying to explain things with inappropriate concepts. The challenge is to go deeper and make sense, to challenge present concepts.

The above issues also confront the COMPAS partners with the question of how to relate to western science. For many of the partners it is clear that it cannot be the only standard for their work. Probably a valuable service to western science would be done if its deficiencies and biases are challenged. These challenges could take place in debates, but in the spirit of COMPAS an open dialogue is suggested where there is also room for respectful disagreement and where suggestions can be made for joint experiments with concepts and parameters from other sources of knowledge.

Self-development and training

Most staff of support organisations have undergone training based on western scientific concepts where it is suggested that the western scientific way of thinking is superior to that of other traditions. There should be an awareness about possible arrogance displayed in the professional situation and possibly a process of 'de-schooling' or 'learning how to learn from the communities' may be needed. Similarly, conviction that traditional knowledge and cosmovision represent the solution to all problems is far from desirable.

Every individual who interacts with rural people has to reflect on his or her own position and ask the question: What is my attitude and behaviour? We have to realise that our own attitude and behaviour can either strengthen or weaken the culture. An example of this would be our presence during the performance of a ritual with a soothsayer or a spirit medium. If we cannot connect ourselves with the spiritual process, we have to be careful and we should ask ourselves what we want: to act as an observer with empathy and respect or to develop our spirituality and participate fully in rituals? We may have to develop skills in intuition, reflection, in flexibility, spirituality and in openness. These skills are generally not taught at universities, but we might find teachers in the communities.

The practical translation of these skills is the capacity to have a good dialogue. Dialogue does not necessarily mean reaching consensus. Sometimes there may be disagreement. The key is to make an effort to understand, agree to disagree or respectfully disagree and remain open to feedback and further information. Many of us have not sufficiently developed the skill of listening! One should be able to understand hidden information: body language, emotional expressions, symbolic language. Rural people will not easily reveal the actual reason for traditional practises or rituals either because they are secret or because they simply do not know. We need skills to understand these aspects. A person who gets involved in a community should be able to identify with the feelings expressed by the people. One should not only be talking and listening with the head, for example, but also be able to feel with the heart. Bridging the heart and the mind and bringing them together is an important challenge. The experience of AGRUCO in the Andes underlines the importance of communication from heart to heart. A field worker should go with an open mind and open heart, not just with the aim of documenting facts and figures. IDEA in India can provide more information on the method of emotional integration. CECIK has developed the concept of Empathic Learning and Action. These (and other) partners may provide important clues on the ways mind and the heart can be linked.

Most field staff and managers of development organisations have been trained in the conventional way. Often it has been suggested that, in order to modernise indigenous knowledge and institutions should be substituted by modern knowledge and institutions for research and extension. Enhancing endogenous development requires a different attitude towards indigenous knowledge and institutions and a different method for technology development. Not a top-down approach of transfer of technology nor the use of PRA techniques during a diagnostic phase, followed by a persuasive phase of technology testing. Rather there is a need to express appreciation for indigenous knowledge and indigenous institutions that is combined with empathy, but which also encourages a provocative dialogue with the community in the search for better alternatives. This requires a re-orientation and re-training. Frequently this training cannot be offered by conventional training institutes, and, therefore, it needs to be developed by innovative NGOs or universities. Often, however, the teachers should be drawn from the communities or from centres for spiritual development. The development of intuition, meditation, learning how to interpret dreams and how to be open to revelations, in short the spiritual development of professionals, may need very different learning locations and teachers.

Networking and stimulating dialogue

Networking is an important activity and allows organisations to exchange and assess experiences and to build coalitions between like-minded organisations for cooperation in domains where the organisation itself would have been too small to carry out the activity on its own. This can be the case in training, technology development and lobbying. Networking is especially important in the context of the COMPAS project, where it is developing a relatively new approach.

Many partner organisations have been engaged in networking. AGRUCO has distributed the COMPAS newsletter in Latin America. AZTREC recently organised a southern Africa workshop and set up a regional network to ensure recognition of indigenous knowledge by government structures and other policy-making bodies. CECIK is producing a newsletter and is stimulating NGOs in the southern part of Ghana to start work on endogenous development. At present it is also involved in teaching the subject of Cosmovision and Indigenous Knowledge at university level. ECO in Sri Lanka has done extensive lobbying in government agencies, universities, development projects and the mass media and has established contacts with Buddhist religious centres to consult them and involve them in field activities. FRLHT proposes to organise nation-wide workshops to share and discuss findings. KPP is part of a national farmers' movement and IDEA is active in lobbying and cooperation with other NGOs. Regional networking has been foreseen in the COMPAS programme and regional coordinators have been appointed and plans can be formulated.

The research, development and teaching agenda of the international and national research organisations and universities generally follow the Cartesian tradition. One can say that these efforts have the tendency to enhance globalisation. Initiatives for supporting endogenous development and cultural diversity may also need the help of these institutions. Globalisation and diversification are not necessarily in conflict with each other. They can be complementary as well. Therefore, the possibility of influencing the agenda at the local and (inter)national level in favour of policies for cultural diversity is important. We should try to influence agendas by meeting with people at different levels, and sharing the results achieved. Cooperation might be crea-

Participants of the COMPAS workshop (February 1998)
gathered around a sculpture which visualises intercultural dialoque.
From left to right and front row first are:
Rukman Wagachchi, Vanaja Ramprasad, Mary Shetto, Backson Sibanda, Maheswar Ghimire,
Gloria Miranda Zambrano, David Millar, Jaime Delgadillo, Kalyani Palangasinghe, Marthen Duan.
Second row: Purushothama Rao, Krishna Prasad, Joke de Jonge, Cosmas Gonese, Shyam Sundar,
G.K. Upawansa, Gowtham Shankar, Bertus Haverkort, Marijke Kreikamp.
Back row: Aruna Kumara, Coen ter Berg, Darshan Shankar, Wim Hiemstra, Ananda and Johan Kieft.

ted with institutions that have a complementary capacity: some dealing with the technical aspects whilst others concern themselves with cosmovision. Influence can be most effectively exerted by finding strategic alliances, persons or organisations that have a genuine interest in the subject and with whom we can exchange ideas and build coalitions.

When lobbying, the focus may be on relating to government agencies and international organisations. Of course, the relationship with the community is very important indeed. In fact, the role of NGOs and development organisations in this respect could be to support indigenous people, spiritual leaders and local groups in their efforts to influence policy and research and development agendas. They are the first interest groups. Development organisations can act as their ambassadors, their coaches and funders.

In order to enhance the dialogue between the COMPAS partners and between these and others interested in research and development, COMPAS will produce a six-monthly newsletter and organise regional and international workshops. With this book, COMPAS partners have set out to share some of their orientations and plans. Time is needed to really include the aspects that are suggested by indigenous knowledge systems and to build a capacity to support the new dimension and making it practical.

Readers are invited to send their comments, suggestions and ideas to any of the COMPAS partners and to share their own experiences in the COMPAS newsletter which will be produced regularly.

Mo! Ye mao mo
by **David Millar**

BIRTH? YES!
You were born of 'three worlds'
Your mental birth was in Europe
Your spiritual and physical birth in Africa
At dawn, when the Moon was setting,
You were taken out, naked! in the cold morning
You were presented to the Ancestors, Spirits and the Gods
They chose for you the name Compas
If you have come, stay well
Mo! Ye mao mo - well done! We give you: well done!

GROWTH? YES!
You have to crawl, to walk and to run
You have to crawl on the earth
make contact with it by eating portions of it
It shall fortify you;
after all the soil you eat
is mild doses of vaccines
for various illnesses that will come your way
You sure will be sick, you will have your ups and downs
Then you will walk

You will learn the Ancestral trade
You will learn from other cultures and Ancestors as well,
but don't leave yours for theirs.
You will be prepared for responsibility and continuity
Then you will run

You sure run! You can run as much as you like
but you can never hide
You can never hide from the Ancestral Spirit
So be careful how and to where you run
If you run, run well
Mo! Ye mao mo!

DEATH? YES!
You sure will die!
For all that has life has death
There shall be crying and disappointments
There shall be sorrow and depressions, even frustrations
But no! That is not the end

Death for us is the beginning of a new life
A Life of higher Lights
You will be transformed by Death to high energies
and then you shall live in this transformed form forever
If you are thus transformed.......
Mo! Ye mao mo!

(a poem made during the second COMPAS workshop, February 1998,
dedicated to COMPAS' life cycle)

Addresses

AGRUCO
Mr Freddy Delgado / Mr Gustavo Saravia
(Latin American coordination)
Agroecologia Universidad Cochabamba
Av. Petrolera km 41/2
Casillla 3392, COCHABAMBA
Bolivia
tel/fax +591 4 52601 / 52602
e-mail agruco@pino.cbb.entelnet.bo

AZTREC
Mr Cosmas Gonese
Private Bag 9286
MASVINGO
Zimbabwe
tel/fax + 263 39 66006
e-mail aztrec@mvo.samara.co.zw

BD Union
Mrs Joke de Jonge
Hoofdstraat 24
3972 LA DRIEBERGEN
The Netherlands
tel +31 343 517814
fax +31 343 515611
e-mail louis.bolk@pobox.accu.uu.nl

CECIK
Dr David Millar
(African coordination)
P.O. Box 607
BOLGATANGA - U.E.R.
Ghana
tel +233 71 22000 / 23240
fax +233 71 23478
e-mail cecik@africaonline.com.gh

CIKS
Mr A.V. Balasubramanian
No. 47-C, Gandhi Mandapam Road
Kotturpuram
CHENNAI 600 085
India
tel +91 44 4451087 / 4450215
fax +91 44 4430033

ECO
Mr G.K. Upawansa / Mr Rukman
Wagachchi
(Asian coordination)
Hyneford
Dekinda, NAWALAPITIYA
Sri Lanka
tel +94 8 223012 / 226082
fax +94 8 232517
e-mail of Upawansa pasasa@eureka.lk
e-mail of Rukman dzp@sri.lanka.net

ECOS
Mr Maheswar Ghimire
P.O. Box 4
NARAYANGARH CHITWAN
Nepal
tel +977 56 23663
fax +977 56 20482 / 20165
e-mail ecoce@mos.com.np

ETC-COMPAS
Mr Bertus Haverkort / Mr Wim Hiemstra
(International coordination)
P.O.Box 64
3830 AB LEUSDEN
The Netherlands
tel +31 33 4943086
fax + 31 33 4940791
e-mail Haverkort b.haverkort@etcnl.nl
e-mail Hiemstra w.hiemstra@etcnl.nl
e-mail Compas compas@etcnl.nl

FRLHT
Mr Darshan Shankar
50, MSH Layout, 2nd Stage,
3rd Main
Anandanagar
BANGALORE 560 024
India
tel +91 80 3336909 / 3330348
fax +91 80 3334167
e-mail darshan@frlht.ernet.in

GREEN Foundation
Mrs Vanaja Ramprasad / Mr G. Krishna
Prasad / Mrs Gowri Gopinath
839, 23rd Main Road
J.P. Nagar II Phase
BANGALORE 560078
India
tel +91 80 663 5963
fax +91 80 663 1565
e-mail nanditha@blr.vsnl.net.in

IDEA
Mr Gowtham Shankar
Flat no. 4c & F, Maharaja Towers
R.K. Mission Road
VISAKHAPATNAM 530 003
India
tel +91 891 535685
fax +91 891 535685
e-mail gowtham@sai.xlweb.com

IDIKS
Mrs Mary Shetto
P.O. Box 1982
MBEYA
Tanzania
fax +255 654421
e-mail ifadsherfsp@twiga.com

KPP
Mr A.S. Anand / Mr Aruna Kumara /
Mr Upendra Shenoy
Chitrakoota no. 14,
I Cross, II Block, I Stage
Vinoba Nagar, Shimoga
KARNATAKA
India
tel/fax +91 8182 56539

TALPUY
Mrs Gloria Miranda Zambrano / Mr Raúl
Santana Paucar / Mr Jesus Lino Revilla
Apartado Postal 222
Jr. 2 de Mayo, no. 336
San Carlos
HUANCAYO
Peru
tel/fax+51 64 216889

TIRD-P
Mr Johan Kieft / Mr Marthen Duan
P.O. Box 116
KEFAMANANU 85601
Timor NTT
Indonesia
tel +62 38831172
fax +62 388 31111
e-mail ytm@kupang.wasantara.net.id

UNEP
Mr Backson Sibanda
P.O. Box 30522
NAIROBI
Kenya
tel +254 2 623387
fax +254 2 623918
e-mail backson.sibanda@unep.org

University of Nijmegen
Third World Centre
Mr Gerrit Huizer
Postbus 9104
6500 HE NIJMEGEN
The Netherlands

Yardi & Sorée
Mrs Prabha Mahale / Mr Hay Sorée
E-110 Saket
110017 NEW DELHI
India
e-mail ysindia@giasdl01.vsnl.net.in

COLOPHON

Concept and realisation
COMPAS / Bertus Haverkort and Wim Hiemstra
P.O. Box 64
3830 AB Leusden, The Netherlands

Final editing
Bertus Haverkort, Wim Hiemstra, Marilyn Minderhoud and Marijke Kreikamp

Photography
The colour pictures in this book were made by:
Bertus Haverkort: cover and backcover, 1-1, 1-2, 1-8, 2-1, 2-2, 2-3, 2-4, 2-5, 2-6, 2-7, 2-9, 3-1, 3-2, 3-3, 3-4, 4-8, 4-9, 4-10, 4-11, 4-12, 5-1, 5-2, 5-3, 5-4, 5-5, 6-5, 7-6, 7-7, 7-8, 7-9, 7-10, 7-11, 8-6, 8-8
Cosmas Gonese: backcover, 6-6, 6-7, 6-8
Wim Hiemstra: 1-3, 2-8, 8-7
David Millar: 5-6, 5-7, 5-8, 5-9, 6-1, 6-2, 6-3, 6-4
Peter Oud: 8-1, 8-2
Chris Pennarts: 8-3, 8-4
Florian Perez: backcover, 1-4, 1-6, 7-2, 7-3, 7-4, 7-5
Vanaja Ramprasad and Krishna Prasad: 1-5, 3-5, 3-6, 3-7, 3-8, 8-5
Gowtham Shankar: backcover, 4-1, 4-2, 4-3, 4-4, 4-5, 4-6, 4-7
Illustration 7-1 made by:
Jesus Perez (AGRUCO), Bolivia
Black and white photos and illustrations were made by:
Sander Essers, Jesus Lindo Revilla, Bertus Haverkort, Joke de Jonge, Hans Levelt, David Millar, Florian Perez, Krishna Prasad, Vanaja Ramprasad, Gowtham Shankar, Michiel Wijnbergh

Graphic Design
Pharos, Nijmegen / Monique van Hootegem

Printing
Ad Process, Bangalore

Distribution
Books for Change, Bangalore (for India)
Zed Books, United Kingdom (outside India)